TALES FROM THE GUTTER

and other
Rock and Roll Shenanigans

MIKE CORCIONE

Instagram @1985roaddog and @talesfromthegutter

YouTube @youtube.com/beforeiforget1985

Email: beforeiforget147@gmail.com

Table of Contents

Who's Who:

Mike Corcione: Aka Mike C., aka DJ, aka Corky Gunn. It's my story.

Scott Levitt: Aka Levitt aka Caligula. The root of the connections. One of my oldest friends. Carrying the torch into the future. He's low!

Bruno Ravel: Aka Bruno Valentino. One of my oldest friends. Danger Danger and The Defiants founder, songwriter, and bassist. Cottonballs!

Mitch "Diamond" Pfeiffer: Old friend, went to high school with me and Scott Levitt. Long Island guitar player.

Steve West: Aka Steve St. Tropez. Old friend. Drummer, founder, and songwriter for Danger Danger. I was there!

Larry Braverman: Old friend and former promotion guru at Elektra Records

Barry Kobrin: Owner of Important Record Distributors (IRD) and Relativity/Combat Records.

Stacey "Shmendrek": Old friend and mischief maker.

P.A.: Old friend who worked at IRD/Relativity/Combat.

Mike Pont: Aka Pont aka Ponty Hall. Photographer, Hotshot lead singer, Trouble lead singer, old friend.

Mike Schnapp: Aka DJ Uncle Mike. Old friend, former Sweet Pain manager, and Combat Records radio promo.

Tommy Lee: Drummer and songwriter dude from Mötley Crüe.

Nikki Sixx: Bassist, songwriter, and biter from Mötley Crüe

Robbin Crosby (RIP): Aka King. Ratt guitarist, songwriter, and founder.

Kelly Nickels: Aka Blade. Hotshot roadie and L.A. Guns bassist and songwriter. I think he's still my friend.

Mick Cripps: L.A. Guns founder, songwriter, guitarist, and keyboardist from 1985 to 1995. Founded The Brutalists and Burning Retna. One of my oldest and best friends.

Alan Jones: Manager of L.A. Guns from 1987 to 1989

Nickey Beat: L.A. Guns drummer from 1985 to 1987. Drummer for The Weirdos and The Cramps.

Phil Lewis: L.A. Guns lead vocalist and songwriter from 1987 to present. Former singer of Girl and Tormé.

Tracii Guns: L.A. Guns lead guitarist and songwriter from 1984 to present. Also played with Brides of Destruction.

Steve Riley: L.A. Guns drummer from 1987 to present. Former drummer of W.A.S.P., The B'zz, and Roadmaster.

Bob Skoro: L.A. Guns A&R man from 1987 to 1991.

Allen Kovac: L.A. Guns manager from 1989 to 1992.

Peter Gatien: Club king of New York City. Owner of The Limelight, Tunnel, Palladium, and Club USA.

Arthur Weinstein (RIP): Lighting director at Limelight and former club owner.

Prologue

Sex, drugs, and rock and roll? Yes. There was lots of that.

But it's all about the songs, man. Always was, always will be.

Yes, I did lots of drugs, partied dangerously hard, met lots of girls, did lots of stupid shit, and put myself in some very dangerous situations. But so did lots of people back in those days. The difference is, I got paid for it. When it's your job to party in "nightworld," it can really get out of hand. I mean, I could just sit here and tell stories about the dark underbelly I lived in nightly, and what went on at four in the morning on a Saturday night in 1982. But you can become jaded just from listening to it all, and it can seem ridiculous to people. Like, come on man, that can't be true; or that's insane, that didn't really happen.

But it did.

This is my story. Who am I? No one really. Not famous, is what I mean. But I lived a wild and colorful life, and worked in a world that gave me first class access to an insane life of rock and roll bands, musicians, drugs, nightclubs, wiseguys, booze, and freaks. And I was in the right place at the right time, lucky enough to experience some great moments in the history of pop culture. But it wasn't luck. It was all meant to be. I look back on it all, and it seems like it happened to someone else. But I know who I am.

And the stories told in this book all happened. That guy you will read about isn't me anymore. I have shed some skin, morphed, and elevated my consciousness since then. I'm thankful every day that I am still here to even talk about any of it. This book is a time capsule about a time and a place that is no more. Herein are the tales of my journey through music, first as a fan, and then eventually working in the music and nightclub business. From my start in 1978 as a disco DJ in an illegal after hours club at 17 years old, to working as a new wave and rock DJ in the biggest nightclubs in Manhattan, Queens, and Long Island, to working for an import record distributor that morphed into a huge record label eventually purchased by Sony, to an on tour backstage Sodom and Gomorrah with the biggest rock bands of the 1980s from Mötley Crüe to L.A. Guns. Here lies my manic history working in the seedy underbelly of what we used to call the music business in the 1970s and 1980s. The other thing is, all of this stuff was going on at the same time! Starting in 1981, I was working full-time as a DJ in huge nightclubs, working at the record distributor IRD, and hanging with Mötley Crüe, Iron Maiden, and all my friends that played in bands. It was all happening simultaneously. I didn't burn the candle at both ends. I melted it with a blow torch. I lived that life. Hard. At the time it felt like home. Not anymore. But it is sometimes fun to look back on it and be thankful that I got to experience it and thankful that I made it through and am still here to tell the tales.

It's also a story about a group of friends that grew up together and were fans of the same bands. We weren't with the Grateful Dead and Hot Tuna crowd, and we weren't greasers or disco guys. We weren't jocks. We were into Kiss, Aerosmith, Starz, Twisted Sister, and Mötley Crüe. We liked rock stars like Mick Jagger, Steven Tyler, Paul Stanley, and David Bowie. Real rockstars that looked cool and flashy. Some of the friends in our crew went on to be in bands that signed major label record deals and toured the world, opening for bands like Kiss and AC/DC. Me? After working at a record label and at the same time working as a DJ in nightclubs three nights a week for eight years, I went to work for L.A. Guns in December 1987 and almost cracked up. I thought I had changed and straightened up when I went to work for them. Who was I kidding. After nine months with L.A. Guns, I was a wreck. But the common denominator with all of us friends is that we were fans first of the bands and fans first of the music, and we were lucky enough to have found a way to support ourselves from music. At least for awhile. We did it. Achieved the dream. No matter what happens in the future, we all got there in our own way.

My dad, who is from New York, met my mom down in Georgia at 19 years old when he was in the Army at Fort Benning. They dated and eventually got married and moved to New York. I was born in Far Rockaway, Queens, and from birth my life was a parade of rednecks and wiseguys—mostly wiseguys, as my dad's family was in the business, but still—I had crazy family on both sides. I didn't have the most normal upbringing, but I got through the abnormalities by listening to music. My family's lifestyle influenced me, sure, but ultimately it was me that chose the path that I ended up on. I was focused on it, and I was meant to do it. I was guided to it. Obsessed. But I suffered for taking that path. I went through a lot of lessons—pain and loss, hurt and trauma, failures and successes—to get to the version of me that exists today. I gained an incredible life experience, and became wise from living a thrilling, but dangerous lifestyle. I carry the scars, but have finally gotten past the pain. That is one of the reasons I am writing this book after all these years—I am ready now. I am ready to face it and accept it and love that version of myself. And also to forgive myself for being an asshole sometimes. I was coming from the ego then. I was self-centered and oblivious to others feelings at times. I was in pain, hurting from a traumatic childhood and acting in the only way I knew to protect myself.

Living that lifestyle and taking that chosen path has made it difficult for me now. I didn't prepare for a future. I just lived and followed the path in front of me. Those choices have made it a struggle today. I did not ever think about going to college—not that going to college is a guarantee to a successful future. I had no steady job path. I went with the flow of things, and I made no real money to save for the lean times. All of those choices are the price I have had to pay. It was the price tag to live that type of a life, but I wouldn't change any of it for anything. Without it, I couldn't be where I am at now mentally and spiritually. Do you have to struggle sometimes to make it in this life? Sure, you do. But so do millions of others. Hell, my life ain't bad. There are others out there that have it really bad. I remind myself of that daily. I moved around so much, from job to job or gig to gig, out of boredom and frustration. I was searching for something. Chasing something. Anytime I was forced to face some internal issue, a programmed response would kick in, and I would leave the place I was in and change the scenery. I was searching for the light. I wanted to be healed. I just didn't know it at the time.

But I'm done hiding. Done denying. It's time to face what and where I came from. I am who I am. But it's not about who I was or what I did, it's about who I am now and what I am doing with my life today. Have you evolved? Shed a layer of skin or two or three? I have. I tempted death daily for ten years and lived to tell the tale, when so many from the same circles I travelled in have fallen. This book is dedicated to the fallen family and friends that were not supposed to be here now. Their journey was meant to be a short one. They were called to the other side way too young and way to early, but that is the way it was meant to be. It's the way the script was written. We all have our time. My brother Jonathan lived a tortured life. Addictions and demons chased him every day, and they got him in the end. He lived longer than my cousins, Caine, Alex, and Donnie, though. They all died very young. Jonathan was very tight with all three of them. My Long Beach friends, Sean and Cap, again, went too young. You look back and you have memories of those days, but it seems like a whole different lifetime. Like it happened to someone else. We are always changing and morphing, or at least I know I am.

This is a story about the music and the times that shaped me. I did lots of different things in the music industry, but at heart, I am a DJ. That is the only thing I really set out to be and to accomplish. It's what I do best: program music. It really is all about the songs for me. When you boil it down, I was and I am inspired and motivated by music. It's what has sustained me, and it never fails me when I need it. I have included at the end of the book a list of my top 250 songs ever. It's my personal list and not meant to be any kind of official data. I was a hardcore working nightclub DJ from 1978 through 1995. I grew up surrounded by music. So in reality, the list could be never-ending, but these are my desert island discs.

In writing this book, I spoke to old and close friends, and we relived the stories of the times when we all came of age and experienced rock and roll, concert tours, nightclubs, and drugs. Their voices throughout the book are noted as such. I want to thank them all for giving me the time and having the stories to tell. I have also been inspired by the many photographs and memorabilia I have collected over the years. Too much of it. I have been weeding through it all. It seems like it all happened to a different person.

I have avoided facing a lot of what is contained in these pages. It was a completely different lifetime for me. I ran and ran, never stopping long enough to confront and heal my past and heal my pain. I was running from it and didn't want to face it. But I have now, and I work on myself daily. I've learned that to evolve, morph, and change is absolutely normal and essential for spiritual growth. Embrace it, be true to your calling, and love yourself.

"Just as a snake sheds it's skin, we must shed our past over and over again" - Buddha

"A mind that is stretched by new experience, can never go back to its old dimensions" - Oliver Wendell Holmes

My life experience is mine alone. I was who I was, and now I am who I am. I am not the same person that I was in 1978, 1984, or 1992. Hell, even 2019. A lot of people remember a person that doesn't exist anymore. I was an idiot a lot of times; I admit it. And I apologize to anyone that I have hurt emotionally or whose feelings I didn't take into account back then. I am writing this book for a few reasons—first, to hopefully inspire someone to just go for it no matter what. Go get it. Be driven. Be passionate about whatever it is that turns you on and excites you. And second, to let there be some lessons here. I was a damaged soul and a wounded child that never grew up, in a lot of ways. I had a lot of fun and experienced so much in my life, but it was a dangerous world I travelled in. I was close to death a few times, for various reasons, but the universe said not yet, you keep going. Those two decades, the 1970s and 1980s are a moment in time that will never return. Thank God. There were a lot of great things that came out of those two decades—and a lot of bad as well, at least for me. The number one great thing was the MUSIC. But trying to recreate the energy in the air? The insanity of the "swinging seventies" or the "me" decade? You can't do it. It is ridiculous to even try and recreate it. The new generations must now do their own thing. Be inspired by the past, the classic music, stories, and imagery, but make your own scene. Just be forewarned: drugs are just the worst. Why do any drugs? The shit they do today is just plain stupid. The opioid thing is so bad. Heroin. That's what got my brother. Terrible. Pills, Xanax, plus the crap they make in the bathtub, the homemade stuff. Meth. Ugh, just so lowww. Whatever the hot drug of the moment is, just stay the fuck away! But weed? Weed is okay. It's not a drug. Vodka is more of a drug than weed. Hell, definitely don't drink. That's the number one brain cell killer and fight starter. I would never recommend any of it today. Way too dangerous. It's a different and scary world, so watch yourself out there. Fly under the radar and make no waves. Be invisible. Trust me.

Ahhhhh, 1979. It was a different time then. You had hope still. Hope for the world and hope for generations to come. Security wasn't an issue. Everything was always going to be alright. It's not that way anymore. Maybe it wasn't that way then, and I just had blinders on. But there was still an innocence back then that has been lost. Social media and smartphones have taken away everyone's attention and everyone's soul. If those things existed in 1984, I wouldn't be writing this book because you would already know what's in it from my social media accounts. Rock and roll is gone with the wind. A vanished relic, like vaudeville, to quote Phil Lewis. The music industry? There isn't one anymore. Its now all about "content" and "branding" and 360 deals. It certainly doesn't have anything to do with what the business used to be. It's like that scene in the HBO show, *Vinyl*, set in 1973, when Richie Finestra, the head of American Century Records, is sitting in his Mercedes buying cocaine from a street dealer. The dealer mistakes Richie for a Wall Street guy and he lashes back at the guy: "Wall Street! Do I look like Wall Street? I'm a record man."

Me? I have the same take on it. I'm a record man.

The business of the thing that they now call "music" is bigger than ever, but the MUSIC business is gone with the wind.

Read on and be inspired by the stories, by the times, and most importantly, by the music.

Once the last of the great rock stars die off and there is no one left, it will be a sad day indeed. All hail the rock stars. All hail the greatness of the last surviving musical pioneers. Go and see as many live shows as you can before there is no one left to go see, 'cause in 20 years there will be no one left. And keep listening to the songs. It really is all about the songs. No matter where you are or what you are doing, if you need to hear a specific song, it's so easy today with Spotify or YouTube. It's comforting to me to know that they are out there still, floating through the sky. And even though that time will never return, I can call on the songs at any time to help me through a moment or inspire me to greater heights.

Those great songs are golden medicine.

They don't change, and they don't disappoint.

Intro - Electric Gypsy

I was standing on an arena stage in front of 18,000 people wearing a wrestling mask, introducing Los Angeles sleaze band, L.A. Guns, in Lexington Kentucky:

Ask me how I got here. How I was talked into wearing a wrestling mask and taking on the alter ego, "Lord Humongous from the wastelands of Hollywood California," to introduce the band.

It was the last night for L.A. Guns as special guest to AC/DC on their Blow Up Your Video 1988 world tour. As tour tradition demands, on the last night on a mega tour like this, the headliner's road crew pulls harmless pranks on the opening act.

Harmless, but embarrassing nonetheless.

As I ran through the intro that I had been reciting every night for the last month, I got shocked out of my too-small leather jacket by not one, but two cream pies in the face. I was the first victim of the night for the revved up AC/DC road crew. I couldn't see that well with the mask on anyway (it blocks your peripheral vision), and now I had cream pie all over my face. I stumbled across the stage, crashing into the big side monitor speaker, and blindly made my way to the wings where I grabbed a towel, ripped off the mask, and wiped my eyes. Did that just happen? We kind of heard that there was going to be some mischief from the crew for the Guns that night, but I had no idea they would start with me! Not to mention, the record label was recording the show for a syndicated live radio broadcast, all while the band were dodging the attack from the AC/DC crew, hellbent on keeping with the rock and roll road tradition.

We had been on the road nonstop for the last four months.

After this last show with AC/DC, it was back to the clubs. Better money and better clubs. Two nights in each club instead of one. Then back to more arena opening slots with Iron Maiden.

L.A. Guns was riding the rock and roll party train, straight off the fucking rails.

It's pretty wild riding the wave, touring the country, feeling the intensity and insanity of it all.

And watching Guns N' Roses become huge.

The "Guns" in Guns N' Roses comes from L.A. Guns, and L.A. Guns (LAG) comes from Tracii Guns. Well, kind of. The connection was deep and emotional. L.A. Guns rode the same train as Guns N' Roses. Hell, my first show working for the band was LAG opening for Guns N' Roses at Perkins Palace in Pasadena, CA, December 1987. L.A. Guns were always in the shadow of Guns N' Roses.

Guns N' Roses rode the train all the way to the fucking top. Mega huge superstars all the world over. Then it all imploded— of course it did.

It was never meant to last. Exploring the roots of it all, you can see why it never could. Dysfunction Junction. Ego and insanity. Mental issues and messy childhoods. Add a healthy appetite for sex, booze, drugs, and destruction and you know how it ends.

In a whiskey soaked fireball.

But first, let's go back to the beginning, to my entrée to the wild side.

This is a story about a specific slice of the rock and roll music scene spanning from 1978 through 1992.

Rock and roll, punk, new wave, heavy metal, glam.

It's a history of that place and time from a particular point of view. Mine.

Is it all 100% accurate?

Who the hell knows, but to my recollection, from what I can remember, this is it.

Chapter One - In the Beginning...1975-1979

When friends, old or new, look at my collection of pictures of the crazy shenanigans that went on in the 1980s, or I tell them a story and they just can't believe it, they always end up asking:

"How did you get backstage?"

"How did you get these pictures?"

"How did you get that access?"

"How did you get to be a DJ in a nightclub that held 3,000 people at 20 years old?"

"How did you start working for L.A. Guns?"

"How did you meet these famous rockstars?"

"How did you get in the music business?"

Well, here is how it all started for me. I'm a lucky fucker to have been born when I was.

And I wanted it. Thats the most important thing. I was driven. I let nothing stop me.

I started my professional life in the music biz as a nightclub DJ. I was a senior at Lawrence High School in Cedarhurst, New York in 1978, while also working at my dad's after hours club, The

Spot, every weekend. He used to have a jazz trio on weekends, but with disco being so big at the time, I convinced him to let me play records, so he did away with the jazz band and let me DJ.

Cedarhurst is one of the Five Towns in the southwest corner of Nassau County, very close to Kennedy Airport and the Queens border. Lots of Italians and our cousins the Jews.

Lots of rich people lived in the Five Towns. Famous people too. I wasn't one of them.

An after hours club is an illegal bar or club that is allowed to exist because it really is a private club. Only "members" or known people were allowed in. What made it illegal was you weren't allowed to sell alcohol without a license, and an after hours club had no license and paid no taxes. That's the definition of an after hours club: outside the law. They stayed open way past the 4 AM curfew. Totally illegal, but still allowed to operate, if you knew how to maneuver. The club was decorated all black and white, silver and chrome, and had a small dance floor. It was very dark. There was blackjack and slots in the back room and an intimidating guy that worked the front door named Joe Kent. The door was thick and steel and bulletproof. It had a peephole so Joe could see who was standing outside the door when they rang the bell to come in. It was secure, that's for sure. All the rich doctors and garment center mavens—people that lived in Hewlett Harbor, Lawrence, and Woodsburgh—would also frequent the

5

place. They knew it was all cool and that it was run right. They felt safe.

My dad used to get all the heavyweight people from the airport to come down to The Spot. If there was a famous actor or musician that had a long layover at Kennedy airport, Dad had some people that worked at the airport that would bring them down to club. One night, one of the guys in Earth, Wind & Fire came down and someone told me he was in the house, so I played "Shining Star." He came over, said hello, and gave me 20 dollars. Man, in those days, in that type of place, people were giving out money to all of the staff all of the time. Bartenders, cocktail waitresses, the doorman, the DJ—everyone was getting cash stuffed into their pocket. There was cash money all over the street. It was a different time. There were a lot of characters that hung out at The Spot. One of which treated us to a song at the end of the night, every night. At around 10 AM in the morning, a stocky guy named Jack would sing "My Way," the Sinatra version, the classic. Jack looked like a cross between Elvis and a wiseguy. He had jet black hair, pompadour style, and always wore Elvis-type sunglasses indoors. I would play the song, or they would play it on the jukebox, and he would sing with the record, karaoke style. No microphone or anything—he was loud. He actually sang it pretty damn good! It was like a scene from the David Lynch movie, Blue Velvet, every morning with Jack. Priceless.

I started work at 2 AM and ended at about noon every Friday and Saturday night. I spent Sunday afternoons at the Sherwood Diner on Rockaway Boulevard with the crowd from The Spot. People a lot older than me and a lot more experienced in life. We would get there after the club closed, eat bad food, and then go home and sleep it off. I was up for school on Monday mornings and started another week. This continued until I graduated high school in June of 1979.

I was exposed to lots of crazy things at that club and in all of the nightclubs I hung out in back then. That lifestyle was unforgiving with soft emotions and weakness and exuded macho male posturing. Very Goodfellas. I learned about drugs, alcohol, sex, violence, and power, developing keen street smarts along the way. I learned from my mistakes. Well, sometimes I did, because I kept repeating bad and harmful behavior, no matter the pain or danger I put myself in.

I had five major car accidents between 1979 and 1986. I totaled cars and walked away. I got pretty banged up in a couple of the accidents and still carry the scars. It's a miracle I'm alive. Truthfully. I should have been dead a few times. But I'm still here. God has a plan for all of us. My time isn't up yet. Thank you universe. But let me back it up a bit.

I was born in Far Rockaway, Queens in 1960. My dad, uncle, and grandfather were in the "life," so to speak. I grew up around the actual guys that were portrayed in the movie Goodfellas. Paulie Vario and Jimmy Burke were sticking folded 20 dollar bills into my pocket when I was hanging around my grandfather's card games in the cellar of his house. I was probably 5 or 6 years old at the time. They would give me the money and say, "Little Mike, go buy yourself some candy." From birth, my life was like the movie Goodfellas. Seriously. I knew the people in that movie. We were at their houses, and they were at ours. When I saw the film on the day it opened in the theaters, it was like watching a home movie. If I was in that world or around those people, I was treated like a prince and looked out for. But in the straight world, or the civilian world, I was looked at differently. My last name was known in the neighborhood, and I was sometimes looked at as being a bad kid or someone that got into trouble. My dad and I shared the same first and last name, so I had a black mark against me from birth. It followed me around everywhere, but I didn't notice it until I got older. By then, I knew that just because of my name, some people looked at me as being trouble.

I listened to AM radio religiously and became a manic music fan. Rock and roll, soul, pop, R&B, country—I loved it all and still do. Music was, and is, everything to me. It's what got me through many difficult times in my life. The power of a great song, one that connects with you deeply, is really magic. I still feel that way. Whenever I hear one of my faves on the radio or on Spotify or wherever it pops up, it brings me right back to that place and time. I can feel the time, the moment, the era, see the movie in my mind, like Marty Scorsese. Its unbelievable. I wish that everyone on earth could feel this way from music. It's the great force that really has the power to bring us all together. If only everyone listened to the right songs! The radio was always on when I was a kid, or my mom or my aunts would be playing 45 records. The hits of the day. My grandfather listened to the old 78s. Caruso and Italian opera. My grandmother sang show tunes and performed sometimes in local productions. Music was everywhere, during every waking hour.

I always felt different from everyone else. I always felt like I never fit in anywhere.

My family and friends were different than me. I don't know how or why, but I felt it. I always felt like I had knowledge that others didn't when it came to certain things, or I felt that I had lived a past life because certain things were very familiar to me. But I felt out of place at the same time. I would zone out at times by myself in my room, totally go into a trance, and I would start hearing a loud buzzing, like I was being transported to another place. It was very strange. I would have to force myself out of it and to snap back to "normal." This happened when I was probably 7 to 10 years old.

After lots of drama, my parents divorced in 1973. My dad had to go away to "college," and my mother couldn't handle it all. I was

12 years old and had to move with my mom and my younger brother and sister to my mom's hometown in the sticks of Georgia right after 6th grade ended. It was like being ripped from civilization and plopped down in the middle of nowhere. But I carried the music with me, as I would do for the rest of my life. All I cared about were my records and my little stereo. The move was very unsettling, as to be expected, but was compounded by having some country hick I never met in my life come in and move us down there. He came up with my two aunts from Georgia to get us moved down. My mom, ever the dramatic, had made them all come up to get us. My dad was not around at this time—he was away—or none of this shit would be happening. They were loading the giant rental truck for what turned out to be a three day drive, and my records fell out of a box and spilled out in the driveway. I got so mad. From that moment on, the records and the stereo rode in the car with me, my mom, and aunts, while goober drove the truck. It took us three days to get there. The truck broke down in Virginia, and we had to stay the night. Torture. As soon as we got to my grandmother's house, I set up my stereo in what would become my room. I was listening to Billion Dollar Babies by Alice Cooper, The Who Sell Out, and Goodbye Yellow Brick Road by Elton John. But the positive was, I saw my first concerts at the 5,000 seating capacity Columbus Municipal Auditorium. My first concert was the Lynyrd Skynyrd Second Helping Tour in 1974. I was 13. An older guy that was a

friend of my uncle took me. He and his girlfriend were about 21 and went to a lot of the concerts in town. They had their wine pouch and weed and partied all night. The Outlaws opened the show, and they got signed that night by Clive Davis to Arista Records, at the urging of Skynyrd vocalist Ronnie Van Zant.

In 1975, I saw the Edgar Winter Group with Rick Derringer and Dan Hartman in the band and saw Kiss on the Alive! Tour with Styx opening. I also saw Kiss in 1976 on the Rock and Roll Over Tour with Tom Petty as the opener. It might be difficult for people today to understand how amazing early Kiss was. There was nothing like it. They were young and hungry, determined to make it. They were the coolest thing ever. They were like nothing that had ever happened before. And they were from New York Fucking City. However, in my opinion, they lost it around 1978 really. Nothing great lasts forever, but they have remained in the game and are still at it, at the time of this writing. The current lineup is not for me—two old guys that look terrible and two replacement fake guys. A band like Kiss, so special and unique, so groundbreaking in so many ways, superhero rock stars dressed to kill, can't have old guys dressed in makeup in it. It just doesn't work. Old guys can work in any other band, just not Kiss, man! I saw the real thing: Gene, Paul, Peter, and Ace at the height of their powers.

Kiss changed my life. For real. There, I said it.

I was blown away by Cheap Trick opening for Foreigner in 1977. Foreigner's first album was just out and "Feels Like The First Time" was a smash radio hit with "Cold As Ice" right on it's heels. I had seen the guys in Cheap Trick in Creem magazine, but had no idea what they sounded like, so when I saw Rick Nielsen on the side of the stage, I recognized him right away as that crazy looking dude that resembled Satch from The Bowery Boys. They were so unique, so individual, so cool, with so much energy on stage, and the best songs. I went out the next day and bought their new album, In Color. I was a Cheap Trick fan from that day forward. I was lucky enough to talk to Robin Zander back in the early 2000s, and we spoke about that show. I think he said that was the first show they did out of their hometown Midwest area of Rockford, Illinois. One of the senior girls at my high school, a hotsie-totsie named Sandra, was first row at that Foreigner show. I was sitting on the side of auditorium in the stands and saw her in the first row. She was flirting with the singer, Lou Gramm, and after the show he motioned for her to come backstage, and I saw her walk back there with him. I knew what that was all about. Automatically. She was a wild senior chick, and I put two and two together. Lou knew what he was doing—so did she.

From 1975 to 1978 I saw Foghat, Elvin Bishop Group, Blue Öyster Cult (I saw them twice, and once was the recording of the show for the live album, Some Enchanted Evening), Rush (twice), Angel, Piper, The Godz, Atlanta Rhythm Section (three times),

Johnny Cash, Gary Wright, James Brown, Charlie Daniels Band, Parliament's Mothership Connection Tour, Starz, Bar-Kays, Marshall Tucker Band, and Joe Cocker. I literally went to every concert that played that beat up old auditorium. On a visit back in 1980, I saw Prince open for Rick James and the package tour of Angel, Mothers Finest, Frank Marino and Mahogany Rush, and Humble Pie. My 9th grade social studies teacher took me to see the Joe Cocker show in 1975. He was just out of college and had played bass guitar in a cover band and was pretty cool. He told me that in his band, they did the song "Touch Me" by The Doors, and when it came time for the chorus, they would sing, "Come on, come on, come on, come on now fuck me babe," instead of, "Touch me babe." Cool, I guess. So he took me to the concert. He picked me up at home and took me to the show. I guess it was kind of weird, but that type of stuff happened a lot back then, especially in a place like Georgia. He ended up secretly dating one of the senior cheerleaders, and they ended up coming out publicly with it, and it was kind of accepted. I can only imagine how that would go over today.

I had no car, so 75% of the time to get to the shows, I would hitchhike (I lived about 20 minutes from the auditorium by car), beg people to take me, or get a ride there but have no way back and walk home. I was obsessed with music and rock and roll and got there no matter what it took. I sometimes got free tickets through the local radio station. My mom knew someone that worked there. If I couldn't get a free ticket, I would save up pennies. I would cash in soda bottles for a nickel. No lie. If you wanted to be in the mix and go to shows, you had to be dedicated! When Kiss played both times, my mom let me cut school, and I waited on line all day. I made a bologna sandwich and put it in a paper bag and took it with me to eat. I waited there, first on line, from 8 AM till they opened the doors at 7 PM. It was a general admission show, as were all the shows at this venue. There were seats up top in the stands, but no seats on the floor; what they called back then, "festival seating." It makes it sound fun and happy, but years later in 1979 there was a stampede at a The Who show with festival seating in Cincinnati, and people got trampled and died. It was a shock to everyone. It had to change at some point, which it did. But when I went to shows at that venue, the floor section was not reserved, and there were no seats, so if you waited all day on line, when they opened one of the four doors that got you into the building, you were able to run like a maniac and get right to the front of the stage. I did that for both Kiss shows. Those Kiss shows changed my life and set me on a course to work in the music business in some way and be around a band, somehow. I was hooked. I watched American Bandstand and Soul Train every Saturday afternoon and The Midnight Special and Don Kirshner's Rock Concert late nights. I listened to the radio at every moment I was not in school. I slept with a little AM radio under my pillow at night. WDAK, or if you had the radio positioned just right, you could get WABC in New York City, very faintly, but you could hear it. I absorbed it all. Music was my escape.

I was relentlessly bullied from 3rd grade till about the end of 8th grade, and music was what got me through it. I got beat up regularly and was forced to help the bullies cheat on tests, do their homework for them, and most importantly, be afraid of them. That's all a bully really wants, is for you to be afraid of them. It made me very introverted, but extroverted at the same time. I longed to be seen, heard, and known, but I escaped to my bedroom and put on the headphones and lived through the music. My dad wasn't around a lot, and once my parents divorced, never. My mom really raised me. She was overprotective and smothering, and all I heard was "Don't fight. Don't drink. Don't do drugs." And I didn't. What I needed to hear from my dad was, "Don't take that shit. Kick his ass!" But neither of them knew I was being bullied because I never told anyone. I think I was ashamed, especially coming from the world I saw at home and around my extended family in New York. The men were in fights every other night and were very tough guys. They would hit you in the head with a pool cue and think nothing of it. Like I said, it was very Goodfellas. So I imagine that the shame of getting my ass kicked every day made me keep it a secret. My mom did have to come pick me up at school once in 3rd grade after I got tripped and thrown down at the bus stop, hitting the back of my head on the sidewalk. I just got up and got on the bus when it came, and when I got to school there was blood all over the back of my hair, and the teacher sent me to the nurse, and they called my mom. I had to have stitches. So she had to have known something. Years later, once I moved back to New York, I was determined that I would never be bullied again. I went the other way and became very loud and abrasive at times. I understand now, that was my way of dealing with the past trauma I went through—being loud, abrasive, a braggadocio. Some of that, though, was my natural excitement and passion for music and the music scene. When I was into something—a new band, a new album, a new song, a new nightclub—you knew it. I wanted to let everyone know about my latest discovery. When I got back to New York, there were times I must have appeared crazy to people because I never had any trouble with anyone ever again. Plus, everyone knew my dad. No one fucked with me.

My first job as an "amateur" DJ was at a 9th grade school dance in the lunch room. 1976 was the year, and I was 15. I owned an automatic turntable whose tonearm would lift up at the end of the record and return to its rest position with a home stereo receiver, 50 watts a channel, and two home stereo speakers. I had a major discussion with the kids in my school about what I would play. The black kids wanted to make sure that I played a lot of Parliament, Bar-Kays, O'Jays, Jimmy Castor Bunch, Brothers Johnson, etc. The white kids wanted to hear Kiss, Aerosmith, Ted Nugent, Led Zeppelin, and Queen. This is how people talked back

16

then. No one called our dark brothers and sisters African American—they were black. So my black friends would come to me and tell me, "Now make sure you play some black folks music," just like that. Same with the white kids: "Make sure you play some white music." It's how people talked in Georgia in 1976. We've come a long way, no matter what the media will have you believe. It was my first lesson in handling requests, but in the end, I was a hit! A natural, everyone said, even with one turntable. You had to wait until a record ended, then quickly take it off, and put on another. But I was fast and kept the party rockin'. Technics 1200 turntables didn't exist at this point, and disco mixers were crude or very high end and mostly unavailable. Even if they were available, I couldn't have afforded that stuff.

The white kids would say, "Hey, DJ....what's with the Soul Train shit? Let's hear some Zep or Kiss or something!" But I tended to play "black" music or soul music because that's what people, black and white danced to! Rock music is mostly not something you dance to. There are exceptions of course, but for the most part, you dance to soul and funk and later on, disco. Most rock music was just that: Rock. As Keith Richards says, "They got the rock, but lost the roll!" Every once in a while there was a rock and roll record that you could dance to: "Walk This Way" by Aerosmith, or "Lowdown" by Boz Scaggs. I just wanted to make people dance, no matter their color.

Once a year, every summer, I would visit New York to see my dad for a few weeks. I lived for this. I would get a taste of the beach clubs and Manhattan life and go to record stores in Manhattan like Bleecker Bob's in the Village and buy the coolest import records and clothes. It was such a lift for me. I felt plugged in and in touch. I subscribed to Punk magazine from New York City that you could only get mail order in Georgia. I could go to the drugstore in town and get Creem and Circus mags, but Punk was serious shit and only available mail order. I lived for the mail order. I started ordering punk 45s from Bleecker Bob's and would get little handwritten notes from Chris who worked for Bob for years and did the mail order back then. He would let me know about cool new stuff they had in stock, or he would throw in a band flyer or something. It's what got me through living in the sticks in Georgia for five years.

At the end of May 1977 I graduated 10th grade and was about to go into my junior year of high school. I hated school. I was glad it was over for a couple months, and I spent a lot of time dreaming of becoming Gene Simmons. I was Kiss obsessed, and Gene was it for me. Remember, back then you didn't know what Kiss looked like without makeup and knew very little about their personal lives. They were still viewed as rock superstars, not money-hungry, uncool egomaniacs. In 1977, they were still like aliens and superhero rock gods. They were still cool, and the biggest band on the planet. No one knew the product-hawking, money-obsessed Gene Simmons of today. So I was a major Kiss fan, but in the summer of 1976 I had discovered the Ramones, and I was also way deep into the punk scene, mostly of the UK variety. I loved the Ramones, but wasn't really into any other American punk bands except the Dead Boys. I liked the Sex Pistols, X-Ray Spex, The Clash, and Generation X. My Uncle Mike worked as a hairstylist in a salon called Town Shepard in Forest Hills, Queens, and he worked with Johnny Ramone's girlfriend. She washed hair there. He knew I liked the Ramones, so he asked Johnny's girlfriend to get me an autograph. That summer he got me this cool sticker of the first Ramones album autographed by Johnny: "To Michael, Johnny Ramone" written in red script. I still have it. Amazing.

I went to visit my dad in July for a few weeks, like I had been doing for the past three years, but this few weeks in New York would alter my life's course greatly. This was a pivotal year for pop and music culture in general, and it definitely was a pivotal year for me. 1977 saw the rise of punk rock into the American mainstream news media, the opening of Studio 54, and the rise of disco. The Son of Sam was loose in New York City and killing people, which was on the cover of all the newspapers almost every day, scaring the shit out of everyone, and there was the great blackout of 1977, coupled with a massive heat wave of 100 degree plus temperatures for two weeks, making that particular summer one I will never forget.

I got the first UK Sex Pistols and The Clash 45s at Bleecker Bob's and bought New York Rocker and Punk magazines. I picked up the free Village Voice newspaper and drooled over the club ads and who was playing at Max's Kansas City, CBGB, and Club 57. I bought clothes at JJ Flash—the rock star boutique on 59th Street where Kiss bought their street clothes—and cool rock t-shirts in little shops in the Village. In the daytime, we went to the beach, and at night my dad would take me around with him to some Long Island discos that he had an interest in, and I would hang out in the DJ booth and watch the DJ. I was in heaven. I had been playing records at my school dances in 9th and 10th grade, and I was very into the whole idea of playing records for people to dance to. The radio DJ was a different breed. I didn't want to talk; I wanted to make people dance and be right there when they did it. I was never one that danced myself, so playing records became my thing. Hanging in the DJ booth of a disco when I was 16 and watching the DJ play records was like heaven to me. People seriously danced back then. It was exciting to watch. They were into it, sweating, for hours. Other people were at the bar drinking alcohol, checking each other out. Discos were pick up joints really. The only people that cared about the music were on the dance floor. It was very much a Long Island, Brooklyn, Queens kind of thing. I checked out the women, who also checked me out. I was 16 and looked even younger. I always had a babyface. They were probably wondering what I was doing there in the DJ booth standing next to the DJ. I was in awe of the whole thing. Hooked.

My dad's girlfriend, who later on became his wife, took me all over Manhattan and showed me the city. She was cool and knew all the spots for records, clothes, Broadway, restaurants, etc. She took me to see *Beatlemania at* The Winter Garden Theater. My first Broadway experience. It was electric. The whole thing.

One day we went to visit her sister in Brooklyn. It was July 13th, hotter than hell, and that night the entire city was thrust into a blackout after a lightning strike at a power plant sent the entire city into darkness. Pitch black. There was massive looting going on, and I heard the glass breaking as the looters rushed the stores, along with the police and fire sirens and people screaming all night. There was no way we could leave—there was no power at all. Plus it was World War Three out there. We spent the night and went home the next morning. It was surreal walking out the door. It felt like a bomb had dropped. We got to the car, which was not damaged, and started to drive home, zigzagging through garbage and the remnants of the looting spree all over the streets. We survived the great blackout of 1977.

It was an exciting summer, that's for sure. Disco nightclubs, punk rock, Manhattan, the beach, a blackout, a serial killer, and a heat wave. As my brother, sister, and I waved goodbye to my dad at the airport, I was feeling great, but knew once I got back to Georgia, it would suck again, so I lived and breathed for every magazine, concert, record, or any band's appearance on *American Bandstand or The Midnight Special.* I was into a lot of music, so the scope was wide. I read every rock magazine I could get my hands on, cover to cover, multiple times. Even the fucking ads. I started my junior year of high school and was hating life. I had an asshole stepdad—my mother had gotten married to the goober—I had no car, lived in the woods, and had five television stations, one being a UHF channel, that all signed off at 2 AM. No cable TV back then. Hell, no smartphones, no NOTHING. Being in New York fucking City for almost a month, and then being dropped back into the woods, was like a shock to my system. I was having withdrawals. I was miserable.

So I put on the headphones and listened to the music. It was what sustained me.

In December of 1977, I went to see *Saturday Night Fever* in the theater, the week it opened. The movie actually opened on my birthday. I was shaken out of my bored existence of school and living in the woods by this film. This movie changed my life in a big way. It set me on a path back to New York, back to the nightclubs I had just experienced that summer, and put me on my path to becoming a real DJ in major nightclubs in Long Island and New York City.

Saturday Night Fever was monstrous: sold a gazillion records and was the top draw in theaters for over a year. It introduced a lifestyle and a music to America and the world that spread like the plague. It was a look at a life that most people didn't know existed in Brooklyn, but it was also a reflection of the small town mentality and macho male posturing that existed in every town. No future except the factory. That kind of life. I have seen it in New York, and I have seen it in Georgia. The only differences are the clothes and the accent. I went to see this movie probably ten times in the theaters that winter. I was obsessed with becoming a disco DJ and obsessed with going to see rock concerts any chance I could.

In the fall of 1977, I took a job at Camelot Records in the mall, which was 30 minutes away by car. But I had no car, which in a place like Georgia in the late 1970s, was essential. Everything was miles away from everything. It's not like in New York where you can just walk around the corner to a store or take the train or a cab. In rural Georgia, you had to drive miles and miles for anything. But I took the job and did the same thing that I did with the concerts. I would beg, plead, or hitchhike to get to work. But I did it, and I spent most of my paycheck on records. Camelot was getting punk import albums that cost a lot more than American albums, but I didn't care, and I bought a lot of them. That fall of 1977 I was buying albums by the Sex Pistols, The Clash, Dead Boys, Ramones, Richard Hell, The Saints, Ian Dury, The

Runaways, and Talking Heads, but also listening to Billy Joel, Con Funk Shun, Kiss, Brothers Johnson, Piper, Rufus and Chaka Khan, The Godz, Harold Melvin & the Blue Notes, Angel, Parliament, Aerosmith, Ohio Players, and ELO. I loved music, not just any one genre, and that's what you heard on the radio: a mishmash of so many styles and genres. Rock, R&B, pop, country, soul, hard rock—you heard it all on AM and FM radio. Radio was so important to me. I grew up with it. I would call into the radio stations and talk to the DJs and make requests. It was the heartbeat of music and of the song. For a musician or band, more than any other medium, it was radio that made you a star. That all changed with the advent of MTV in the mid 80s, but radio was where it was at in 1977. That and concerts, and I was a student of both.

Around the same time Saturday *Night Fever* premiered, I heard via the local TV news channel that the Sex Pistols were going to do a US tour, and the first show was going to be in Atlanta in January. I was a big Pistols fan and had the UK singles of "Anarchy in the UK" and "Pretty Vacant" and had gotten the Never Mind the Bollocks album the week it was released. I was hooked early. I had to go see this. How could I not?! They were changing music, pop culture, and the world. The songs spoke to me, they looked like no one had before, and the "normal" world hated them. Hated what they looked like, and what they represented. Johnny Rotten was so smart, and so clever. He just gave it to 'em—"Bollocks to you and piss off." No one knew what to say to that. Rock music would never be the same after the Sex Pistols. This was also a major mainstream media event. The hype about the disgusting Sex Pistols that launched from the UK had followed them to America. The news media were all over it. Atlanta was about two hours from where I lived, and I had no idea how I was going to get there. I had only been to Atlanta once before for a concert—Shaun Cassidy at The Omni—that I took my sister to 'cause she loved him. I went with some other friends, and their parents drove us all up. Hitchhiking to Atlanta would be tough, so I had to rely on someone that would drive me, and no one in my town had any clue who the Sex Pistols were, and those that did know and knew that I liked them thought I was a crazy person. I finally got the older brother of a girl I knew to take me. I didn't really know him, but my girl friend begged him to do it because I think she liked me. Her brother was into music and had heard about the Pistols. He was curious, as was 90% of the audience that night. They wanted to see the "car crash." This gig changed my life. Again. We drove to Atlanta and the show not talking a lot 'cause I didn't know him. He listened to Black Sabbath 8-tracks the whole way there. We got to the show, and the venue was in a shopping center: The Great Southeastern Music Hall. We didn't have tickets, and it was a crazy scene outside. I never had an issue buying a ticket at the box office for any show in Columbus because none of them ever sold out. This was Atlanta, it was different, and it was a major media event. TV crews everywhere; pretend punks running around. Long-haired rock guys and girls listening to the Ramones and the Sex Pistols blasting from car stereo 8-track players. We got up to the box office and were told the show was sold out. I could see through the window that there was a girl in the box office that was wearing a Warner Bros. Records t-shirt standing in the back. I had my Camelot Records badge with me that I wore at work and pulled it out and showed the guy in the window my badge asking him if he could get the Warner Bros. girl for me, which he did. She came up, and I showed her my work badge and said I worked at Camelot Records and just did a Pistols display at my store (which was a lie), and I was told that there would be tickets here for me to buy. I gave her my store manager's name and some other random info and looked in her eyes like, Hey, *I'm supposed to be here.* She must have liked me, and I guess I sounded convincing because she said there were no more tickets to buy, but here are some press passes to get in, thanking me for supporting the band with an in-store display in a major chain. I couldn't believe it! We were in! There was no way I would have been allowed to put up a Sex Pistols display at my store! It was all ELO, Barbara Streisand, the Bee Gees, and Billy Joel. My "ride" was shocked that I got us in! He thought we drove all that way for nothing! We walked in, and I tried to get as close as I could to the stage, but it was packed tightly, and there was a hostile vibe in the air. Once the band took the stage, the place erupted. I had never felt this kind of energy at a concert before. A Kiss show had incredible energy, but it wasn't like this. This was scary and real, like a bar brawl. I was in a trance watching it all, as bottles, glasses, and ashtrays careened around the room and at the stage. The crowd had heard about what was expected at a punk show from the relentless media propaganda, and they gave them what they wanted. People were just generally being rowdy and wild and acting nuts. Sid, Rotten, and Steve looked like aliens, leering and thrashing at the lip of the stage, all attitude. TV cameras filmed the carnage, only white light shining on the stage, the better to light it all up for the cameras. They played what I thought was a short set, and then it was over. We stumbled out, ears ringing, found the car, and drove back home in silence. I couldn't get to sleep for two days. My life would not be the same after seeing the Sex Pistols at The Great Southeastern Music Hall, Atlanta, GA, January 5, 1978.

The combination of hanging in the DJ booth at New York discos the previous summer, Saturday *Night Fever*, and seeing the first US show by the Sex Pistols put me on a course back to the action in New York. As soon as my junior year of high school was over, early June 1978, I had my dad drive down and pick me up, and move me back to Cedarhurst. It was like moving back to the heartbeat of life. I finally got a car: a 1969 red GTO with a white top.

I felt like I was let out of prison. I was 17.

I was a serious rock and roll fan, having worshipped at the altar of Kiss, Aerosmith, the Stones, and The Who since I was 12 years old, so I was never what you would call a disco person. I just enjoyed discos and nightclubs and the whole decadent vibe of it all. I was a disco DJ, but still attended dozens of rock concerts and rock clubs a month. I was the DJ at my school dances in 9th, 10th, and 11th grade; bar mitzvahs and sweet sixteens at real deal Long Island discos like Twigs, Buttons, and Club 231 on Saturday and Sunday afternoons; teen discos like Shuffles and Our Gang on weekends; and filled in for established DJs when they needed a night off, usually on slower nights like Monday or Tuesday at places like Club 147. I learned and studied constantly and was always hanging around in the DJ booths of every club I could. I was obsessed with becoming the DJ that could rock a big crowd from 9 PM till 4 AM and have a line of a thousand people waiting to get in all night.

And I did. I became that guy. I worked my way up and got into the real clubs—the big clubs on Long Island with capacities of 2,000-3,000 people that were filled five nights a week. 2,000 people out on a Tuesday night. Of course, the drinking age was still 18, and a New York State driver's license had no picture on it, so everyone went out to the clubs. Everyone. It was glorious.

My first day of Senior High School in New York 1978, I walked into health class and saw a guy with a shorter version of the Punky Meadows haircut and a Kiss guitar pick earring hanging in his ear sitting across the aisle from me. This was Scott Levitt. I was wearing an Ace Frehley t-shirt, and he asked me if I liked Kiss, and of course I said yes—I was wearing a Kiss shirt. From that day on, we bonded. He ended up getting me in trouble on the final test day when he was sticking his tongue out like Gene Simmons, and we were both laughing and goofing around. The teacher, Mr. Gulley, told us both to shut up and gave us a failing grade. I had to go to summer school to make up the credit. Luckily the summer school warden was cool . Some of the guys in the class put brakes on his '72 Camaro for him, and he let us skate through the class. Once a week for an hour wasn't bad, and I just showed up and drew Kiss and Sex Pistols logos on my notebook.

Through Scott, I met future Danger Danger mastermind Bruno Ravel, who lived in Rego Park, Queens. What the three of us shared was a love of Kiss, Angel, Starz, and Aerosmith. We were rockers who liked cool looking bands, glam, pop, rock, nightclubs, Capezios, satin jackets, and chicks—but we were all obsessed with Kiss.

SCOTT LEVITT: *"This is how Bruno and I met: In the summertime, I went to sleepaway camp, and I knew Scott Gelfand (a mutual friend of Bruno and myself) from camp. Scott and I both* *liked Zeppelin, ZZ Top, Trower, and Mountain. When camp ended, I would go visit Scott at his house in Queens, and one time when I went he said, 'My friend Bruno's here, you should come meet him.' Bruno lived near Scott. Bruno had a boombox and was playing the first Kiss record. I had Hotter than Hell and I didn't like it, but Bruno had Dressed to Kill and Alive! too, and he was so excited about presenting it to me. And that got me into it, the way he was so into it. He really got me into Kiss because I liked Bruno. This was 1975. And then we tried to make a band together. He played the cello, and I played the guitar. I'm not sure if he was playing the bass yet. He would come over my house in Long Island, and we would play.*

Then, two years later, Bruno and I played at my high school jam night. We were probably 16 or 17. We were already going to Gildersleeves [sleazy Lower East Side rock club], defining how to dress with Capezios and satin pants and stuff. We went and saw Kiss at the Garden when we were 16 before we ever went to Gildersleeves in February 1977 on the Rock and Roll Over Tour. Bruno had already seen them out at the Nassau Coliseum."

Those two guys introduced me to the New York City rock scene and nightclubs like The Great Gildersleeves and Trax, but mainly Gildersleeves. That's where the coolest bands played, or at least bands we thought were cool. Bands like Hotshot, The Brats, Lover, Falcon Eddy, and Wowii. Now at the same time, you had the CBGB punk scene going on, but we were not punks (well, I kind of was and still am sometimes). The Great Gildersleeves was on the Bowery in Manhattan, a couple blocks away from CBGB. Back in 1979, the Bowery was a rundown, fucked up place where bums would sleep on the street and piss against buildings. That's what attracted these clubs and bars to that area: cheap rent. The street was surrounded by hookers, drug dealers, bums, psychopaths, criminals, and garbage. It was pretty much free reign on the Lower East Side of Manhattan then. No one gave a fuck about what went on most nights. It was a fertile ground for the exploding punk scene out of CBGB that had been going on now for a few years already.

Bruno was the first of us to go to The Great Gildersleeves:

BRUNO RAVEL: *"In high school in the late 70s, I took a class called 'Plays in Production,' which included a few class trips to see Broadway and Off-Broadway shows. One of those trips was to see Shakespeare's Hamlet at the Jean Cocteau Repertory, a theater that just happened to be on the Bowery right across the street from The Great Gildersleeves. I had already been to Max's Kansas City and had heard of The Great Gildersleeves, but had never been.*

I first heard about it and the whole Lower East Side scene from a photographer who sold buttons outside the venues at all the rock shows named George. He was super friendly and would tell us about all the cool bands and cool shows, clubs, etc. Through our connection with George, we discovered Rik Fox, a fixture on the scene. He looked cooler than anyone I had ever met! He was at pretty much every show that mattered and always had a backstage pass. When I looked across the street and saw the lit up marquee reading: 'Tonight! Murder Inc. and Dina Regine,' I thought to myself, 'Whoa! There it is! Gildersleeves! I gotta check this place out!'

The next semester, I made sure to select that class again as an elective, and after we attended another performance at Jean Cocteau, a friend and I made our way across the street and were able to get in, even though we were underage with some fake IDs. Of course, I immediately told Scott about it and that we had to go together."

I first met Bruno when we all went to Gildersleeves together one night. Scott and I drove to Queens in his mom's giant Cadillac and picked up Bruno. He walked out of his apartment building and got in the car. Scott introduced us, and we talked about music and stuff on the drive to Manhattan. I was wearing a pullover, long sleeve American flag t-shirt that I inherited from my hippie uncle. A leftover from the Woodstock days.

Bruno on meeting me for the first time:

BRUNO RAVEL: *"I thought to myself, 'Who is this guy wearing that shirt?!' Corky [Corky Gunn is my nickname and Sweet Pain stage name. "Corky" comes from a mispronunciation of my last name by a teacher in grade school, and "Gunn" comes from Tommy Gunn, the guitarist in Piper] was bouncing off the walls. We were sitting at one of those long tables in Gildersleeves, and Corky was talking a lot and going nuts."*

I was definitely a hyper kid and teen and pretty much still am. I naturally have a lot of energy. I get jacked up when I am involved in something that excites me—music, bands, films, nightclubs, records, books. etc. So I was blowing their cool, I guess. I was too excited to be at this cool rock club in Manhattan that members of Kiss and Starz hung out in, but we bonded and became great friends right there and then. Bruno and I went to so many shows together. Concerts like Kiss, Judas Priest, Aerosmith, Pat Travers, Van Halen, Rainbow, Journey, Bryan Adams, Iron Maiden, Mötley Crüe, Loverboy, Duran Duran, Ratt, W.A.S.P., and of course, many nights traveling the tri-state area to see Twisted Sister. We both loved Twisted Sister.

BRUNO RAVEL: *"The first time I went to Gildersleeves, I was 15 or 16 years old. I had my brother's driver's license. There was no picture on the ID back then. From going to see Twisted Sister at Speaks, I knew how it worked with the ID thing already. I tried to get into Speaks one summer night, and the bouncer nailed me* on the ID. I had to wait outside for hours because the guys I went with that drove me, didn't want to leave. The bouncer wouldn't let me try to find my friends or go in to make a phone call or anything. I stood outside and had no clue how I would get home—I wasn't gonna wait out there all night until 4 AM. I either took the railroad home, or I called someone and got them to take me home. I can't remember. The bouncer nailed me on the height. My brother was shorter than me, 5'7, and I'm well over 6 feet tall barefoot—and I was wearing heels.

The second time I went, I wore Capezios, and I kind of hunched over. After that, I got it down. They asked me for the matching zodiac sign to the birthday on the license, and I learned that too. We would test each other so we got the ID questions down. So I learned the ID ropes.

Gildersleeves was totally underground in 1978 and 1979. It was not the hip scene. It was almost like a dinosaur kind of leftover scene from the New York Dolls days. Elvis Costello and short hair and skinny ties were the hip thing. Gildersleeves was not that. Manhattan was a real scene, though. You had to dress the part, and you wanted to be part of the culture. It was driven by the musicians. Long Island was about cover bands and people that wanted to just party. People didn't go to see the bands—they were there for the party and to get drunk, not necessarily the band.

Bands that played in Manhattan were trying to get signed to a record deal. When Hall & Oates played Gildersleeves, Paul Stanley was there with Cher's sister. When Trigger played at Gildersleeves when they got signed, Gene Simmons was there. Gene got them their deal. You could see rock stars at Gildersleeves. When Hotshot played, Billy Squier was there. Everyone in Gildersleeves knew who he was. Even though he was only in Piper at the time, and he hadn't gone solo. But he was a star already at The Great Gildersleeves.

You went there for the culture and the scene and maybe you would like the band—you would take your friend's advice and either you got into it or you didn't. Like, 'Hey, you have to see The Brats,' or 'You have to see Murder Inc. Go check em out.' It was a nightclub, a speakeasy. That's where you went to get together and meet people. It was a meeting place for like minded people. A club where you would go at night to congregate and see what was going on. You didn't hear The Brats or Hotshot on the radio. They played original songs, but didn't have record deals. They weren't cover bands that played songs you already knew. You maybe discovered them in the club after going for the scene, not necessarily the band, and maybe you liked them after you heard them. It was a weird way to discover music. You didn't go see The Brats because you heard a song on the radio or someone gave you their album and said, 'Check this out, and oh by the way, they are playing at Gildersleeves.' No. It was like, 'Hey, did you hear this *band, The Brats, are playing Gildersleeves and they're really cool.' You would have to take your friends word for it, and then you would go and make your own decision about it.*

I was dressing up and wearing makeup and heels. To go to Gildersleeves, you had to look the part! We dressed like chicks. Glam-y. On the subway! It was crazy. I took the train like that! I stole money from my parents to go see Kiss and other bands. That's terrible! My brother caught me and ratted me out. I was obsessed. I might have committed crimes to go to those concerts. What if my parents didn't have money for me to steal? I might have done some crazy stuff! I had to go! Obsessed!

My friend, Peter Mercurio, was rich and always had money. Mitch Pfeiffer also had money. His parents would buy him a ticket to go see someone for 100 dollars. I had no hookups for tickets. My parents weren't giving me 100 dollars for a concert ticket. That was a lot of money! We weren't rich. I was lucky if I got 20 dollars to do anything. I stole from my parents four or five times. I just took it! The fact that I would do that—it was just crazy! That's why I'm so obsessed with locks and safes and stuff now! It's not gonna happen to me! Steve West [future Danger Danger drummer and Bruno's songwriting partner] didn't steal money from his parents like me! He was a goody-goody. His parents didn't let him out!

After Gildersleeves closed for the night, we all used to go to a place called Phebes, a restaurant down the street from Gildersleeves that served great French onion soup. Classy!"

SCOTT LEVITT: *"We saw in Rock Scene Magazine that Ace Frehley from Kiss produced The Brats' demos. So we knew about The Brats and Gildersleeves that way too.*

Gildersleeves was like artists showcasing their record—on the Island it was about selling drinks and packing them in, making people drink. We saw Hardcore. After Starz broke up, Richie Ranno and Joe X. Dube did Hardcore. We saw The Flying Tigers with Dennis Dunaway and Neal Smith from the original Alice Cooper band. T. Roth and Another Pretty Face. Wowii used to pack Gildersleeves. The Brats were the biggest band, and Wowii was second biggest. Falcon Eddy played every week. Also Hotshot and Murder Inc. They were the house bands. They played every week.

The Brats were so big, they were like rock stars. The audience for the bands came from Brooklyn, Queens, and New Jersey. It wasn't a Manhattan crowd, really, at Gildersleeves.

The band Susan was great, but Susan was too good for Gildersleeves. They had graduated from that whole scene. They already had a record deal on RCA when they were playing Gildersleeves, but they really didn't have a draw. During the week, it was a showcase type thing. The Brats were a big draw, so they played on the weekends, and during the week, the club was more experimental. But The Brats looked like stars man, they looked professional and groomed, played good guitars, and had good equipment. Very cool. The bands that played Gildersleeves played to get signed, not to make money. Twisted Sister was making crazy money playing covers and packing them in on Long Island, but the Manhattan bands were just trying to get a record deal. Gene and Paul from Kiss were there when Hall & Oates played. They were standing right next to us. Paul had a beard and mustache, and Gene had the handkerchief in front of his face. They had the JJ Flash clothes on, the boots. They had the limos outside. It was unbelievable. It was their peak. I went to the bathroom one night at Gildersleeves, and I'm standing at the urinal next to Joe X. Dube from Starz. He had his leather jacket on, and it's him! Right next to me! That guy's like a Kiss guy. Their manager, Bill Aucoin, was all about advertising and promoting, Circus and Creem magazine had ads for Starz, Angel, and Kiss every issue, so you could see guys and bands that were coming up. It was all right there. They were young guys, rock stars. It was very exciting, cool stuff. I'll never forget that. And Rock Scene was a local New York-based magazine, New York City stuff, but it got national distribution. It was all the Lisa Robinson, Richard Robinson thing, New York Dolls thing—the cool people. The Kiss guys were New York guys—Italian,

Jewish—it was a real homegrown thing. It's all New York. You're right there. It's amazing. It was a special time."

We had to be at any hot club, concert, or event. We were obsessed. At least Bruno and I were. To give an example of what we went through to get to Gildersleeves, when you "had to be there," to not miss a "hot night," a "hot show," etc., I'll let Bruno tell the story about the "gay" truck driver.

BRUNO RAVEL: *"One night there was a benefit for the band Hotshot to help with the cost of replacing their equipment, which had been stolen a week prior. All the bands played: Hotshot, The Brats, Lover, Murder Inc., Wowii, Moonbeam—everyone. I had to go. I begged my parents, "Please let me go? I will do anything!" They replied, "No way! You're 16 years old! You're not taking the subway by yourself! You aren't going. Forget it!" So what did I do? Well, of course I waited until my mother fell asleep and stole my her car, like any good son would, and went to Gildersleeves! Mitch Pfeiffer and his friend Lance went too. I hung out with them all night and had a blast.*

At around 2 AM, I realized that I should go, so I leaned over to Mitch and said, "I gotta leave and get home before my mother knows I'm gone. See ya later." I left, got into my mom's car, put the key in the ignition, and...nothing. It wouldn't start. My heart sank. I was dead! I tried again. Nothing. I was fucked. Luckily, I had some money on me, money I had saved. I had like a hundred bucks on me, which was a lot of money back then. I ran back into the club and Mitch was still there, thank God! I asked Mitch to please come outside and help me jump my car. He said, 'Alright, alright, I'll come.' Mitch pulled his car around and we hooked up the jumper cables and tried to start my car. Nothing. Completely dead. Now I was really fucked. 'What the fuck am I gonna do?' I said. 'I don't know what to tell ya man, but I gotta get home,' Mitch said. 'Can you at least hang out with me long enough to make sure I'm gonna get home alright?' I asked. He agreed and stayed with me an extra half hour before he had to leave.

There was that gas station that used to be across the street from Gildersleeves that was open 24/7; I went in there. I was fucking 16 years old, I didn't have a driver's license or any ID, and I walked in and said, 'I need to get my car towed.' Meanwhile, I had my puka shells on and my heels and satin pants and a fucking huckapoo shirt on. The whole 70s Gildersleeves outfit, makeup and mascara and shit. Everything! That's how we used to go to Gildersleeves. We used to dress up like rock stars! I went into the gas station, and the attendant told me the tow truck driver is gone and he'll be back in 45 minutes or so and to come back then. I went back into Gildersleeves totally dejected. I was just gonna have to wait and worry. After an hour or so, Gildersleeves was emptying out, and the club was closing. I walked back to the gas station, and now it's four in the morning. I waited and waited and finally the tow truck driver arrived, He said to me, 'Alright, *where's your car?' It was literally around the corner from the gas station.*

We drove around the corner to my car, and he tried to start it, and said, "Yep, your starter is gone." Whatever, I didn't care I just wanted to get home, so I told him to tow the car. He hooked the car to his tow truck, I got in the front of the tow truck, and he started driving. I'm shitting my pants. There was that famous corner of Houston and Delancey Street where that dry cleaners used to be; it was a known hangout for hookers and right near Gildersleeves. We drove down Bowery and made the left on Houston Street going towards the Williamsburg Bridge. I gave him my address and told him that I knew exactly how to get home: Williamsburg Bridge to the BQE, blah, blah, blah.

We approach that famous corner, and of course there are hookers standing right in front. The tow truck driver said, 'Hey man, look at those fucking hookers!' I was so scared, I said, 'Yeah man, that's where they always stand, ha ha ha.' He said, 'Yeah man, sometimes I go over there and get a blowjob.' I was trying to be cool, so I nervously said, 'Ha ha yeah man ! Cool!' We continued driving, and he starts talking about sex more and more, about chicks and hookers, and he's asking me all about the rock scene. 'You look like you get a lot of girls,' he said. He had no idea I was 16! 'You know, I pick up all kinds of customers. I tow cars all over the place. Sometimes people don't have the money to pay me, and

41

I might have to fuck 'em up,' he said. Then, he leaned over, opened the glovebox, and showed me his gun. 'Just in case there's any trouble,' he said. 'Oh wow! That's fucked up,' I replied. He continued, 'One time, I towed a guy and he didn't have the money to pay me, so I let him blow me.' When he said that I froze up. 'Is that something you'd be into?' he said. 'Ha ha, no man! I have cash, I'll pay you! I'm not into that sort of thing,' I replied. 'Okay, well, you might want to think about that. You could save yourself a lot of money,' he replied back.

From that moment on, I was silent and on edge. Scared shitless. He was this big fucking dude. He showed me a fucking gun, and he told me about guys that blow him when they don't have the money! Insane! So now we made our way over the Williamsburg Bridge, onto the BQE headed toward my apartment, and all of a sudden, he got off at the wrong exit. That's when I lost my mind. 'Hey! What are you doing, man? This is not my exit," I said. 'I got to make a quick phone call. It will be a minute,' he replied. He pulled the truck off the highway onto the service road of the BQE, and there was a payphone there, and he got out and makes a phone call. I was sitting there looking in the rearview mirror, looking in the side mirrors, looking at him, freaking out, wondering what I should do. Should I run? I was sweating. Cut to the chase—he came back to the truck and thankfully drives me home, but the story isn't over yet.

The driveway that led into the parking garage was under my apartment building, down an incline. He left the car in the driveway, but not in the garage because the tow truck couldn't fit through the door. I paid him, and he leaves the car right there. At that moment, I was so relieved, but then I realized that the sun is starting to come up and I'm standing outside in the street with my mother's car! Shit! How was I gonna get this car into my mom's parking spot? There was no one to help me, but I had nothing to lose, so I just went for it. I opened the garage door, used all my might, and pushed the car and it started to roll down the driveway. I ran, jumped into the car as it's rolling down the driveway, shut the door, and steered the car. It glided into the garage and it got close to the parking spot, but not nearly close enough. It was getting close to the time that my mom was gonna wake up to go to work. I pushed the car again with all my might and got it close to the parking spot. The spot was on a slight incline. My mother would always park it close to the wall. I had to get the car close to the wall, and I just couldn't do it. I had my JJ Flash boots on—my red shoes! I kept slipping! I put my arms underneath the bumper, in the back of the car, put it in neutral, used all my strength to push it as far as I could with the car in neutral, and then tried to run around to the driver's side to slam it in park, but when I ran around the car, it would roll back down the incline—back to square one. I started to cry out of frustration. I didn't go through all this shit, almost get raped at gunpoint by a gay tow truck driver to get caught now! I gathered my strength and tried a few more times. The insides of my arms were bleeding 'cause the metal bumper was ripping my skin every time I would push it. So I said, fuck it, and gave it one last shot. I got it close and it started rolling back down the hill. I jumped in and I threw it in park again. That was it. I couldn't do it anymore. I was drenched in sweat. I was done. It was like 6:30 in the morning. I took my shoes off and went up to my apartment, not making a sound. I quietly opened the door, got in my room, put my shoes in the closet, took my clothes off, and got in bed. I made it!

Ten minutes later, my mom wakes up. Now I was freaking out again. I pretended like I was asleep. About a half hour goes by, and all of a sudden, my mom comes in my room and shakes my shoulders. 'Bruno? Bruno,' she says. 'What mom?' faking being woken up from a sound sleep, I replied. 'The car won't start! What am I gonna do?' 'Uhhh, ehhh...I don't know mom,' I said. In the end, they never caught me. My parents never knew. They were shocked when I told them years later."

BRUNO RAVEL: "In the summer of 1980, I started working the Dr. Pepper Central Park Music Festival. My dad was connected with people in the stagehands union and got me the job. I saw amazing bands that whole summer. Eddie Money and Pat Benatar, Devo, The Pretenders, The Cars. That's where I got

44

into Utopia. I saw Cheap Trick on the Found All the Parts tour. Amazing."

I went to some of those Central Park shows. It was the Dr. Pepper Central Park Music Festival. Bruno would get me in early before the doors opened, and I'd run to the front. There weren't reserved seats; first come, first served. Once, I went with a girl I was way into named Dana. I met her at a Lipstick (Bruno's first band) show in Huntington at some bar, and we were a thing for the summer of 1980. I was so into her. I took her to The Pretenders at Central Park, and Bruno let us in the side gate right before the doors opened, and we were front row for The Pretenders. That show is in my top 20 concerts of all time. They were so good. It was the original band with Pete Farndon and James Honeyman-Scott. There was a crazy girl in the row behind us, freaking out on acid, and pulling her dress up and fingering herself. Insanity. I took Dana to see what we thought was a "rare" club show for Starz at Gildersleeves on September 6, 1980. We didn't know it at the time, but it was the end of Starz. But they were so good that night. After the show, I drove Dana back to my house singing Starz songs all the way. She spent the night. We were kids. But I will never forget that summer. Good times.

STEVE WEST: *"I remember Eddie Money and The Babys at Central Park, and The Records opening for The Cars there, also. Those were incredible shows. I remember when Corky gave Rick*

Nielsen from Cheap Trick that giant guitar pick at the Palladium, around the same time. Corky got some promo pick from one of the companies, and it was oversized—bigger than his hand! Bun E. Carlos played with those giant drumsticks on the last song, and we knew that, so when they started that last song, Corky gave the giant pick to Rick, and he played with it! That was so cool!"

BRUNO RAVEL: *"Gildersleeves pretty much ended after the fire. The Brats played one night, and they always had a great stage show. They had TV screens everywhere and threw out 'Brats money,' and used lots of flashpots like Kiss, for the smoke and flash bomb effect. I'll never forget it, because I smuggled my boombox into Gildersleeves and recorded the whole thing on cassette. The Brats were on stage playing Sweet's 'AC-DC,' and in the chorus, there was singing and then out of nowhere, BOOM! Everyone started screaming and rushed outside. No one thought it was a big deal. It didn't seem like anyone was seriously injured.*

Ten minutes later, my friends and I were outside talking, looking at the commotion; police, fire trucks, etc; and that was it. They told us to go home, and that the night was over. What we didn't realize was, that was the end of the club and The Brats for awhile. One of the club's patrons had been burned by the faulty flash pot, and they sued the club and sued The Brats, and that was the end of it. The club reopened eventually, but it wasn't the same. The Brats reformed as The Secrets, but it was the end of an era. That's when Steve started going there. That scene is long gone and will never ever, ever happen again. It's like classical music or something. Never coming back. It's crazy."

Bruno and I went to Gildersleeves and to Twisted Sister concerts all through 1978, 1979, and into 1980. I graduated high school in June 1979 and started my quest to work as a DJ and to work in the music biz.

That summer, I was always hanging out at the local, cool record store in Cedarhurst called Platterpuss. Platterpuss supplied the neighborhood with black light posters, records, cheap promos, cool bootlegs, and weed. I was always yapping away and bugging the owner, so looking for a way to get me out of his hair, he started telling me about a warehouse that was looking for help—a record distributor across the street from Kennedy airport, ten minutes from my house. The distributor imported records from Europe and sold them to stores in the US. He told me I should go there and ask for a job. He gave me the guy's name and number. I called the guy, and he told me to come down to the distributor address. I drove down to New York Boulevard by the airport and met the owner, Barry. Barry hired me to work in the warehouse. Man, I just got the sweetest job ever, working days at Important Record Distributors (IRD). I had access to the hottest and newest import rock, reggae, dance, punk, and new wave records, plus UK magazines and music newspapers.

I had received test pressings of "Dancing with Myself" by Generation X and "Dreaming of Me" by Depeche Mode. Every day, amazing records came through the doors. Records I was holding in my hands for the very first time that would go on to become classics. This was such a fertile time for music and to be a DJ. Disco, rock, punk, reggae, and this new thing, rap, were all coming together to create the biggest and hottest dance club scene in Long Island history. For a DJ, this connection and the ready access to the hottest records before anyone else, was like hitting the lottery. I played some of the new stuff at the clubs I worked at, but most of the crowd didn't really dig the progressive new music. Yet. But one club, Malibu, had the hippest scene going on Long Island. Located on the ocean in Lido Beach, it was the biggest and hottest new wave dance club on the Island's South Shore, near Jones Beach. It was one of the top five live music venues and nightclubs in the New York City area. I was there Halloween night 1980 for The B-52's. Their new album, *Wild Planet*, had just come out, and it was super packed, probably 3,000 people. I met a girl there that night who I dated for awhile. One night while she was driving us home after Malibu and a stop at a local motel, we had a head-on collision. I was super drunk and passed out in the passenger street, and she was driving her little Toyota Corolla. She wasn't sober either, and she fell asleep driving hitting a Lincoln head on. I went through the windshield and was out of commission for about a month—stitches, plastic surgery, broken teeth, crushed chest plate, lacerated legs, and busted knees. I was in the hospital for a day and then went home, going back and forth to the doctors for weeks. I laid up in bed at home, and my grandmother took care of me, nursing me back to health. Scott came to visit me, and I had a big bandage on my head. He said I looked like Peter Criss from Kiss on the *Spirit of '76* poster.

I started bringing the house DJ at Malibu, Bart Dorsey, all the hottest import records from IRD, and we became friends. When he left Malibu to go manage a club in Manhattan called Youthanasia, he suggested me as his replacement, and I was in.

I started working at Malibu in 1981. Malibu held 3,000 people packed to the rafters and featured all the big new wave and post-punk bands of the day. There were concerts three to four nights a week with shows by the Ramones, the B-52's, Squeeze, U2, Siouxsie and the Banshees, the Plasmatics, OMD, Todd Rundgren, The Knack, Adam Ant, etc. I would DJ before, after, and in between the bands.

STEVE WEST: *"Bruno and I used to go to Malibu, and we asked Corky to play the OMD song 'Enola Gay.' We loved that song. We went to see The Knack at Malibu, and we got backstage and met Sharona. We couldn't believe it!"*

49

After awhile, the DJs who hung out at Malibu all the time from the local radio station, WLIR, started asking me what certain records were. Guys like Ray White, Larry "The Duck," John DeBella, and Denis McNamara. The station sponsored a local band competition at Malibu on Sundays, and the jocks were at the club a lot. We got tight, and I invited them to come by IRD and pick up their own copies of the songs I was playing. They would then play them on the air, making them hits. In response to this new boom of music coming over from the UK, and the turning of the tide as far as what the "hip" thing was at radio, they started a new format for WLIR, "new wave." "Dare to Be Different." It worked big time, and WLIR became one of the leading stations in the country, as far as breaking new music, a lot of it only available as UK imports.

Naturally, all the US record company promo reps started showing up at Malibu and giving me records, asking me to play them and report them. By this time, I was sending my weekly playlist to stations such as WKTU, WABC, and Billboard magazine. I also joined Rockpool, the first and only rock, punk, and new wave record pool. I drove my '69 GTO over the Williamsburg Bridge onto Delancey Street to Rockpool's offices to pick up my weekly box of records religiously. I reported to Rockpool and had my playlists featured in their nightclub reporter section. They had charts and playlist sections for radio, retail, and club play. Reporting to the stations and Rockpool was a big deal. I got so many free records from all the labels and Rockpool, it was insane. I think now about how hot vinyl is again, and if I saved every record, I could have had an insane collection! Those records got abused though, in more ways than one! I also would go to all the major record labels in Manhattan once a week. I would have boxes of stuff to lug home on the train. It was an incredible period. The golden days of the record labels. You walked in the door of the CBS Black Rock building or the WEA building, and the energy was off the charts. I had the desire to turn the club crowds onto new songs and new sounds, and I was excited to play them. I had so many promo records given to me in any given week, plus the imports I was getting daily from working at IRD, plus the stuff I actually bought every week. Being able to play that music for a crowd of 2,000 people every night was a high that I have never matched in all my time working in music.

One night, Larry Braverman from Elektra Records came to Malibu and knocked on the DJ booth door, asking me to play a record he thought would be a hit there: "Johnny Are You Queer?" by Josie Cotton. I played it for Larry, and we became friends. He added me to the mailing lists for promos and always took great care of me with things like concert tickets, etc., so, naturally, when Elektra signed Mötley Crüe, I was excited. I already had Mötley's debut record Too Fast for Love that was released on their own label, Leathür Records. I loved Mötley Crüe from my first listen and turned Bruno and Steve and the guys onto them. When

Mötley Crüe came to Elektra's New York City offices one day, shortly after their signing, I happened to be there picking up records and met them briefly. I didn't see them again until January 1984 when they were opening for Ozzy Osbourne.

It was at Malibu that the DJ groupies started. Now, working as a DJ, I had met girls at the clubs I worked at and taken them out to the car after work or maybe to their house or something—kids stuff—but it was not what I would call a groupie-type encounter. Malibu was a very big club, both in size and prestige. There were big bands playing every week and crowds in the thousands every night, so it was on a large scale. It was 1981, and the drinking age was still 18. Thousands of people came to Malibu every night. This was my first experience playing records in a club this large. I had access to drink tickets and was able to put people on the guest list. This brings power. I started noticing girls really coming on to me at Malibu. It got really crazy. You get in that zone, and it just happens every night, and it's your job. It's what you do for a living. How could I not want to do this forever? I worked five days a week at IRD and was a DJ four nights a week at Malibu. On my nights off, I went to see numerous bands, both in concert and in nightclubs. I didn't sleep a lot. Things were starting to get out of hand.

Chapter Two - Local New York Bands, New York Friends, & Drugs - 1979-1992

In 1979, Bruno Ravel started playing in a local band called Lipstick. They were from Queens and had a girl drummer. They did cover songs and played the bars on Long Island and Queens. Joe Jackson, Lou Reed, The Cars, Alice Cooper, and Thin Lizzy was the setlist.

I went to see them as often as I could between working day and night and partying the rest of the time. Bruno and I became good buds and went to a lot of concerts and clubs together, mainly seeing Twisted Sister or The Brats. Bruno played in a lot of bands over the years. One of which, Hotshot (they took the name from the Gildersleeves band after they broke up), was a new wave cover band from Long Island, and they were my favorite. They played all the hot clubs, performing songs by Duran Duran, The Cars, Thompson Twins, The Police, and all the new wave hits of the day. That band also featured Steve West as the drummer. Steve and Bruno would eventually form Danger Danger in 1987. Danger Danger were signed to Sony/Epic Records and had a successful run in the hair band era, released multiple records, and are still active to this day.

Bruno also played in Talas, White Lion, and Michael Bolton's band for the Everybody's Crazy tour. Yes, Michael Bolton used to rock! The roadie and light man for Hotshot was Kelly "Blade" Nickels. Hotshot was a springboard to so many opportunities for all of us and supplied so much reckless insanity—heavy, crazy, partying with Hotshot.

STEVE WEST: *"The first guy I met from the crew was Mitch Pfeiffer. I met him through these South African guys who lived in Great Neck, my neighborhood. I went with them to the club Speaks one night, and they introduced me to Mitch. They were into Deep Purple and so was Mitch. This was 1978. I had just started playing drums for about a year and Mitch said to me, 'Hey, I'm a guitar player. Everyone said we should jam.'*

Then I went to see Cheap Trick at the Calderone theater in Hempstead, and Mitch was there in the second row. He was with a guy wearing a Trigger satin jacket. I said, 'Who the fuck is that guy wearing a Trigger jacket?' And he introduced me to Bruno. Bruno says it wasn't a Trigger jacket, but a black satin jacket with pink sleeves."

STEVE WEST: *"Bruno was the coolest. He looked great, and he was a cool looking guy. Mitch said, 'This is my friend, Bruno. He's a bass player. This is Steve. He's a drummer.' And we said we should all get together one day and jam. We watched Cheap Trick and then after the show, we chased their limousines into Manhattan to their hotel, the UN Plaza. We hung out in the lobby and met and took pics with Cheap Trick. I got to know Bruno a* *little better, and we were all hanging out. I was hangin' in the same clubs and concerts as the whole crew before I even knew who anybody was. We were all there, but didn't know each other yet. Then Mitch said, 'Bruno is in a band called Lipstick, and they are playing at the club US Blues in Roslyn.'*

I went down to the show with my friend from high school, Chris Buttner. I walked in, we were hanging out, and then Bruno came in carrying his bass, and he had on his sunglasses and Capezios and satin jacket, and looked like the coolest guy. I said, 'That's the coolest guy I've ever seen!' He was like a Gildersleeves guy; he looked so cool. I said, 'That Bruno guy is the coolest!' We said hello, and he was really nice. He was like, 'Hey man, how ya doin'.' He remembered me, we hit it off, and everything was nice. Corky, I remember, was onstage and nailing down a piece of wood in front of the drummer's kick drum so it wouldn't move. The kick drum was moving. Corky was banging it down. I was like, 'That guy's crazy!' And then we went into the bathroom and Corky was helping the guys with their makeup or clothes or something like that."

Bruno and I had taken quaaludes. I was out of it on 'ludes nailing down a four-by-four piece of wood in front of the kick drum so it wouldn't move.

BRUNO RAVEL: *"Mitch came with Chris Buttner to US Blues to see Lipstick and brought Steve to see us. Steve said that he saw* me and was afraid to talk to me because I looked cool. He said when he saw me, I was wearing my satin jacket, and he thought I looked so cool. He was too scared to say hello to me. Hahahaha!"

Diamond

BRUNO RAVEL: *"Through Scott Levitt, I met Mitch. Levitt and Mitch went to school together. It was 1977. How do I know this? The first time I went to Mitch's house, Mitch was wearing a custom Van Halen t-shirt that he had made, the kind that you would get at the mall with block lettering. It was a black shirt, white letters, that said, 'Van Halen' on the front, and on the back it said, 'The Atomic Punk.' Very cool! I started hanging out with Mitch a lot 'cause he went to all the concerts. Scott stopped going to concerts by this time. He had to move on to 'real life.' Mitch got me tickets to all the shows because he was friends with the big-time local ticket scalper. I bought tickets from Mitch at face value, but they weren't shitty seats—they were primo first row seats! Cheap Trick, AC/DC, Rush, etc. Every cool show. You name it, we were there!*

STEVE WEST: *"Diamond was my first band ever and my first ever interview. Corky interviewed us at the club February's for his Metal fanzine."*

BRUNO RAVEL: *"I started jamming with Mitch, and then me, Steve, and Mitch started jamming in Steve's basement with no*

56

singer. Then, Mitch said, 'I got a singer,' and we went to a famous rehearsal studio in Flushing near Booth Memorial Hospital to jam with him. It was Bob Ring. We hired him, and that became Diamond. We jammed Judas Priest, the Scorpions, Cheap Trick, Rainbow, etc. And 'Delilah' by Tom Jones! Diamond lasted about a year. We played maybe a dozen times."

STEVE WEST: "After Diamond broke up, Bruno and I went our separate ways. I was done with doing cover songs. Bruno stayed in Diamond, and I left, and then Lance Kovar became the drummer. I then joined this band, Kid Blue, doing originals. We opened for The Specials at Malibu, and we played The Ritz in Manhattan. I think the Ritz gig was like a local band type of night. The band had a girl singer—she loved Tom Petty—a guitar player and a bass player. We were a four-piece. We played CBGBs on June 17, 1981. Bruno came to see me at CBGBs. He sat there in the front row, and I remember him going, 'What the hell are you doing in this band?' So for about six months or a year, I was not playing with Bruno.

Kid Blue had a kind of manager guy who lived with the lead singer in Alphabet City on 4th Street and Avenue A. It was all burned out buildings and shooting galleries down there. Scary as shit. I used to have to go down there and pick them up. The manager was Michael Alago. The singer and him shared an apartment. They weren't dating, obviously. When we opened for

The Specials at Malibu, at the end of the night we got paid, and Alago paid me my cut of the money. I was like, 'Wait a minute, what's this?' He said, 'That's your cut of the money.' They lied to me about what we got paid. They each told a different story. She said we got 400 dollars, and Alago said we got 300 dollars. Someone was lying, and I was like, 'Wait a minute. You said you were paying me one amount, and now you are giving me less.' She finally broke down and said, 'I'm sorry I lied. I got no money. You live with your parents—I can barely eat and pay rent.' I was like, 'If you would have just said that to me, it would have been fine,' but she lied to me and stole money from me. Michael was cool. He felt bad. He said, 'I'm sorry. She didn't mean it. She has no money.' So I quit that night. I said, 'I'm out of here,' and then I got in touch with Bruno. He had left Diamond, so then we auditioned for The Kidds."

The Kidds

BRUNO RAVEL: "Steve and I were writing songs, trying to get something together, trying to be a Gildersleeves-type band— but we didn't have any songs."

STEVE WEST: "The first song we ever wrote together was at Bruno's house, and it's called 'Tighter.' We also recorded 'Without You,' and two or three other songs with Brunos' friend, Mara Mellon, singing. Mara was a crazy Kiss fanatic that Bruno knew

58

from the scene. She lived down the road from Bruno in Queens. It was our first time in a real studio. It was a great experience."

BRUNO RAVEL: *"In 1982 we auditioned for Arion Knight and The Kidds. When I auditioned for The Kidds, Blade [Kelly "Blade" Nickels, future L.A. Guns bass player. Why he was called Blade is still a mystery to me.] was auditioning too. That's how I met him."*

I brought black beauties to a Kidds show in Oakdale way out in Suffolk County and gave some to my friend, Mike Pont, and we went crazy. I got really drunk and so did Pont. He was throwing up in the dressing room and was a mess. I was out of my mind, going crazy. Loud. Wild. And I drove home that night, an hour away. Insane how many times I drove drunk and fucked up on drugs. I thank God every day that I never hurt myself or anyone else. We were just crazy about music, the scene, and getting fucked up. It wasn't malicious. We were just idiots.

STEVE WEST: *"After Diamond and Kid Blue were over, we auditioned for The Kidds. The audition was in their warehouse. Don King, the sound company guy, had a studio in a warehouse. Bruno and I showed up, and there was a guy waiting with his bass to audition for The Kidds. It was Blade. He was there before us. We showed up and went in before him, for some reason, and auditioned. We thought we would play two or three songs. We were in there for an hour. They really liked us. Arion was really*

59

excited. We kept playing more songs. He pretty much told us we were in the band, and I felt bad 'cause I knew there was another guy out there waiting to audition. We came out an hour later, and Blade was still sitting there. We just walked by and left. I felt bad. He was still waiting to audition. I don't even know if he got to audition. They probably said, 'We got the guys.' We did REO Speedwagon, Tom Petty, John Mellencamp, and Billy Squier. The second set was always the Rod Stewart set, 'cause Arion looked like a Rod Stewart guy with the blonde hair sticking up."

Arion looked like a cross between Vince Neil and Ric Flair.

MIKE PONT: "When Bruno's car got hit that time and knocked onto the sidewalk, it was in Rockville Centre. The show was at that club, Apples. It was after a Kidds show. We were all sitting at Lenny's Clam Bar eating, we heard a loud crash, and went outside and Bruno's car was sitting on the sidewalk faced the wrong way!"

Hotshot

MIKE PONT: "Me and Joey 'Sykes' Chechi were in a band called JayCee with John Cappadona. They both had names with the initials J.C. The tag line was, 'Ceeing is Believing.' We did everything: The Police, The Kinks, U.K., Genesis. We opened for Vixen [Long Island new wave cover band] one time at Beggar's Opera. Steve had come to see us at one point, and started hanging around. When The Kidds were ending, they decided to do their own thing, Bruno and Steve. They started Hotshot. Joey was big at the club February's, so he also might have met Steve at February's when Diamond was playing there. Joey was probably 15 or 16 then. I would also go to see The Kidds, so I started to get to know them. Joey got in Hotshot first, then it was between me and that other singer, Rudy, but I got it. Vito Romano was the first keyboard player. He lasted a couple months. Then, Joey knew Bobby Guy, and he became the keyboard player. April 19, 1983 at Mad Hatter with Vixen was the first Hotshot gig. The third gig was April 23rd, at the Holiday Lounge in Wappingers Falls, the same town the Tawana Brawley thing later exploded in."

STEVE WEST: *"The original Hotshot was around for a year or so, and three fifths of the band were dealing blow. I went to see Joey Sykes play with the band JayCee at some small club on the Island. That was the first time I met Mike Pont. They did the Genesis song, 'Abacab,' and Billy Squier stuff. The Kidds fell apart, and Bruno and I teamed up with Mike and Joey and started Hotshot. Bobby Guy and Pont were dealing blow. Pont used to carry the blow in his sock, and he was all hot and sweaty one night, and the blow melted. We were doing three sets a night. By the third set, we were all shot. It was three in the morning, and we were like, 'Pont, break it out.' Pont pulls out his plastic baggie of blow from his sock, and it was all liquid. It melted!"*

Then, Hotshot hired Kelly "Blade" Nickels to be their roadie.

STEVE WEST: *"Down the block from my house was a Goodyear tire place. I went in one day—I had a flat—and this guy came out to check out my tire, a long-haired guy. I was thinking, 'This guy looks interesting. Who is this guy?' He came out in a Goodyear jumpsuit with his long hair, and he looks at me, and says, 'You look familiar.' I went, 'Yeah, I kinda think you look familiar too.' He said, 'Did you audition for that band, The Kidds?' I went, 'Yeah, I was in that.' He recognized me. I said, 'Oh right, you were that guy, right? You auditioned also.' I told him we got the gig, whatever. We were talking about it. I said, 'What are you doing right now?' He was like, 'Nothing. This.' He said, 'This blows.' I said, 'Hey, you want a job? You want to be a roadie for us?' He said, 'Sure, anything to get the fuck out of here.' I got his number, and I hired him. I told the band, 'I got a new guy for us.'*

Blade was living in Little Neck, a mile away from me. He became our roadie and set up everyone's equipment. He did the lights. He started growing his hair. He wanted to be like a Crüe guy.

One day, he came in to one of the gigs and he said, 'I just found the coolest band.' I went, 'What band?' He said, 'I just saw their video. They're the coolest. They are called Candy.' I was like, 'Candy?' He said, 'Yeah. They are like Mötley Crüe with sneakers.' So I learned about Candy from Blade. Candy featured

Jonathan Daniel and later Gilby Clarke. I've since met Jonathan and have been friends with him for many years. Jonathan now manages Green Day, Weezer, Fall Out Boy—a bunch of bands. But Blade knew about Candy first. Blade worked for us, and he was also like a beginning bass player."

STEVE WEST: *"We all went to see Blade play for the Penthouse Pet of the Year, Sheila Kennedy's, birthday party at Studio 54 and Blade's band, TNA, played. It might have been their first gig—I think it might have been their only gig. We went down there, and it was all Penthouse chicks, and it was nuts. We were going nuts. We never had seen anything like that. I was hitting on Sheila Kennedy, and Blade was hitting on Lisa Schultz. Blade got Lisa's number, and I got Sheila's number. I told her I was in a band also. They were digging us rock guys. I said, 'Me and Bruno have this band, Hotshot,' and I said she should come down to a gig.*

Later, I called her up, and she was living at Bob Guccione's in the Penthouse mansion in the city. We had a gig at the Country House in Banksville, New York. I drove into the city to the mansion to pick her up. I knocked on the door, the butler opens the door, and Sheila came out looking slamming. My mind was blown: the Penthouse Pet of the Year. I was 19 years old. I picked her up, and we drove up to the Country House. She hung in the dressing room with us and watched us play all night. She loved it. After the gig, we were driving back home from Upstate, and I was so nervous. I was like, 'Fuck man, what am I gonna do with this chick?' I wanted to hang with her. I was driving and I put my hand on her leg and with my right hand I started fingering her as I was driving. I was like, 'I'm making the move!' For like a half hour, I was fingering her driving down the Hutchinson River Parkway from Upstate. I got to hang out with her, so I said, 'Why don't you come to my house?' I was not gonna pass this up. I still lived with my parents. I was a fucking teenager. It was like five or six in the morning, and I snuck her into the house. I brought her into my room, and we were fucking around, getting crazy, ya know, and she's making noise, and I'm fucking shitting thinking my parents are gonna wake up, and she's moaning, I was sweating and nervous. I was like, 'Oh my God, I've never brought a chick to my house at night.' So anyway, we fucked around, and the next morning we were in bed, and all of the sudden, my dad opens the door and sticks his head in, and we're in bed with the covers over us. She was sitting up with the covers over her tits, and I said, 'Hey dad, what's going on?' I didn't know if he was gonna kill me or what. He just looked at me and looked at her and just closed the door. I said, 'Oh shit.'

We hung out for a couple of hours and fucked around a little more. She only had her clothes from the night before, so my sister lent her some sweatpants and stuff, and I drove her home that afternoon. I never saw her again for years. I called her every day

64

for a week after that, and she never spoke to me again. I got the brush off. The mansion told me to leave a message. It was so out."

At the Penthouse party, I was up in the balcony all night with Pont doing blow and never once saw any of the Penthouse chicks.

STEVE WEST: *"Hotshot was doing all the new wave songs. After Diamond broke up, we all cut our hair; we had the new wave haircuts. As Hotshot progressed, we started dressing like Mötley Crüe. When the first Mötley record came out, Too Fast for Love, Bruno and I came to Corky's fucking house in Cedarhurst. We came in—this is one of my most vivid memories—and Corky was going, 'Look at this fucking record I got. Look at these guys. They are like Sweet guys with crazy hair. Look at this guy's hair.' Corky showed us the first Mötley record. He got it first. Corky got us into Mötley, and we started growing our hair again. Mötley started getting big, and we started dressing like them. We were new wave guys playing new wave songs, but started wearing the ripped stockings on our arms and ripped shirts like Mötley.*

At the Country House one night, we played 'Cum On Feel the Noize' and 'We're Not Gonna Take It,' and the owner of the Country House grabbed us after the show and said, 'Don't you ever play that heavy metal shit again, that's not why I hired you.' He went nuts on us. He got so mad at us and that was when we pretty much said, 'We are done with this shit.' We said, 'Fuck this.' We wanted to rock again."

BRUNO RAVEL: *"I let Blade play bass on those two metal songs at the end of the set. I remember that 'cause it was the last set of the night. The club was emptying, and he wanted to play really bad, so I said, 'Go for it!'"*

MIKE PONT: *"I remember crashing on a pile of laundry at the dry cleaning place Corky's dad had. Corky had to manage the place in the daytime for a while, and we used to go there after being out all night. He had to open the store at like six in the morning or something, and we would just stay up or sleep for a half hour in a pile of dirty clothes! That's where we got those mesh bags we cut up into shirts! They were mesh laundry bags, made out of like football jersey material, and they were in all kinds of colors. Corky would give them to us, and we would cut them up and wear them as shirts onstage with Hotshot!"*

BRUNO RAVEL: *"Play Duran Duran at night, sell blow on the side, and fucking go see Mötley."*

New wave, Mötley, Ratt, and the new heavy metal sound were all big at the same time. Hotshot were out there playing Duran Duran and U2 and stuff. Then Mötley came out, and everyone was like "Whaaaat??!" What is this! But Duran Duran was so huge—insanely big. We went to see them at the Garden in 1984, they had the big screens up. Nick Rhodes would come on the screen, and the girls would scream so loud, you couldn't hear the band. That Duran Duran show and the Journey Escape tour were the only two shows I've ever been at where the crowd screaming was louder than the band. True mania.

MIKE PONT: *"Hotshot was very competitive with Vixen [the bigger new wave cover band on Long Island]. We wanted to do the hot new songs before them. We asked Corky what the hot new songs were because he got all the new wave imports first."*

Bruno, myself, Mitch, Pont, Blade, and sometimes Steve would go see concerts together all the time. Van Halen, Aerosmith, Kiss, Rainbow, Def Leppard, Judas Priest, Ted Nugent, Journey, Bryan Adams, Pat Travers, Duran Duran, AC/DC—you name it. We saw every rock band that we thought were cool. And living in the New York City area, you got every band. Everyone played New York City, Long Island, and New Jersey. Every band, no matter the size of their success played, and we saw almost all of them.

We were all experimenting with drugs (not Steve, no matter what he says to the contrary)—mostly quaaludes and speed—and drank whatever was available. Cocaine started creeping in by 1980 and started to become the drug of choice. Through my nightclub work, I had all the underworld connections and was able to get drugs for free a lot. We paid, or shall I say, everyone else paid, but I got freebies regularly because I hooked up everyone at the clubs. The lines to get into the clubs I worked at would be a half mile long, seriously, a thousand people on line

67

waiting to get in, so I got all the dealers in first. They could jump the line and got in free. Same with the bar. They never waited when it was six people deep. They got taken care of because they took care of us. The bartenders, the bouncers, and me, the DJ. Everyone wanted to hang out in the DJ booth and party. I developed quite the connections over time and used it to good effect when partying with bands, girls, record company friends, and our crew. I was a facilitator. But how many times we drove home from Hammerheads, Malibu, Speaks, or Manhattan half asleep, drunk, on 'ludes at five o'clock in the morning—too many. I'm not saying its a good idea. EVER. But it was different back then. I'm thankful I never hurt myself really bad, or anyone else especially, in a car accident. I was very lucky. I had my guardian angel on my shoulder my whole life. I know people, better souls than I was, who died so young. Lived their life like a saint, and stepped off the curb one day to get hit by a bus. You know what I mean? Me, I tempted death every day, and I am still here. When it's your time, it's your time. I really believe that.

MIKE PONT: *"Hotshot played French Charley's in the Bronx, an old school bar with sawdust on the floor, and Blade did a handstand on a bar stool and fell right on his head. We played Gurney's Inn in the Hamptons and back-to-back proms on a Friday and Saturday. The chicks' boyfriends wanted to beat us up because the chicks liked us. We played the Princeton, New*

Jersey prom, and Brooke Shields was at the prom. Blade was so drunk, he passed out at her feet."

Guys wanted to kick my ass there at French Charley's. At the Bailiwick too. I was drunk all the time and going crazy. Guys wanted to kick my ass every night I went out. I was wearing pink boots and screaming and yelling, drunk. I didn't care though. I would have fought anyone back then. I'm lucky I didn't get killed! I was a fool, but I forgive myself now!

MIKE PONT: *"Bobby Guy was going out with this chick, Angie, whose mother was dating a Peruvian drug lord. They got caught in Hicksville doing a million a week out of the house. Bobby was getting us the blow. He went to jail while he was in Hotshot. Gary Bevona took Bobby's place. Then Joey Sykes quit to join Vixen, and Blade's brother, Duke, replaced him. After I quit, George Tibbet came in right at the end. Blade and I went out to Hollywood for a month, and George took over singing."*

STEVE WEST: *"Me and Bruno continued Hotshot with George Tibbet, and then Billy Douglas who wound up in the band Shooting Gallery. Billy was also in the cover band Vixen, at one point. Billy would do one set with us—only Prince, Bowie, and The Psychedelic Furs."*

MIKE PONT: *"Blade and I got back from L.A. in the summer of 1984. I dyed my hair black, and then I quit Hotshot. It was* always gonna be Ravel/West. I was in my new band, Trouble, by 1985. Trouble was right after I left Hotshot. George Nastos was in the band, and he now plays with Rick Springfield. Johnny Jinx was in the band. He ended up in that band Big Mouth on Atlantic—half rap kind of band. Rob Carlton, who is now a sound man, and Danny Drasser, who passed away, were the other members."

Michael Bolton

BRUNO RAVEL: *"I was friendly with Tony Bruno, the guitar player from the local Long Island cover band, Swift Kick. I was in with all the cover bands on the Island. I knew Chuck Bonfante. I knew these guys from the clubs. Chuck was dating a chick that was friends with a girl I was dating. That's how we got friendly. Tony was trying to get out of the Long Island circuit after Swiftkick ended. He's a hustler, and he became friendly with booking agents, managers, etc. He was friendly with Louis Levin, Michael Bolton's manager, and he heard that Michael Bolton was looking for a band to back him. Tony played with Billy Squier, and he had auditioned for Kiss when Ace left, so he was plugged into that scene. Tony put together the band for Bolton. It was Chuck, Al Pitrelli, Tony, and Scott Fishkind as the keyboard player. The bass player was Ricky from Swift Kick. They auditioned as a band, and Bolton didn't like Ricky. Chuck mentioned me to Tony, and I got the call to audition. I was already a Bolton fan anyway, so I knew all the songs. Of course, I got the gig. We toured for a* *few months, but the Bolton record didn't do well, and he immediately went back into the studio to do a new record. So that ended."*

I flew up to Rhode Island to see Bruno play with Michael Bolton with a girl I was dating. She worked at the place where I got my hair cut. I was in my usual crazy party mode, and we had a blast. Bruno was the first one of us to do something on that level. It was the big time. He played a small arena and was playing in a band with a guy on a major label.

Bang Zoom/Cintron

STEVE WEST: *"I did this short-lived band with Tony Bruno, Tommy Farise, and Bruno called Bang Zoom. This was after Bruno's Bolton gig ended. That's where I fucked up the Aerosmith song 'Lick and A Promise.' I knew I shouldn't have played it—I could never play that drum intro. We also did Ratt songs like 'Lay It Down' and 'You're In Love,' and also did some Zeppelin."*

Bruno and Steve also played with renowned Long Island guitar virtuoso George Cintron after Bang Zoom ended.

STEVE WEST: *"Cintron was this crazy double bass drum thing. I was a new wave guy, and it wasn't the right fit. I wasn't into it, and it wasn't my scene really. I fucked up some songs, and George was like, 'Later.' But while we were playing in Cintron, Bruno cut his hand and had that crazy blow scene. Bruno called* me screaming, 'My hand, my hand, my hand!' He was screaming like a nut. He said, 'There's blood everywhere,' freaking out, and then the phone just goes dead."

BRUNO RAVEL: *"The story goes like this: My hairdresser I had met months prior in a Forest Hills salon, got fired from his gig one day. Over time, he transitioned into one of the biggest drug dealers in New York. He supplied all the big clubs in New York with coke in the 80s. He drove around in a limo all the time—a real player. Even though he was dealing with some real shady people, he always looked out for me, and from time-to-time, he'd give me a free haircut or put some streaks in my hair, if I called him.*

One time, I went over to his apartment to get my hair 'frosted,' and he asked me if I wanted a hit off the pipe. They were 'freebasing.' 'No man! I don't do that. I'm not gonna end up like Richard Pryor!' He kept after me and said, 'C'mon, just try one hit. It's great,' and I caved. The next thing I knew, I had stayed at the guy's apartment for a day and a half freebasing. There were kilos of coke in the closet and guns all around. Crazy fucking people laying on the floor in the corners of the rooms.

After a day and a half of being high, I finally had a moment of clarity, and left. When I got home, to my surprise, I was hungry. I hadn't eaten in a day and a half. I grabbed frozen hamburger patties from my freezer and tried to break a patty off, but the patties wouldn't budge, so I grabbed a big knife to attempt to pry them apart. The knife slipped, and I punctured my hand with the knife. As soon as it happened, blood started pulsating out of my hand, and I freaked out. Almost simultaneously, my phone rang, and I answered it. I started screaming into it, "My hand, my hand, my hand!" It was my mom! Ouch! She screamed back, "Go straight to the hospital!" I grabbed a towel and wrapped my hand and drove myself to St. John's Hospital, running red lights, blood everywhere. I ran into the emergency room screaming, 'My hand! my hand!' I looked in the waiting room, and there were guys in there with their arms hanging off, shot in the head, bullet wounds. The nurse took a look at my wound, slapped some gauze on it, and told me to go wait in the waiting room. I was like, 'What!'

A few days later, I had to have surgery to repair the tendon I had severed. The surgery went well, and of course, the doctor prescribed lots of physical therapy. I was worried I wouldn't be able to play bass again. The doctor told me not to put stress on my hand for three weeks to a month, but I didn't listen. I had to play a gig with Cintron two weeks after my surgery, so I played with my hand in a sling with only three fingers. I didn't use my pinky. This was right after my stint with Michael Bolton. I played in Cintron with Steve. That didn't last long. George had a reputation as a great player and always played with solid musicians. He was worried about Steve because he wasn't a

'Carmine Appice' heavy metal type powerful drummer. We were playing heavy rock. Zeppelin, Deep Purple, etc. A couple of times, he ended up screwing up the songs, and we had to stop and restart them. This happened one too many times, and George was so embarrassed, he got rid of Steve. This was right before I joined White Lion."

I was living with Bruno at this time. I came home, walked into the apartment, and no one was home. There was a knife on the floor, blood everywhere, and hamburger patties thrown around. I was like, *Okkaayyyyy*, what happened here!

White Lion

BRUNO RAVEL: *"After Bolton, Greg D'Angelo [White Lion's drummer and good friend] called me to audition for White Lion, and I did that for a little bit, then quit because they wouldn't let me contribute to the creative process."*

Talas

BRUNO RAVEL: *"Billy Sheehan left Talas to join David Lee Roths' band. Al Pitrelli called me so we could audition for Talas together, which we did, and we both joined the band. Original vocalist, Phil Naro, was singing, Al was on guitar, Gary Bivona was playing keyboards, and drummer Jimmy DeGrasso [Y&T, Megadeth, Suicidal Tendencies] joined later. A few months and a* few dozen gigs later, Phil left. We tried to keep it together, but it just wasn't meant be"

Hotshot 2.0/Danger Danger

BRUNO RAVEL: *"From the ashes of Talas, I started to put together what would soon be the original version of Danger Danger. Jimmy DeGrasso left to join Y&T. Steve West came in to play drums. It was me, Steve, Mike Pont singing, Al Pitrelli on guitar, and Gary Bivona. Then Kasey Smith came in to play keyboards after we parted ways with Gary. Our A&R guy at Sony, Lennie Petze, wasn't very fond of Al's playing. Al was having issues executing his parts in the studio. It became clearly evident what we had to do, so we parted ways with Al, and held auditions. In the end, we chose Andy Timmons. We had originally asked Tony Bruno to join, but he had a conflict with the band he was in, Saraya. Both bands had development deals at the time. Tony recorded the guitars on our first album, then halfway through the record, he decided to stay with Saraya full time. Andy Timmons joined and recorded a few tracks for the album. Steve and I were so desperate to get a record deal, we had two sets of demo tapes circulating at the same time. One with Mike Pont singing, and the other with Ted Poley [Danger Danger singer]."*

STEVE WEST: *"Bruno wore that shirt, 'Who the Fuck is Billy Sheehan,' and Billy got mad and said, 'You can't use the name, Talas, anymore.' Now they needed a new name.*

Bruno called me up one day and said, 'We need a new name for the band. Sheehan won't let us use the name.' He said to me, 'You got anything? We're probably gonna call the band Hearts in Armor.' I'm like, 'Alright, whatever, Hearts in Armor.' I was hanging out in L.A. with Pont, and I made up a name as if I was in a band in L.A. I was reading BAM and LA Weekly, the bands in L.A. had cool names. I told Bruno, I said, 'If I started a band, I'd call it Danger Danger,' and he goes, 'That fucking blows.' I said, 'Whatever, you asked me. Don't use it. That's all I got.'

A week later, he calls me and said 'We're using your name, Danger Danger, but it's the Talas guys.' Bruno, Al, Phil Naro singing, Jimmy, and Gary, but they are calling it Danger Danger. Then DeGrasso left to join Y&T. Bruno then asked me, 'Do you want to join the band?' I said, 'I don't want to be in that band playing those kind of songs. If you want me to be in a band again, let's write some great songs, some catchy things, and try to get a record deal—I don't want to play these metal songs.' He said, 'Alright, fine, let's do it.' So I joined the band, and they had already booked a gig at L'Amour.

In the meantime, Bruno and I were writing songs, 'Naughty Naughty,' a lot of the songs that wound up on the first Danger Danger album. We were writing songs, and Phil Naro was up in Canada. We kept writing. They had booked the L'Amour gig as Talas, but now it's gonna be a Danger Danger gig. I went, 'Alright, whatever. *When is Phil coming to rehearse? We got to learn all these songs.'* We were gonna do half Talas songs and half new Danger Danger songs Bruno and I had written, and it was a week away, and we hadn't rehearsed. Phil kept going, *'Don't worry, I'll be there, I'll be there. I'm coming.'* We hadn't rehearsed at all. I said, *'Bruno, we have to cancel this gig. We never played with Phil. I never played with him.'* We were sending him demo tapes of the new songs. Phil didn't know the new songs. He said, *'I'm learning them,'* whatever. He never came to New York. I said, *'We have to cancel this show.'* Then Mike Pont ended up singing. Phil quit. Bruno wanted to get Pont, and I was against it. I said, *'Cancel this fuckin' gig. What do you want Mike for?'* We were done with him after Hotshot. I was against it—it just wasn't the right voice. Mike came down to rehearse the first time, and right away, he was being Pont. He was singing however he wanted, making changes, and trying to change everything we were working on. We just asked him to be in the band, and he's coming in trying to change everything! Bruno said, *'Why don't we have both Ted Poley and Mike Pont sing, and whoever the label likes, that's who we will go with.'* I said, *'That's not cool.'* Mike was a really good friend of mine. We were really tight. I didn't want to do that to Mike. I was against it. So we ended up getting Ted to sing on the demos, as well, behind Mike's back. I said, *'Why don't we just go with Ted, and tell Mike he's out?'* Bruno said, *'Why jump the gun? Maybe someone will like Mike, and we'll get a deal* with him.' Again, I was like, 'That's not cool. Mike is our friend.' I felt bad, but I'm just as guilty because I went along with Bruno. I said, 'I'm not for this, but your my partner, so whatever.' Mike then found out about Ted, with the two demos, and that was the end of our relationship with Mike. He said, 'You guys are being sneaky and sending out two sets of demos with me and Ted.' Mike was pissed. I was bummed. Then we were in the studio doing demos, and the A& R guy said we have to get rid of Al—he wasn't playing well, so that was another tough call. Not take the deal and stay with Al? We let him go. Al understood. We said, 'They aren't gonna sign us if we keep you.' He was cool. We were in a bad position, and he said, 'Fine. Do what you gotta do.'

Ted knew a guy that owned a lighting company that knew a manager. Ted brought the guys down to a photoshoot, and they said give us a tape, and we will get you a record deal. They brought the tape to Lennie Petze at Sony, and we went with them, but they were half-ass managers. They didn't know what they were doing.

I always felt bad about Pont. I never wanted him to be in Danger Danger. It was all Bruno. I was guilty 'cause I went along with it; I never wanted to lie to Pont. I never wanted to have Ted sing behind his back. I felt bad. I lost a good friend. I didn't speak to Pont for like five years or more. I always tried to help him. I would always write songs with him after we became friends

78

again. I always wanted him to have the shot like we had and Blade had. He was always the guy that kept missing. If Mike gets his one shot, I'll be happy. I helped write the later Hotshot songs for Mike, and Bruno helped too. I felt bad that we couldn't take him along with us."

MIKE PONT: "Talas/Danger Danger had shows coming up in two weeks. Bruno and I were at my mom's house. He called Phil Naro, and Phil said he wasn't doing it. He quit. Bruno asked me right there if I wanted to sing. That was my first Danger Danger show. It said on the flyer: 'Formerly Talas.' The show was at L'Amour East. Everyone was raving about the show, so we kept doing it. We did demos at Al Pitrelli's house. Then they kicked me and Al out of the band. They were sneaky about it—you know how Bruno is.

Ted Poley was at that first show, and he came up to them and told them, 'If I sing with the band, we will get a deal tomorrow.' He brought the whole package. Management, bookings, etc. Ted knew the manager from New Jersey. Ted got Danger Danger the deal, pretty much. Ted was in Prophet, and they had a record out on a subsidiary of RCA.

After I was kicked out of Danger Danger, I moved to L.A. After I got to L.A., Al called me and said he was kicked out too! My mom was sick, and I had to come back to New York, so me and Al started playing in a new version of Hotshot. Teddy Cook was *playing bass and Kruken was on drums. This was the end of 1988. In 1989, Al got offered the Alice Cooper gig, and he did that. In that same month, Teddy Cook got offered the Dio gig, and he took it. Hotshot was obviously on people's radar as being a good band. Then we got Timmy and Spike into the band. That's the version that got the attention of Nikki Sixx and Tommy Lee. In 1991, I gave our demo tape to Mike Amato, Mötley Crüe's tour manager, who I knew from Sondra at Enigma Records, when Poison was on Enigma. She's in the "I Want Action" video. I got a phone call from Nikki one day, and he left me a message on the answering machine saying he wanted to possibly produce us. Throughout the next couple of months, we spoke a couple times a week. Then he said we should come out to L.A. to do some shows for them. They booked a rehearsal studio for us, and we also booked some shows at Spice in Hollywood and FM Station in the Valley. We went out and rehearsed and did the shows. Everything was fucking great. They loved it. Then in February 1992, we got a call from Doug Thaler saying they just kicked Vince Neil out of the band, and they didn't have time to deal with us."*

BRUNO RAVEL: *"Danger Danger released our debut record, Danger Danger, in 1989. On our first tour we opened for Warrant, and then did double-bill club tours with Faster Pussycat, Alice Cooper, Extreme, Lita Ford, and Kix, and then we opened for Kiss. First time we opened for Kiss was on the Hot in the Shade Tour in America, and then we did the Revenge Tour in Europe.*

For our second album, Screw It!, we headlined our own tours with various support acts. After 1992, when the grunge movement killed us, it was every man for himself."

STEVE WEST: *"We did our second record, and we toured on our own headlining tour doing little 1,000-seat theaters, and it was not good. We were dying, We weren't on MTV, and it was over, pretty much. Grunge was happening. We were pretty much over, but the saving grace was the Screw It! record started getting big in Europe. We didn't even know. Kerrang! magazine and all these other guys there are loving it. It was a huge import, and then they released it officially in England. We were done, but we were getting action in England, so they booked us to do the Astoria Theatre in London, and it sold out. 'The American Dream Series,' it was called. That was a legendary gig. Kerrang! was saying we were the best band ever, and we were huge in England. It's 1992. We had three singles go Top 50 in the charts in England. Then we booked a UK headlining tour. As this tour was being booked, Kiss was doing their UK tour, and they asked us to be the opening band. We cancelled our tour, and we opened for Kiss. We played Wembley and all the big places in the UK. We started breaking in Europe, yet in the States, we were dead. Then we went back to Japan, grunge kicked in, and it was over from there. Europe kept us alive when grunge was happening—barely. We fell apart on the third Sony record, Cockroach, in 1993. After the record was done, Ted came to us with all kinds of crazy demands:*

wanting publishing and money, etc. He made all the demands on me and Bruno, and we said, 'That ain't happening,' and then he said, 'Fuck you,' and we never heard from him again. He didn't quit, and we didn't fire him. Sony was like, 'Fuck Ted, get a new singer, and re-record the record.' We were like, 'Fuck, are you kidding?' They were gonna keep us on the label! We got Paul Laine to sing and re-recorded the vocals, and then Ted sued Sony and sued us for 10 million dollars each. Sony said, 'We aren't gonna deal with this.' Instead of dealing with the lawsuit, they just didn't put the record out, and that was it. The end."

MIKE PONT: "When Nikki and Tommy backed out of that deal in 1992, I did the Platinum Posse with Petey—a long-haired white hip-hop thing. We opened for House of Pain at Industry Nightclub. Then I got the topless DJ gig. Corky came in all the time at Texas Gold 'cause he worked down the street at Limelight. Then it changed names to Silverado, then VIP Club. That was a crazy grind, but I did it.

Look at Joey Sykes. Joey went from Hotshot to Vixen and then eventually was in the Elektra band Coward. He got a record deal. After that, he played the Garden with Meredith Brooks when he was in her band. He's an angry guy, which is his problem really. He gets so depressed. I tell him, 'Joey, you've been doing exactly what you wanted to do your whole fucking life. I gave up singing

30 years ago. I did well at it, but at the time, I didn't want to do that DJ thing. But I did it! What are you depressed about?!'"

Chapter Three - Twisted Sister - 1978-1982

Many moons ago, back in the early 1970s through the mid 1980s, there used to exist a rock and roll cover band circuit on Long Island and the tri-state area in New Jersey, Connecticut, the upper New York State Westchester County and Orange County, and all the boroughs of New York City, *excluding* Manhattan. Manhattan was never really about rock and roll. It still isn't. It's about fashion, art, and celebrity, Wall Street, the United Nations, Broadway, and disco.

Disco. It started in Manhattan. Sure, maybe it really came from some Parisian palace before that, but on a "Wake up world, it's DISCO TIME!" level, it started in Manhattan. The nightclub that made it famous all over America, the holy Mecca of disco, was Studio 54. Studio 54, being what it was, influenced nightlife in general throughout America from that point onward. Studio 54 defined the history of Manhattan nightlife. Disco is Manhattan nightlife.

Disco—and now hip-hop, house, and techno. NOT rock and roll.

Before Studio 54, you had Max's Kansas City as the cultural hub for those influential players. Max's was a rock and roll place. It had live acts, some with record deals on their first stop into Manhattan—some rock, some country. Disco, not really being "born," in the national sense of the word, until the mid to late 1970s, was not what the ultra hip and cool fashionistas took to when it was time to musically express themselves. It was rock and roll—their version of good old time rock and roll. Elvis, Chuck Berry, and a little Ronettes thrown in. The band that epitomized all of it was the New York Dolls. Even though the New York Dolls are one of the most influential rock and roll bands to emerge from the tiny island called Manhattan, they didn't mean shit anywhere else. They never sold any records. That doesn't make them any less important, but it never translated an hour east to Long Island—forget places like Tulsa or Birmingham. Yeah, a few people here and there, but never a real bulldozing, record selling, getting airplay rock and roll monster. Manhattan was and never will be a true rock and roll city—rock and roll in the true rock and roll sense. I understand and respect what the Andy Warhol version of art and rock and roll has contributed: The Dolls, The Velvet Underground, Lou Reed, Nico, the Ramones.

All great, all influential, but never sold any records.

The Great Gildersleeves, along with Trax and a couple of other Manhattan rooms, all had the same type of clientele: people that were in that suit and vest bracket. Women and men in platform shoes, suits, high heels, and hot pants sitting at tables, ordering drinks, and smoking cigarettes and chatting. For a band, it was very hard to get a real reaction because everyone was busy being cool. Cool is the correct word—the only word. The bar crowd—the audience for the most part—liked the bands they went to see, but not enough to stand up and go nuts. Hell, that wouldn't be cool.

Rock and roll is 100% blue-collar. Rock and roll isn't a guitar tone, a drum sound, or just the right outfit. Rock and roll is all attitude, baby. Don't believe me? Ask Nikki fucking Sixx! Those 9-to-5 workers all across the country are the people that buy CDs, t-shirts, and tickets to the shows. They are truck drivers, carpenters, teachers, cops, firemen, hairdressers, strippers, bartenders, secretaries, auto mechanics, and cable installers—even some Wall Street traders can join in from time to time. They are the weekend warriors with Budweiser courage, and they rock their asses off. A little suds, some girls or guys to have sex with, and A LOT of rock and roll. After working all week or all day, you want to go let loose and not try and make any statements—just party. And if a local band was playing some great songs that you knew and were familiar, then it made it all the better. Cover bands working hard to make you have a good time. Not a band trying to prove that they are cooler than you—that they too, could be the ones millions of kids idolized. Cover bands just wanted to make the room party and get paid. You didn't have nightclubs in Manhattan that hosted cover bands. Original bands, yes, but not cover bands that played a cover band nightclub circuit. That's why bands like The Velvet Underground, the New York Dolls, and the Ramones were able to get noticed. Max's, and later punk temple

CBGB, allowed and encouraged improvisation and originality. A band like the Ramones would never be given the chance to play their own original material at a nightclub in Long Island or New Jersey in 1976. They would have cleared the place out empty.

The club owners in the tri-state area did not want a band that would clear the club. Are you kidding me? We are talking New York State, New Jersey, Connecticut, and Long Island. Most of those clubs were wiseguy connected. Nightclubs in general, one of the boys always had his hand in somewhere. The name of the game was to make money. The people with the money—the spenders, the hardcore drinkers, the people that wanted to party their asses off, the "weekend warriors"—wanted to hear their favorite songs. The bars and clubs in the mid to late 1970s through the mid 1980s wanted cover bands to play the top hits, the Top 40—familiar songs.

Some bands leaned more R&B and funk, some more rock and roll. As the scene and circuit progressed onward, toward its death in the mid 1980s, one band emerged as the king of all cover bands. A band that worked nonstop, three sets a night, five nights a week, for ten years. A band that eventually started working in their own original material to the set, with their own original material becoming as well-known as the rock and heavy metal hits they were covering. This band went to England and got themselves an independent record deal that led to an even bigger deal with a major record label. That record deal afforded them a national presence—hit videos and hit songs. A face and a song people will remember into rock and roll heaven. Rock and roll glory and the big time—or so they thought.

The record deal, sadly, was the beginning of the end. It was the end of what made them the incredibly successful and kick ass rock and roll band in the first place. The main songwriter and frontman, the main reason the band became successful writing their own material, got all the music publishing money because he wrote the songs. The frontman's ego exploded, and some of the other band members did not like it one bit. The frontman did not start the band—the guitar player did. The guitar player formed the band, ran it, kept it going through numerous personnel changes, and managed it's business from the beginning in 1973.

The balance had changed. The other players were reduced to sidemen.

They probably made more money in the clubs than they did when they got signed to a record deal. That golden period right around 1980, a couple of years before they got signed, was when they ruled the roost. They were the king of the hill of that tri-state nightclub and bar circuit.

They were outdrawing every band in the tri-state area, with clubs like Hammerheads on Long Island and the Fountain Casino in New Jersey cramming 3,500 to 5,000 people in every time they played.

They were Twisted Sister.

Jay Jay French was, and is, the heart and soul of Twisted Sister. Dee Snider was the bands rocket to stardom: the star, the personality. But Jay Jay French is what made Twisted the bar band kings.

My earliest memory of seeing Twisted Sister was at Speaks in Island Park, New York, summer 1978. Speaks was owned by the real club king of Long Island, Phil Basile.

Phil owned that building going back to the late 60s when it was first known as the Action House. All the 1960s rock bands— bar The Beatles and the Stones—made their way through there on their tours. The Doors, Jimi Hendrix, Alice Cooper—you name it. The Young Rascals were the house band at one point. Phil also managed Vanilla Fudge, so this club was a big deal to play. Over the years, it's name changed a few times. In the mid 1970s, it hosted all the disco bands, not because the club liked disco per se, but because that was what brought people in.

Then the tide shifted. Punk, new wave, and heavy metal started to change the musical landscape. Speaks was forced to turn back to rock as disco subsided a bit. Twisted Sister took it upon themselves to bring rock back to the clubs. Twisted wanted to make money too, and they weren't about to let disco take over the clubs and ease them out, so Twisted Sister started the "Disco Sucks" campaign. At every club they played, they led "Disco Sucks" chants. They broke disco records and took a cardboard standup of John Travolta, in full disco pose, and hung him by his cardboard neck. For Dee Snider, it was real. He hated disco.

Born and raised in Baldwin, Long Island, Dee was a bit of a geek in high school. Danny Snider was never a good-looking, all-star jock kind of guy. Dee himself has admitted, "Twisted Sister aren't a bunch of good-looking guys." He was tall, had curly, kinky reddish brown hair, and was what they call on Long Island: a dirtbag. But he wasn't into alcohol and drugs. He was straight as an arrow, but he still had that "fuck you" rebellion in him. He loved his Black Sabbath, AC/DC, and Led Zeppelin. The heavier the better.

Jay Jay French, on the other hand, was from Manhattan, but started his career with Twisted in New Jersey. He loved the whole glam thing: David Bowie, the Dolls, and that whole lot. Before Dee joined the band, Twisted Sister was a straight up glam band, dressing glam and playing glam rock covers—no heavy metal—and there was no real "star" in the band. There was no frontman that would take them to the top. When Dee joined the band in 1976, he was to become that star.

He could also write songs, and his songwriting eventually developed to the point where he was able to write rock and roll anthems that will be on classic rock playlists forever.

But first, he had to learn the ropes, and he learned the business from Jay Jay French. Jay Jay had been playing in Twisted Sister since 1973, and had been through every shithole club there was in the tri-state area. He'd been ripped off and burned, threatened and harassed. Twisted even used the AC/DC song "It's a Long Way to the Top (If You Wanna Rock 'n' Roll)" as their intro. When you go through that rock and roll battleground, and come out with scars and wounds, that experience teaches you. You either learn from it, or you die. Dee learned from Jay Jay how to work a crowd, and how to hold them in the palm of your hand. But Dee took it even further. When you went to see Twisted Sister, you'd better party, or Dee would make sure you did. And you didn't want that. You definitely didn't want Dee Snider pointing you out in the crowd as being someone who was an "asshole," standing there with your arms folded, trying to be too cool. No one was so cool that they couldn't boogie their asses off at a Twisted Sister show. No fucking way. Dee would point you out, and harass the shit out of you until the whole crowd in the club would be on your ass. After awhile, people got the point. You'd better rock out hard at a Twisted Sister show.

Twisted Sister broke through that sitting down and being cool barrier, "waitresses bringing you drinks to your table" type of thing, and standing there with your arms folded. Dee demanded you react, or he would single you out and humiliate the shit out of you in front of a thousand people. Twisted Sister had a very loyal following. Dee would welcome them, "How are all of our sick motherfucking friends tonight?" There weren't a lot of tourists at Twisted Sister shows, and if so, they stayed way in the back. Better to hide from Dee. Me? I was always up front. Always.

Bruno Ravel and I went to see Twisted all the time. I saw them over 50 times. We were there for the opening night of the Bad Boys Tour on Memorial Day weekend 1980, at the club, Detroit, in Port Chester, New York. WLIR broadcast the show live on the air. The first 100 people on line got a t-shirt, and we were two of them. We would drive an hour and a half or two hours to see Twisted Sister. We were so into it.

From working at Important Record Distributors, I met Twisted's road manager, Joe Gerber. I met him at a Twisted show and gave him my card. By this time, I was a salesman at IRD and had an official business card! I told Joe we could distribute the Twisted singles at IRD, and I would try to help them because I was a fan—I was a superfan. I would go see Twisted by myself in a snowstorm if I had to. I went a lot by myself. I was a fan, but I was also able to help sell some fucking Twisted singles. Joe would bring IRD records, and we would try to sell them across the USA, but no one really gave a shit, so I started sending some to all the music papers in London. Working at an import record distributor, we got all the weekly UK music papers. Melody Maker, *NME and Sounds—Sounds* was geared a little more hard rock. I sent some singles to Sounds and all of a sudden, a few weeks later, Twisted starts popping up on the charts. I was so excited! This was great! I called Joe and told him what was going on. He said that Twisted were playing at Hammerheads that weekend, and I should come down and show him what I got. I went down with Bruno and Steve West, and Joe got us in early before doors opened. We walked in and were hanging out by the entryway game room, and Joe brought Jay Jay over. I showed him the Sounds charts and told him we were starting to export singles to distributors overseas in the UK because there was a demand. We couldn't move them in the States, but in the UK things were starting to happen. Sounds magazine then sent a writer over to do a story on them, which led to Twisted signing an indie record deal with Secret Records in England, which then led them to being signed by Atlantic Records. It wasn't that simple, easy-peasy, or stress-free, believe me, but the mighty Twisted Sister got there. Their full story is told in the amazing documentary, We Are *Twisted Fucking Sister!,* directed by the late Andrew Horn. Andy was kind enough to include me in the doc, and I told my story of how I helped Twisted get signed. It was a long ten-year odyssey for them, and

I am proud to have played a part in it. Make sure to watch the doc for the full incredible story of the greatest bar band in the world!

I miss those days. Some of the greatest rock and roll sets I have ever seen were at a Twisted Sister show. They had unbelievable energy, intensity, and attitude. The sets were tight and furious, like a tank rolling over you—clubs packed like sardines. 2,500 people at Speaks on a Thursday every week in the summer, 5,000 at the Fountain Casino, 3,500 at Hammerheads, all sold out. They were funny and entertaining, always, with souped-up high energy versions of classic rock songs that would rip your head off and send you to the bar for an ice cold "green monster"—a Heineken beer. You won't see the likes of a band like that again. Ever.

So for us there was Twisted, and there was Gildersleeves.

Complete opposite ends of the spectrum.

But we loved them both. And Bruno and I both took a lot from them—from their success, and their coolness. They inspired us to do it, to get there, and to make it happen.

Chapter Four - IRD/ Relativity/Combat, Iron Maiden, Speaks - 1979-1985

In the summer of 1979, I was working as a DJ in a few different discos on Long Island and going out to other clubs as much as I worked—discos, rock clubs, and punk clubs on Long Island, Queens, Brooklyn, and Manhattan. I was a regular at Platterpuss Records in Cedarhurst, and one day as I was annoying the owner as usual, he told me about a job opening he had heard about. There was an import record distributor in Jamaica, Queens by Kennedy Airport that was looking for a warehouse guy. He gave me the phone number for the distributor, and I called up the owner, Barry, who was the head guy at Important Record Distributors (IRD). The company was also partly owned by Steve Mason at Windsong Records, an import/export in London. Steve would get all the hottest UK records first and had all the good connections in Europe to get the product to America fast.

I asked the receptionist for Barry, and she connected me. I made an appointment to meet him at the distributor, and I got hired right away. My job was to pack the orders in the warehouse and get them ready for pickup by UPS. There was also an export division run by another guy named Brian—there were boxes of US records being exported to the UK as well. There were about eight or nine people working there. It was a small little warehouse with an office with maybe four desks and a photocopier. Records were stacked all over the floor in the offices. The building was maybe 1,500 square feet, not counting the small loading dock.

In the summer of 1979, I started working Monday through Friday, 9 AM to 6 PM, packing up records. This was the middle of the punk boom and post punk boom and into the early days of synth-pop, new wave, and the new romantic period. You had rockabilly happening with the Stray Cats and the two-tone ska stuff as well, not to mention, the new wave of British heavy metal, which was starting with Def Leppard, Iron Maiden, and Saxon. As a music junkie, I was in heaven. Every day boxes would arrive from Europe loaded with incredible stuff. There was also the remnants of the prog rock stuff, and the Brian Eno records, Holger Czukay, Tangerine Dream, Robert Fripp, Captain Beefheart, and all the great roots reggae. There were The Beatles and Stones imports too. It was like Christmas everyday. One Saturday, Barry asked me to come in and help him put together some more metal shelving for the records that were piling in daily. I went down to the warehouse and was working on the shelves with him when Kenny Laguna came in the door selling Joan Jett albums out of his trunk. Kenny was Joan's manager and was working her first album, pressed on their own indie Blackheart Records. Kenny wanted Barry to distribute it, and he did a deal with Kenny and took the record in. This was the very beginning of Joan's solo career. I got a free promo copy, and we ended up selling that record to every store. Every store took at least one. That's how you get started. Some accounts took more, and it sold better in certain markets, but when you can get at least one copy in every store, then you are on to something.

One night around Christmas, we stayed late, past normal business hours, because there was a big shipment coming in from London at around 11 PM. There were some big records released that week that were highly anticipated. At this time, these records were either not released in America at all, or there was a delay of six months or longer before an album or single would be released in America. The stores were drooling for the imports. I remember it was the The Clash's Sandinista! triple album plus various other hot singles, 12" singles, and albums—huge shipment. That night, all the big New York City record guys were at the warehouse waiting for the records to arrive so they could grab their orders, get back to Manhattan for the weekend, and be the first to start selling these releases. Bleecker Bob, Arnie Goodman from Zig Zag, the guys from Sounds, Free Being—they were all waiting for the delivery. It was very, very competitive; they all wanted to have the hottest store in the city. Having these records first made you the man. Bleecker Bob was always a nasty prick to everyone, but nice to Barry and the girls in the office. He would go on and on with Arnie Goodman, and it was hilarious banter. Insults, curses—it was insane. They would argue, fight, and call each other names. It was an insane scene. The cream of the crop of the New York City record store owners were in this warehouse, and it was hilarious shit. I was getting an education, for sure. This was the beginning of the end of the golden days though; the last days of the import vinyl record boom before the labels in America got their shit together and started signing this stuff for the states. Huge releases would come in from the UK, Germany, Holland, and Japan. Records like Blondie's 12" single mix of "Rapture," Joy Division's Still album, Grace Jones' "Pull Up to the Bumper" 12" single, Human League's "Don't You Want Me" 12" single with the long version, and Ozzy Osbourne's first album, Blizzard of Ozz. These records were not available in the US, and IRD sold tens of thousands of these records all over America. The list of import classics released from 1979 to 1985 is in the thousands.

I started bringing records down to the DJ at Malibu nightclub in Lido Beach. Malibu was a huge live music venue and nightclub on the water and was a beach club during in the day. There was a swimming pool, cabanas, beach, and a huge ballroom-type club on the property where they used to have weddings and bar mitzvahs and stuff. A nightclub group came in and leased the ballroom and turned it into a live music venue and nightclub. The capacity was legally probably 1,500, but they would put 3,000 people in there.

I arranged it so the DJ at Malibu, Bart, could buy records at a discount. I would call him up and tell him what releases came in that week, and he would ask me for some of the other records he was looking for. He was getting stuff right off the plane delivered down to him at the club. He loved the arrangement, to say the least. I hung out with him in the DJ booth. He would give me drink tickets. It was a lot of fun. After a few months of getting to know him, he told me he was leaving Malibu to manage a new club in Manhattan called Youthanasia, and he recommended me to the owners of Malibu to take his spot. He told them I had all the hot records, mixed great, and I should take over his spot. I got hired and was in heaven, again. Now I was working in a new wave club where I could help break some of the new records I got during the day at IRD. I was getting UK test pressings to play before anyone else. Malibu had all the bands that played in Manhattan at clubs like The Ritz, Danceteria, the Mudd Club, and the Peppermint Lounge. Bands like Siouxsie and the Banshees, Adam Ant, 999, the B-52's, Squeeze, The Psychedelic Furs, Joan Jett, Joe Jackson, Iggy Pop, Bow Wow Wow, Hall & Oates, The Go Go's, the Ramones, The Specials, the Plasmatics, and U2 all played Malibu. I remember when U2 played, it was a cold rainy Wednesday night in December, and there was only like 300 people there. It is pretty wild to have seen them like that, and then to see them now, still going, a huge supergroup, popular, and respected all the world over.

At IRD, the records were coming in by the truckload every day, plus all the UK music magazines and weekly papers—*NME, Sounds, Melody Maker, etc.* It was such a fertile time. I got all the early NWOBHM (new wave of British heavy metal) records. 1979 started a whole movement out of the UK of young, working-class heavy metal bands like Iron Maiden, Saxon, Def Leppard, Angel Witch, Raven, Samson, Tygers of Pan Tang, and also Budgie and Motörhead. Being a huge rock and metal fan, I naturally gravitated to this hot new scene. Having access to the newest releases right off the boat kept me very plugged into everything.

In 1980, I started a fanzine called Metal while working at IRD. Everything was hand-drawn and handwritten by me. I wrote the articles, cut and pasted the images, and copied the whole thing on an old-school copy machine, then collated and stapled each copy by hand. I gave them out at shows and clubs and put them in every record store's box that was shipped out at IRD. I also sent one to Iron Maiden's management in the UK. The cover of my first and only issue (hey, I had a lot going on!) was Iron Maiden, focusing on the new *Killers album.*

I got a letter back from Maiden's manager, Rod Smallwood, saying thank you for the coverage and letting me know they were coming to the US for the first time to support Judas Priest on tour. I was super excited, as I loved the first Maiden album and the first EP, The *Soundhouse* Tapes, which is extremely rare and now worth big bucks. I had received the advance UK copy of the new album, *Killers*, and couldn't stop listening to it. The shows were in July 1981 at the legendary Palladium in Manhattan supporting Judas Priest, who were on tour for *Point of Entry* (one of my fave Priest albums). They did four nights at the Palladium. I drove over to meet the band at the Gramercy Park Hotel before the first show, and the first person I saw down at the bar was Iron Maiden's lead vocalist, Paul Di'Anno. I introduced myself, and we immediately connected. I ordered us both a drink, we talked about how the tour was going, and I gave him a copy of my fanzine. We felt at ease with each other quickly. They were doing the first show of four that night, and all of them were sold out. He asked me if I knew where to get some "krell" (cocaine) and I said, "Why yes." We headed upstairs to his hotel room and hung with Maiden guitarist Dave Murray for a bit. I think Dave and Paul were sharing a room. We drank some Jack Daniel's, and I was able to get a friend that lived on 9th Street to get me some krell for Paul before heading to the show in cabs. Paul walked me through the stage door and gave me a pass, and we headed to the dressing room. I was wearing a very rare, city-specific Kiss t-shirt from a 1976 gig in Georgia. Iron Maiden's bassist, Steve Harris, really liked it, so we swapped t-shirts, and I got his Iron Maiden *Killers* Canadian tour shirt. Paul motioned for me to follow him, and we went into a room upstairs. I gave him his package, and he hit the krell. He was about to go onstage, and he was hitting it right before going out—behavior that possibly led to his ouster from Maiden. But, I must say, it was very rock and roll. We then went back downstairs, and the band walked to the stage. I followed and sat on a road case in the wings for Maiden's set.

They were so good—tight, heavy, and fresh to the ears. It was a whole new sound. I still like the first two Maiden albums with Di'Anno more than anything else they have done. I know I'm in a minority here, but those first two Maiden albums are like punk rock metal—tough and streetwise. I never got into the later Maiden records, and I've never been into the dungeons and dragons stuff, myself. After the show, Paul and I met up with legendary Humble Pie vocalist and guitarist, Steve Marriott, at a club called Nobody's in the Village where we talked, drank, and did krell till sunrise.

In between the Maiden shows in New York City, I helped set up an in-store record signing at Zig Zag Records in Brooklyn for the band. I headed over in my car and met them there. I watched after Paul at the in-store appearance and made sure he was okay. It was hot as balls in there, and there was a guy filming a video with a super hot light focused on Paul for most of the in-store. Paul was sweating and not in good shape from the night before. He finally asked me to get the guy to turn the light off. The guy didn't turn it off, but moved to a different spot. The in-store was mayhem. It was super packed, people crammed in all over the place, with a line around the corner. Zig Zag's owner, Arnie Goodman, had put my name as "presented by" on the poster hanging on the door of the store to advertise the event, so that made me happy. Arnie was always a good guy. After the in-store, we went back to the band's hotel in Manhattan since they were playing that night at the Palladium again. Paul rode back with me in my 1969 GTO, and we talked and listened to cassettes on the ride. We did more krell before I dropped him off at the hotel. I would have loved to have seen all of the shows, but I had to DJ that night. I saw two out of the four shows and felt really good about the in-store and about helping Maiden become successful in some small way. I loved being a part of helping to break a band or a record. I loved it.

At IRD, Barry liked all the vices that came with being the boss at an import record distributor. Some of the salesmen—besides selling Joy Division, Spandau Ballet, and Captain Beefheart records—also sold blow, weed, and 'ludes, and probably 75% of the staff was doing some kind of drugs. Friday payday was a crazy scene as everyone was swapping money, drugs, and records back and forth. Barry had an Israeli woman with a heavy accent as the bookkeeper and office manager, and she was wound up like a top. She ran the place as much as Barry did, but she was forever moaning about this and that, whining, yelling, and berating. She was like a cartoon. The salesmen were Jimmy Matt and John L.— with Barry handling a few accounts. There was Brian who ran the export department, and there was also a receptionist. I was in the warehouse packing boxes with George Q. Jimmy and John, the salesmen, called the stores. Jimmy and John picked their own orders and put them in the warehouse for us to pack up and send. One by one, as things grew, Barry hired more and more salespeople. They would start in the warehouse picking orders and packing them with me and George. Then, once they got that down, they would start selling to stores over the phone. Koz came in to sell and so did P.A. Cliff C. came in to start working in the warehouse, as he was an old friend of Barry's and needed a job. Cliff played in the original funk rock band, Material, and some other avant-garde groups out of Manhattan and was a good guitar player. I eventually became a salesman, but I never liked that part of the business. It was a grind.

A lot of the salesmen came from other record distributors, mostly Record Shack in Queens, where Barry, Alan B., and P.A. had all worked. The Shack sold a lot of R&B, soul, pop, and Top 100 albums and singles. Almost no imports—the very few coming from Jem, another import distributor in New Jersey. Jimmy Matt had worked at Jem. All of the record distributors were very competitive, and most didn't like one another, so there were a lot of territorial loyalties. If you were a salesman and had some of the small chains or some of the really big and famous stores, you were set. There were thousands of record stores in 1980—thousands—all competing to get the hottest releases every week before anyone else or at least not get shut out and get, God forbid, none of a hot record. You would call the store and read them the lists of records, one after another: new releases, yesterday's releases, the day before that's releases, catalog titles, magazines, newspapers, etc. The stores would buy the new titles and also restock on older stuff. Sometimes you had an order going out to Wax 'N' Facts or Bleecker Bob or whoever, 3,000, 4,000, or 5,000 dollars worth, two or three times a week. You got commissions on sales on top of your base salary. But being a record salesman wasn't for everyone—it was a lifestyle.

I mean, when we brought in *Sandinista!* by The Clash, we brought in probably 5,000 records every other day. Grace Jones 12" single, "Pull Up to the Bumper" was a HUGE record— thousands sold weekly. I remember the first Phil Collins solo single of "In the Air Tonight." It was an import single way before the American release. It sold a bunch. The records either weren't released here at all, or there was a gap of months before the American release, even with The Clash being a very big, influential band—on CBS no less. It was crazy thinking about all the imports that were sold while the US labels were scrambling around trying to decide if they wanted to release it or when. We were also carrying a lot of US-pressed indie record releases from 99 Records in Manhattan, Celluloid, Bomp!, Ralph, 415, Nugget's stuff—loads of great labels. They had 45 singles, EPs, 12" singles, and albums. All the US indie stuff was usually brought in on consignment, unless you had a good catalog and some clout. That meant we dealt with hundreds and hundreds of small indie labels. They would give you their product to sell up front and only got paid for what we sold. At the end of 60 or 90 days, the accounting office would run a report to see what we sold and then pay the label or not. Everyone wanted us to carry their releases, and we took in a lot of records. It was endless.

When John Lennon was assassinated in December 1980, it was right before Christmas, and the distributor smelled blood. They started bringing in Beatles records, Lennon records, UK-only pressings, and boxsets. We were deluged all through the holiday with everything Lennon. I remember the morning after he was killed, John, the head import buyer, was at the telex machine typing like a lunatic. Barry was also on the phone, and within 24 hours we had tons of Beatles and Lennon records to sell, stuff that was not released in the US. Stores were buying everything they could get there hands on. It was a good Christmas at IRD. RIP John Lennon.

At Malibu, the local radio station DJs at WLIR started hanging in the DJ booth and asking me about the records I was playing. WLIR had been doing an FM rock format for years, playing southern rock, progressive stuff, The Allman Brothers Band, Led Zeppelin, etc. Now, with the exploding import scene and new music out of Britain, they were changing to a "new music" format—essentially new wave. I arranged it so they could come down and buy records or get freebies from IRD, and they would play them on the air. I would start the ball rolling by playing the hottest and newest stuff at Malibu, and then the radio jocks who were hanging with me all the time would pick up on what was a hit on the dance floor. It was a great time.

Things started growing very fast at IRD, and we had to move because there was no more room for records, desks, or people. We moved down the street onto Guy R Brewer Boulevard (formerly New York Boulevard), and the new IRD was born with a bigger warehouse and offices and a drive-in loading dock. This building was around 20,000 square feet, and things were really blowing up. We started doing pressing and distribution deals with labels and bands—P&D deals. We started working with a lot of hot new labels and great bands. We did a deal with the Beastie Boys around 1983 for the "Cooky Puss" EP. They were just coming out of being a hardcore band, and they did this silly hip-hop-y type comedy dance record. They came in the offices, walking around and asking if they could take stuff, wandering through the place just drooling. There were always records, t-shirts, magazines, fanzines, cassettes, and all kinds of stuff just EVERYWHERE, so everyone walked out with stuff all the time. You were supposed to pay for stuff at a discount, and people did, but they usually walked out with more than they bought.

Towards the middle of 1982, I had gotten suspended from Malibu for partying in the DJ booth. That was the official explanation. The group running Malibu as a nightclub leased the property from the Town of Hempstead. It was on county land, so they were very strict there, as far as making sure everyone had proper ID and there were no drugs on the premise, etc. I was in the DJ booth working one night. The booking agent for the club was in there with me, and we were smoking hash and drinking, girls in and out of the booth. I guess it got to be a little much, so they suspended me, like high school. Anyway, I eventually came back a week later, but then a few weeks after that, I had a car accident and was laid up for a couple months. Once I healed, I heard Speaks wanted me to come work there. One of the bartenders there (he would become one of my best friends, Michael "Spud" Chandler) always came to Malibu, and he loved the music I played. He told the manager at Speaks that they needed to hire me. Speaks was Malibu's competition, except that Speaks was a dance club only and had no live bands. Speaks held about 2,500 packed out. It was on the water and had a huge outdoor deck. The music format was new wave, rock and roll, disco, funk—pretty much everything—but was heavy on the new wave dance stuff and the early electronic club music dubbed freestyle. It was the first nightclub owned by the mob-controlled Long Island club king, Phil Basile. Phil was backed and protected by Paulie Vario, a capo in the Lucchese family. Paulie was a family friend since I was a baby, and he and my dad and grandfather did business together. Speaks was Phil's cornerstone club, the longtime party palace in Island Park, New York. Speaks, at the time, was still in its glory. It had been around since the 60s. First, as the Action House, and everyone played there—Hendrix, The Doors, The Who, and The Young Rascals, who were the house band. When disco exploded in the mid 70s, they hosted The Trammps, Gloria Gaynor, and all the early disco groups. When disco started dying, the club changed again and became a rock palace in the late 70s, featuring Twisted Sister, Zebra, and even Aerosmith at their low point. When I started working there in 1982, it was called Speaks: The Dance Club, open five nights a week, featuring the top DJs on Long Island. Guys like Steve Thompson and Johnny Ace and now me. Speaks was not like Malibu. No, no. The owner Phil wasn't there a lot, as he had three other clubs that he owned—classier rooms. Speaks was his first club, but by this time, he had the big Channel 80 supper club on the water, which was the hottest disco on Long Island: 23 and up to get in, and you had to be dressed. Goombahs and guidettes, New York Mets and Jets, coke dealers, and other nightclub workers frequented the place.

Phil's brother-in-law, "Uncle" Ralph, managed Speaks officially, but Phil's son Frankie ran amok there and did whatever he wanted to. Frankie gave Ralph lots of agita, let me tell you. Frankie would pass out pills, weed, and lines of coke for the staff

109

right before we opened. We would all drop a shot glass of Wild Turkey in a mug of beer and chug it, snort a line, and get to work. All the bartenders drank all night. So did I. Everyone that worked there was dealing or doing or both. I worked at Speaks two nights a week from spring 1982 to mid 1985, and then off and on from 1985 to the end of 1987. It was pretty crazy at Speaks, and I have seen a lot of craziness over the years. I mean, anything went, pretty much, if you worked there or knew someone that worked there. From all the things I've done in this business, working at Speaks was where I hit the peak as far as the amount of crazy girls and drugs coming at me. There was no AIDS, and cocaine hadn't become the dreaded, dirty crack yet. It was still very much like the 1970s in a lot of ways. You couldn't find a condom anywhere, unless you went to a drugstore and asked the pharmacist to get you one. They kept them behind the counter. They weren't hanging on a rack next to the ChapStick like today. Every girl that went out to these clubs was on the pill. Sex wasn't that big of a deal—people just did it. Quickies, parking lots, bathrooms, wherever. Cocaine was a currency in the nightclubs. It was passed around and used as payment for all kinds of things, so it was everywhere. They both were: girls and drugs. If you worked for the club, you drank free all night anyway. And being the DJ, I was never without any of it.

I met one of my best and dearest friends at Speaks, Shmendrek. Shmendrek isn't her real name; her name is Stacey.

Shmendrek is a yiddish word for a pain in the ass or a joker. That's what her grandfather called her: "You little shmendrek!" The license plate on her car said "SHMENDRK." One night, she came up to the DJ booth and banged on the door. When I opened it, she loudly proclaimed that the music sucked and to play something else. I told her to go fuck herself and shut the door. A few minutes later, she showed up with a beer for me, and we have been friends ever since. We had our time when we were "dating," but she never nagged me or minded what I did with the guys or other girls or whatever. She was just cool about it. She is like one of the guys. She was the only girl that could hang out with the guys, and they wouldn't mind. She liked to party too—and we did! She made me laugh a lot! We have been the greatest friends since 1983 when she banged on the DJ booth door, and I told her to go fuck herself!

IRD was where I met P.A. He was a salesman there and had previously worked at Record Shack with Barry. He became a good friend and party buddy—and boy did we. We did a lot of drugs, saw a lot of shows together, and went out to a lot of clubs. We went to see The Who at Shea Stadium in Queens in 1982 with The Clash supporting. David Johansen was also on the bill as the opener. We did some heavy pre-show partying at P.A.'s apartment in Corona, Queens and then walked to Shea Stadium so we didn't have to drive. As you would expect, it was sold out, and the hype was high. The Clash had a big album with *Combat Rock,* and The

Who's new album was big as well. It was packed out, around 80,000 people, everyone ready to rock. My memory of that show is standing in the lower tier, listening to "Eminence Front," and doing blow out of an Excedrin bottle with a spoon. Good times. No security cameras anywhere, no social media, no cell phones—a 10 dollar bill would make a guard look the other way, every time. You brought in booze, drugs—anything. Security wasn't an issue then, really. No psycho was trying to gun everyone down or ignite a bomb. Shit, it was just a party! "Eminence Front" is one of the great later period Who songs. It's on the album *It's Hard*, which also had the big radio song, "Athena." When I hear "Eminence Front," I get chills, to this day. What a track. It is so The Who and so 1982.

I was working at Speaks at night and at IRD in the daytime. The new import music that I had access to weekly made every day exciting. There were so many genres and styles and so many great records released in Europe that were not out in America at the time. Eventually, the bigger labels, like CBS, WEA, etc., started getting their release dates tighter and issuing cease and desist letters to all the import distributors in America, but especially IRD, as we were moving the most volume. The two records that started the crackdown were both CBS records: A Santana album and a Journey 12" single. CBS sent a cease and desist letter and said we had to stop carrying those records. It eventually started getting tighter and tighter. The natural move was to do more US

P&D deals and start our own label, Relativity Records. We started doing a P&D deal with a label called Megaforce and did the first Metallica record. We released a lot of heavy metal, thrash metal, and speed metal that was our own later on the Combat label. Our Relativity label also released all kinds of fringe music and artists. Some of the earliest records we put out were from bands like Talas, Private Sector, Cargo, Roman Grey, Alien Sex Fiend, Tangerine Dream, Gene Loves Jezebel, the Dancing Hoods, Cluster & Eno, Joe Satriani, Scruffy The Cat, Wiseblood, Coil, Cocteau Twins, Circle Jerks, Thelonious Monster, and The Brandos.

The import boom at IRD went from 1979, the year they were founded, to 1984 or 1985. After 1985, the release dates for the big import releases and the big labels were pretty much the same or, at the most, a week or two apart. Because of this, the Relativity label was born. IRD still was distributing imports from all over the world, new stuff, as well as the vast amount of catalog that was not available in the US—stuff that the labels tried to stop, but couldn't or didn't want to because they had no label to release them in America anyway. They just wanted the sales. Records from The Beatles and the Stones catalogs; European and Japanese pressings; avante-garde electronic, jazz, reggae, folk, experimental, and punk records—there were plane loads arriving every day, but the days of bringing in The Clash or Journey records was dying fast. And now IRD, the distributor, was set up perfectly to start distributing their own labels, Relativity and Combat, to the stores.

Then came CDs, another huge shot in the arm. IRD carried loads of import CDs that were, again, not out in America! However, the focus started to be on US indies, P&D deals, and the Relativity/Combat family of labels, starting with small releases that sold next to nothing.

One of the first records we did was a 12" dance single called "Like A Ton Of Bricks (It's Hit Me)" by Private Sector that we licensed from the UK. We did a The Cure deal for the single of "Let's Go To Bed" and some other dance, club-type things. Eventually, there was staff for the label that was originally one or two people doing it all. They started hiring radio promo people, publicists, art directors, sales managers, etc. I eventually became Director of Promotions for the Relativity/Combat labels in 1987. It grew into a major company that was eventually bought out by Sony for millions.

Chapter Five - Mötley Crüe, Ratt, Hanoi Rocks - 1983-1985

When Mötley Crüe released the album Shout at the Devil in September 1983, we were all over it. I had turned everyone in our crew on to the first Mötley album, *Too Fast for Love,* when the band released it on their own Leathür Records, so we knew who Mötley were, but were completely blown away when we saw the new album cover. My friend from Elektra Records, Larry, gave me the advance tape and promo vinyl when it was released, and we all freaked. He sent me a monstrous 5 foot tall stand-up promo display of the inside of the album cover. We were in awe. They were the most over the top looking band with great, classic, pop metal tunes. We were yet to find out how much cocaine they liked to snort. This was like a bomb had dropped. Rock and roll was back! Not heavy metal, it never left, but kick ass, crazy rock and roll—Keith Moon style: throw TVs out of windows, screw a million chicks, drink Jack Daniel's from the bottle, and do tons of drugs. ROCK AND ROLL!

Through Larry at Elektra, I got two comp tickets and two backstage passes to the first area show of the Bark at the Moon/Shout at the Devil Tour in New Jersey at Brendan Byrne Arena (Meadowlands Arena) in East Rutherford, New Jersey on January 22, 1984. Mötley was opening for the king of the crazies, Ozzy Osbourne. This was the very beginning of their first big tour, and they were opening for Ozzy, sold out every night. Everything was fresh and exciting for the band. They weren't burned out yet, but jacked up and ready to rock and roll! Ready to conquer the world! My party buddy Bruno Ravel and I drove to New Jersey and did the pre-show party bumps (cocaine) on the way there. We hit traffic and got there late, grabbing the ticket envelope from will call. We walked in, and they were onstage already doing "Bastard," the second song of the set! I will not go into a deep description of what Mötley Crüe were like in 1984, musically or otherwise. I assume if you are reading this book you must know something about them and their absolutely wild reputation, but if not, pull up a live YouTube video from that tour and hear Vince Neil, the master of ceremonies, like a strip club MC, ask that age old question, "How many guys here tonight like to eat pussssssaayyyyyyyyy!!"

They were just pure, "I don't give a fuck," dirty and dangerous idiots having a fucking blast, no matter the consequences, rock and roll. Unfortunately, the consequences would come back to bite them hard later in the year. I had never seen anything like this before or since. It was like watching cartoon character rock stars. The drug and alcohol intake was ridiculous. No one, I mean no one, partied as hard or as recklessly as Mötley Crüe. How their road crew, road manager Rich, manager's Doc and Doug, and security guard Fred dealt with it all is unbelievable.

On stage, the energy was off the charts. We watched the show: "Red Hot," "Too Young to Fall in Love," "Ten Seconds to Love," "Knock 'Em Dead, Kid"—they just killed it. The crowd was like a tornado unleashed, all Aqua Net and spandex, denim and Budweiser, screaming at the stage like possessed zombies. They finished the set, and we started to make our way backstage. We saw Larry from Elektra walking in the same direction and followed him past the security guard, while saying hello to anyone we recognize—mainly staff from Elektra, local radio DJs, groupies, etc. We walked into the dressing room, and Larry introduced us to the band. They gave us bottles of beer and asked us how we liked the show, what we thought, etc. They didn't remember me from our first meeting a year or so prior, but they were so pumped up about opening for Ozzy that it didn't matter. Tommy Lee and Nikki Sixx treated us great. Mick Mars too. Vince is Vince. Tommy liked the t-shirt I was wearing, a picture of Mighty Mouse, the old cartoon character from the 60s. He showed me that he had Mighty Mouse tattooed on his arm, flying through a drum. He started calling me Mighty Mouse, and Nikki picked up on it too.

The dressing room was packed and loud, loaded with "industry" people, and the band was making the rounds. Bruno and I grabbed some more beer and checked out the scene, jacked up and ready for anything. We ended up with Tommy again around the corner in the giant locker room shower (to get away

117

from the insanity). He taught us the Mötley handshake (many steps), and we did some bumps, took a few pictures, and off he went, being pulled away to meet the guy that ran the merch company (not really but it was something like that). Nikki stumbled through, and we chatted a bit, took some pics (I always had a little pocket Instamatic camera with me) and headed to the shower for some more bumps. Then he got pulled away, while Bruno and I are wired and drinking beer.

Vince Neil was not around much, and I'm sure you can guess why. It was only about the chicks for Vince, understandably, being the lead singer. Mick was chatting to someone intensely, and we didn't really speak to him. We were wired and half drunk, but keeping it cool. We kept going into the shower to do bumps with Nikki and Tommy. This pattern continued for an hour or so. It was dizzying. Things were starting to wind down, and we said our goodbyes to Larry and the band and said we would see them in two nights at their show in New Haven. Larry let me know there would be tickets and passes for the show at the box office will call window for me. We didn't even see Ozzy play, but were super excited that we connected with Mötley.

We headed to the car and drove an hour and a half back to Queens. We hit the Sage Diner on Queens Boulevard for a burger deluxe and an egg cream. Mötley were everything we thought they would be and even crazier than we could imagine. They were rock and roll in the flesh. Crazy insane attitude. We were both hooked. We finished eating, and Bruno drove back to his apartment. I got in my car and headed home to crash for a bit. I woke up at 8 AM and worked all day, then went home and collapsed into bed. I woke up at about noon the next day, then headed to Queens. Bruno and I had to head to New Haven for Mötley. We always called them Mötley. Some people call them Crüe. It's like Judas Priest. We called them Priest, and I know guys that call them Judas. Take your pick.

I got through the abysmal traffic on the Van Wyck Expressway and got to Bruno's. I parked, and then hopped into his car for the two and a half hour drive to New Haven, Connecticut. Same thing happened—we hit traffic. We finally got there, parked, grabbed the ticket envelope from will call, and walked in on second song, "Bastard"—again! I guessed we would get to see them do the opening song, "Shout at the Devil," eventually. The show was great, and the crowd was loving it! Tommy held it all together, Nikki the maniac twirling around like a banshee, Mick destroying your ears with dive bomb wailing, and Vince telling you this story: "Our hearts are broken tonight. Do you know why are hearts are broken *toniiiigggggghhhht??* 'Cause we can't eat all the Connecticut *pussssyyyyyy tonite*! But we're gonna try!" They slammed into "Ten Seconds to Love," and the place went nuts! The Crüe were on fire, pumped. You could literally see the energy, like lightning shooting around the stage. Tommy Lee is an incredible drummer. His intensity is unmatched. His long arms were flailing around behind the kit like an octopus. In my opinion, he is one of the top five hard rock drummers of all time. Nikki was like a caged animal let loose. Jacked up on whiskey and blow, he twirled and kicked like an evil Muppet, keeping those in the front rows glued to his every move. He is the heart of Mötley Crüe, if there is a heart in there. Mick Mars was the veteran: experienced, wiser, and louder, he keeps the band groovin'. He's the Sweet by way of Duane Allman. And Vince Neil had taken the David Lee Roth lead singer model and taken it not just into the strip club, but the gutter of the strip club. He liked to talk about eating pussy, getting high, being out at 3 AM trying to get laid and only finding ugly chicks to fuck, and called the crowd "bastards"—the more he talked like that, the more chicks he got! All while prancing around like Peter Pan onstage. The 80s were a unique time, as far as everyone just going to the extreme. The 60s and 70s were wild, sure, but the fucking 80s were over the top. Greed, excess, money, fame—it was the ME decade. Everyone got in as much as they could, as fast as they could. And we were no exception!

We made our way backstage after the set, and there was not one person backstage except me and Bruno. It was just us and the band. There were immediate cries of, "What's up dude!" and "Dude! What's up!" high-fiving, etc. After a couple of tries, we got the Mötley handshake down with T-Bone! Like I said earlier, the tour was still new and fresh for them. They were pumped to just be doing it, playing rock and roll for a living, and partying their asses off. Tommy was what, 21 years old? They loved what they did, and they made sure you knew it! I brought my Mighty Mouse t-shirt to give to Tommy, and he freaked! I explained that I didn't have time to wash it, but he said he didn't care and threw it in his bag, giving me a high five.

We broke out the krell (cocaine) and started the party. Out from the hallway, entered famed British photographer Ross Halfin. He was there to take some pics of the band for Kerrang! magazine, and he joined in on the krell party. I had been loving Ross's pics in Kerrang! and Sounds newspaper for years already and was excited to meet him. We took some pics with Mick and Vince, then they drifted away somewhere, leaving Tommy and Nikki in party mode.

We took pics, the guy's posed, we did more krell, took swigs from bottles, took more krell-face pics, took more swigs, more krell, more pics, etc. Then, in walks Jon Bon Jovi. This was January 1984, a few years before the mega fame of *Slippery When Wet.* Jon had just signed with Mötley's manager, Doc McGhee, for representation and was hanging around on tour. He was all eyes: observing and watching. What to do and what NOT to do. I had no idea who he was, but Bruno knew him from the song "Runaway," which was on the local New York City radio station

WAPP's compilation album of local New York City area artists. Bruno took a pic with him, and he actually looked cooler than Bon Jovi! Ha! Anyway, JBJ was in the mix, but not in on the krell party. Smart, that JBJ.

Having partied with and been around many crazy rock bands, drug dealers, nightclub freaks, strippers, wiseguys, etc., I have never seen anyone party like Mötley Crüe—or specifically, Nikki Sixx and Tommy Lee. Completely wide open, jacked to the nines, and the best part was, they were very cool and nice to us always. Yes, we always came bearing party favors, but deep down, we were fans. We were fans of the music and their lifestyle and fans of the fact that no one else was even coming close to them as far as pure, unbridled, decadent, rock and roll insanity. Mötley opening for Ozzy in 1984? It doesn't get crazier than that.

Everyone decided to split for the hotel. When we walked in, we saw Bon Jovi in the lobby and ended up hanging with him. He invited us to his room to hang and have a beer. Bruno was talking to him about music and his new record he was working on, etc., when all of a sudden Nikki started pounding on the door with "I'm gonna break it down" force. He was in the hallway yelling through the door, "Bon Jovi, give us your chicks!" Bruno and I looked at each other like, What! Jon opened the door, and Nikki came in for a minute, looked around, looked at us, saw we were not chicks, looked puzzled, and then started pouring a drink from a bottle of

Jack he was carrying with him. He sat down with me and Bruno while Bon Jovi took a pic of us. We gave Nikki a bump, and off he went out the door, looking for trouble. We talked a little more, then said our goodbyes to Jon and headed to the hotel bar. We ran into the band's manager, Doc McGhee, in the lobby, and he kind of recognized us from the last show. He asked us what we were doing. We explained we were going to see Nikki. He knew what for. He said, "Hey, I uh, need to test that stuff, need to make sure its good." We gave Doc a bump, he smiled, and on we went to the bar.

When we walked in, it was empty except for the bartender and Nikki and a girl sitting at a table at the far end of the room alone. There was a crazy look on Nikki's face, so we kept our distance and sat across the room, ordering drinks. After a few minutes, Nikki looked at us smiling, and motioned for us to come over by touching his nose. I wonder what he wanted? Duh. We headed over and gave Nikki a bump, noticing that the chick he was with is giving him a handjob at the table. Nikki said, "Bark at the moon, dude," and asked for more krell by touching his nose, smiling that twisted evil smile that he used to smile. His eyes were pinned and glassy. The chick then slid down under the table and started giving him a blowjob. This was rock and roll! We gave Nikki more bumps, the chick was working away, and Nikki's smiling. Bruno looked at me, wired, like, *Time to leave.* I was in worse shape than Bruno and just nodded my head. We told Nikki we had to go and that we would see him the following night. We didn't know where Tommy was, Nikki was getting a blowjob, and it was 2 AM, so we drove back home to Queens, two and a half hours away, knowing we wouldn't sleep at all, because that night they were playing on Long Island at Nassau Coliseum—home turf.

Once I got home, I didn't sleep, passing out on my bed instead fully clothed for an hour. The alarm rang at 8 AM, and I pulled last night's cobweb of cocaine, beer, vodka, and weed off my face. My head was on fire; last night was crazy. I headed to work at IRD, and dragged myself through the day. Bruno drove out from Queens after work, and we hooked up with our friends from the local cover band Hotshot, singer Mike Pont and roadie Kelly "Blade" Nickels, and headed over to the Crüe's hotel in Westbury in the midafternoon to connect with Tommy, and it started all over again.

We headed to Tommy's room. More krell, taking pictures, Mötley handshake, etc. Tommy was rooming with Vince at the time, and old Vinnie was in a bad mood—something about a girl and a phone call, and if she calls back, tell her "I'm down at the bar getting a blowjob" type of thing. He couldn't find his wallet and accused us of taking it, but we kept saying we didn't because we didn't! Tommy was defending us saying we were cool, etc., and

Vince was still going on about it when he finally found the wallet buried in his suitcase.

He didn't say another word and just walked out the door. See ya! Tommy's roadie, Clyde "The Spyde," came in, and we all hit the krell, took more pics, and hung out for a bit, before saying we would see them tonight. We left the hotel in a puff of blow and adrenaline and headed to the diner on Old Country Road, trying to eat, gagging a lot, giving up, and then heading to a bar by the arena. We were psyched up and pumped for the show. Since the Long Island show was close to home, a lot of friends showed up and met us at the bar. The word was starting to get out that we had the hookup with the band, so we had a lot of extra friends that night.

Mötley and Ratt were always very nice to us. They were nuts, but great fun. Great times. Robbin "King" Crosby, Nikki Sixx, and Tommy Lee, I should say, were always nice to us. That's the thing, those guys were nice to us; they weren't dicks to us. And we were crazy, man. We were all over the place. How do you think I have all these pictures?! I was breaking out cameras—we took pictures of them doing cocaine! They didn't give a fuck. They did not care. There's a lot of guys in bands that would do your drugs and be a dick to you. Not Tommy, Nikki, and King. They were very nice to us. And we were hyped up like speed freaks—nervous adrenaline, excitement about the music and the scene—cocaine made us crazy people. It was the times: the 80s.

Elektra were starting a big push at radio and MTV for the first single off the Shout album, "Looks That Kill." Earlier that week, Larry had asked me if I could help get some friends to distribute flyers at the Long Island show. The flyers were asking fans to call MTV and radio and request "Looks That Kill." Of course I could help! I made some calls and got some friends to help distribute the flyers to fans at the Coliseum for Elektra and Mötley. Larry met up with us at the will call window, got me my ticket envelope, and we all started handing flyers to the crazed fans as they entered the arena. The building was ready to rock, fans yelling, screaming, "Ozzy! Mötley! Crüe! Ozzy!" Everyone was pumped up and ready to go crazy! We had about a dozen people who handed out flyers for an hour to all the fans coming in. The energy was off the charts. The place was electric. You could smell the scent of the pregame parking lot alcohol and Aqua Net at every turn. Once the flyers were fully distributed, our work completed, we all headed into the show. I had Bruno as my plus one, and everyone else in our crew already had tickets, but no passes. Before we all split up, I thanked Larry for the tickets and backstage passes, and we saw our third show in a row. The crowd was crazy, ears were bleeding, and the party was on. This time, we saw the opening song, "Shout at The Devil." Finally! It was, and is, one of the greatest kick ass opening songs in the history of rock and roll. The show was great. They killed it again. Vince's raps were hilarious, ridiculous, and cool all at the same time. Long Island was eating it up. Everyone we knew was there, and everyone was loving it. After the set ended, Bruno and I started to head backstage. We were all pumped and primed, but we couldn't find Larry, and it was a repeat of two nights ago in New Jersey. The entry to the backstage was a gridlock; everyone trying to get backstage. People with passes and without passes, people begging for passes; Nassau Coliseum security guards not really sure what to do—who belongs and who doesn't? It was mayhem.

We were held outside the entrance to the backstage area in what we call "the pen," a barricaded holding area, like cattle. Everyone in the pen with a sticky pass waited to be escorted backstage by someone with a tour laminate—or not. It's a very desperate scene. We were quickly grabbed by Mötley's road manager, Rich Fisher. Rich was cool with us and tolerated us because we always brought drugs with us. In later years, I would come to know the road manager game well, and Rich was a good guy and always cool. He motioned us around the barricade of the pen, and we followed him to the band dressing room. We entered and there were a few people hanging out, but it was not overly crowded—yet. Once again, we were met with cries of, "Dude!," "What's up dude!," "What did you think of the show?," and "You ready to get nuts?!" Of course! We grabbed a beer from the bin and started to get...nuts! Bumps all around, high fives, and the

Mötley handshake with T-Bone signaling the start of the fun. I asked Tommy if we could get some passes for our friends who were back in the pen. He said, "Sure dude!" He called over a crew member who we didn't know and asked him to get some passes from Rich. We talked with Tommy, and Nikki came over smiling that crazy smile of his, wanting the obvious—bumps! We took some pics, did some bumps, downed our beers, and yakked away a mile a minute. The dressing room started getting more crowded, and Rich appeared asking why we needed more passes. I explained we would like to get some friends in who also might be "holding." He gave me the talk about "Make sure they are cool and not idiots," etc. This was road manager college. I used a lot of what I learned hanging around Mötley, Ratt, Iron Maiden, Twisted Sister, etc. years later in my time as road manager for L.A. Guns. Rich gave me two passes, and I went out towards the pen, looking for Pont and Blade. I made sure not to get too close to the pen, lest I be grabbed back into it!

I saw Pont, who was also looking for me, of course, and handed him the passes, and they both walked backstage with me. I suddenly had some power because the Nassau security guards let me do it.

We all got blasted as usual, yakked loudly into the night, and finally said our goodbyes to the band, Rich, Larry, etc. Mötley Crüe definitely were the hot band to like if you were into wild rock and roll mayhem and an over-the-top image. Call it what you want—rock and roll, heavy metal, glam, whatever—they were unique and the real deal. They gave a hard kick in the ass to the rock and roll establishment, and they became the band you listened to in the high school parking lot before first period in cities and towns all over America. The more the parents hated them, the bigger they got.

The Crüe were out of the area for a couple days and then returned to New York City to meet with record label execs, media, and MTV, and to get primed for their show at Madison Square Garden with Ozzy. The night before the show, the band attended a record company party at Limelight nightclub for their gold album presentation. Larry told me about it and invited me, and I went solo. It was mainly a media event and wasn't a crazy party night, at least for me! I said hello to the guys and let them do their thing. Hung out for a drink or two and then went home to try to rest. The Crüe was playing Madison Square Garden tomorrow night.

The next afternoon, I took a train to Penn Station and met everyone at the Garden. There was probably about 15 of us altogether. I headed to will call, and Larry, the wonder man, had left me an envelope. I can't say enough about the generosity from Larry during the "Crüe years." He left me two tickets and passes. Bruno and I headed in and got to our seats as the lights were going down with "In The Beginning," the Mötley Crüe intro from the Shout at the Devil album, was blasting. We took our seats, good loge, and when the band exploded into "Shout," the Garden went nuts. It's hard to explain how different Mötley were at the time. They were similar to a lot of things and other bands, but completely original at the same time. That's why they caught fire. They were a new era of rock and roll, not heavy metal, but rock and roll. A new chassis on the classic rock frame.

The band was in rare form that night, as this was the first time they were playing the world's most famous arena, Madison Square Garden. They were on fire. Nikki was twirling and thrashing around, Tommy was beating the shit out of the drums, Mick was wailing, and Vince was always the leader of the party, "New York City! How the fuck ya doing *toniiiiight?!*" The band was awarded platinum albums onstage for *Shout at the Devil* for selling a million copies, and they were pumped up! The Garden is a big arena, and it was sold out, 17,000 plus. The energy was insane.

After the show, Bruno and I started to head in the general direction of the MSG version of the pen. Back in the 1980s, the backstage entrance at the Garden was still set up the old school way, like Sinatra would walk out from the curtain on the side of the floor, where the hockey players went into the locker room. The walkway to the pen area started in the middle of the arena floor.

You walked towards the side where there was a curtain with guards, and in front of that, was a barricade aka the pen. The floor walkway was a gridlock. All of our crew who didn't have passes were in the walkway and descending on the pen at the same time. Everyone was yelling at me to get them backstage. It was madness. We pushed our way through, and eventually Rich got us in again. We were dragged through the insanity and into the tunnel of the dressing room area and sports locker rooms. There were a lot of girls backstage, record company peeps, industry people—it was crowded. The dressing room was off limits, as the band were in there with their girlfriends. Huh? Girlfriends? This was Mötley fucking Crüe! Raping and pillaging America night after night! What girlfriends?! The "girlfriends" flew in to celebrate with the band in New York City for getting the platinum awards for *Shout at the Devil.*

Tommy emerged from the dressing room and saw us outside in the hallway and came over with his usual hyper, positive energy, "What's up dudes?! Mighty Mouse, what's up!" We talked about Shout going platinum, the insane crowd that night, etc., and he gave me the nod, so we snuck away into the bands dressing room for a quick bump.

I asked him if it was possible to get us some more passes, as there were friends outside again.

He was so happy about *Shout* going platinum, so happy that he just played Madison fucking Square Garden, so happy I just gave him a bump of top grade blow, and so happy to see us, he said, "Come with me, dude!" We walked out onto the floor of the Garden, in plain view of everyone in the pen trying to get backstage and all the fans in the crowd. He said to the MSG security guy, "I just played onstage, and these are my friends, and I want them in." He told me to point them out, and as I did, they trampled each other to get backstage before the security guard changed his mind. People were screaming for Tommy and hollering his name, and he just gave everyone the thumbs up as ten of our crew were just walked backstage, led by Tommy Lee!

I couldn't believe it! Tommy was always so nice and cool to us, but this was wild! We all headed to the backstage hallway outside the dressing room area and looked for a beer somewhere. We said hello to the guys whenever they popped out for fresh air from the dressing room full of girlfriends. Tommy and Nikki grabbed me and Bruno and dragged us into the dressing room for bumps, as the hallway outside was packed.

STEVE WEST: *"Mötley Shout at the Garden. We were all hanging out backstage in the hallway, and Tommy and Nikki were grabbing Corky and Bruno and bringing them into the dressing room, and they went into the showers to do blow while we were just hanging out like idiots."*

We wouldn't see the band again for about 5 months when they were off the Ozzy tour and starting to headline their own shows. They came back to Manhattan and played two nights at the Beacon Theatre with Ratt as the openers in June 1984. This was probably the peak gig of that time and that scene for us. Ratt opening for Mötley Crüe: Sunset Strip had arrived in full effect in Manhattan.

Ratt were on Atlantic Records and I had good friends at that label as well, so I got hooked up for all the Ratt shows. I had Ratt's first EP on Time Coast Records, a small indie, so when Atlantic signed them and released *Out of the Cellar,* I already knew who they were. Robbin Crosby was good friends with Nikki Sixx, so there was that connection as far as Robbin knowing we were cool and that we liked to party. Robbin and Stephen Pearcy really ran Ratt, so we were in with the Ratt camp. "Round And Round" shot out of the cannon and was a monstrous radio hit. Ratt had a bigger radio song than Mötley, but Mötley were a bigger band. The first time we saw Ratt was when they headlined L'Amour Brooklyn the day before they opened the two nights for Mötley at the Beacon Theatre. That was a crazy week! I drove to the show with my friend Stacey aka Shmendrek. She drove and I partied the whole way. When we got there, we did some lines in the car. We walked to the entrance and it was insanely packed outside. You could barely get in the door. As soon as we were able to get inside, I asked the box office guy to please find my name on the list, which took a bit of time. He had scraps of paper everywhere, names written on pieces of cardboard ripped off a Budweiser carton, unalphabetized handwritten lists a mile long—it was comical. Once my name was found and we got through the entryway, I immediately ran into a friend of mine from high school who told me that Tommy and Nikki were in the VIP area at the back of the room. To get to the back of the room through this thick wall of probably 2,000 people was going to be an adventure in itself. We pushed our way through, and at the very back was an elevated VIP area, about 3 feet high, surrounded by a metal railing. There was security everywhere, and no one was being allowed up into the VIP area. I saw Tommy and called out, "T-Bone!" He spun around and saw me, physically grabbed me, and lifted me over the railing into the VIP area. It was all, "Dude!," "What's up dude!," as he handed me a beer and we did the Mötley handshake. I got Shmendrek into the VIP area and introduced her to Tommy. As I was talking to Tommy, I looked over his shoulder and saw Nikki leaning against the wall, in full view of everyone, getting a blowjob from a chick sitting on a chair. He was also swigging from a bottle of Jack Daniel's. Insane. Once he was done with the chick, he came over and shoved the bottle of Jack in my face and demanded I drink. "Drink it!" he said. This was his way of acknowledging me and saying hello. I grabbed the bottle and drank a healthy swig. As I was drinking the Jack, he smiled and leaned down and bit the fuck out of my shoulder. It started bleeding. I was screaming and Nikki was just smiling. Tommy grabbed me and said, "He only bites you if he likes you, dude! You're good!" Jesus, that fucking hurt! But at least he liked me!

SHMENDREK: *"Once Corky pulled me into the VIP area, I saw Nikki getting blown by some chicks in front of everyone. I was shocked! Tommy asked Corky if I was a member of the Crüe yet, and he said no. Tommy then nodded to Nikki, and he bit me too! I was black and blue for three weeks! I remember that night at L'Amour, it was one of the hottest nights of the summer. I was sweating to death, and Nikki looked like a monster in head-to-toe black leather. I don't know how he didn't pass out. I remember feeling very small, even in heels. All those guys were so tall and had such big hair! They were showing us their new tattoos they had just got that said 'Mötley Crüe,' with like a bat flying near it. The whole band got them."*

A photographer came by and snapped a pic of me, Tommy, and Nikki. Nikki, Tommy, and I did some bumps and partied partied partied. We passed the bottle of Jack around and looked for cold beers. Ratt hit the stage and tore it up. We watched from the VIP area with T-Bone and Nikki. I kept an eye on Sixx to make sure he didn't sneak up and bite me again. My shoulder was fucking hurting, but I just kept drinking to kill the pain. I hooked up with Bruno at the VIP area and got him in to watch with us. After the show, I headed with Bruno to the backstage area to meet the Ratt guys.

BRUNO RAVEL: *"We were standing outside the dressing room waiting to party with Ratt.*

We got in the dressing room and were nervous! That was the first time we met Ratt."

The Atlantic Records crew was there and we waited outside the dressing room door with them. It was a small room, and people filtered in and out. We got introduced to Robbin and Bobby Blotzer (who also loved the bump game), and the debauchery continued until the club closed at 4 AM. Shmendrek and I staggered out of there feeling like a truck hit us. She got me home, and once I hit the bed I fell asleep instantly.

When I woke up, my arm was bloody, oozing puss, and it hurt like hell. I dragged myself to the doctor and he insisted I get a rabies shot. "Human bites are very dangerous," he told me, and it could get badly infected if I didn't get the shot. Ugh. I got the shot and they covered it with a bandage. I headed home and waited for Mike Pont to pick me up. It was night one of Mötley and Ratt at the Beacon.

It's hard to describe how important these two nights were. This was the peak of the L.A. scene to me. Everything the new rock scene was, was right here. The two biggest and best bands

136

that came out of the L.A. scene in that second wave were playing together. The first wave was the Van Halen era. They started in 1975 and got signed in 1977 with their first album released in 1978. Mötley was the second wave with a 1981/1982 start. Same with Ratt. These were THE two big L.A. bands at the time bringing a completely fresh new approach to hard rock and roll and punk metal pop. Ratt called themselves "fashion rock." It was something that could only exist in 1984.

The Beacon is a theater with a capacity of about 2,900. The vibe was much different than an arena concert. It was much more intimate. The Crüe stage set looked bigger, but somehow more compact on the Beacon stage, more intense. The energy was even crazier than the last show we saw at the Garden opening for Ozzy. The Beacon not only sold beer, but had a full bar in the lobby. Everyone was drunk or on their way. We did constant bumps and drank vodka all through Ratt and Mötley.

I don't remember who I got the tickets from for these Beacon Theatre shows, but the passes came directly from the band this time. Clyde "The Spyde" handed them to me right after the show both nights. Pont and I met Clyde at the side stage door, he gave us the passes, and then he handed us off to security man Fred. Fred saw my bandaged shoulder and asked what happened. I tell him Nikki bit me and he replied, "Fuck that. They tried to bite me once, and I cracked a rib. They know not to bite me now!" Fred is the man!

Backstage, the small stairway leading upstairs to the small rooms that were used as dressing rooms were gridlocked. Fred led us up, and we fought our way up through the crowd. Pont and I got pulled into the Mötley dressing room by Fred. Tommy and Nikki were sitting there in their sweaty stage clothes, and we started giving them bumps. Tommy grabbed a fresh bottle of Jack Daniel's, opened it, and threw the cap out the window. Won't be needing that! We passed the bottle around and did more bumps. We looked out the window of the dressing room down to the street and saw a lot of fans outside by the backstage door. Bruno and Steve West were down there too, yelling up at us to come and get them in, but we couldn't get them in, as it was just too nuts. The Beacon is a small theater that seats a little less than 2,900, and the Crüe were doing two nights. Each night, there was hundreds of people that can't get in. Pont and I were pumped up and partying. We kept getting dragged into rooms by Mötley and Ratt's road managers and security guys, and we partied with Nikki, Tommy, Blotzer, and Crosby all night.

I posed for a pic with Nikki and Tommy, and Nikki started biting my hand. You can see in the picture I'm wincing like, owwwww! Fred told me Mötley were going downtown to a club called Heartbreak on Varick Street. Pont and I headed over there and met up with the guys. We got in the club and it was not very crowded at all. The band were sitting at tables drinking, chicks were hanging out, but it was pretty mellow. We grabbed a table and got some beers, but it was pretty chill. Eventually, we all headed to the basement. Fred asked us if we had some blow. I laid out an 8 ball on the pinball machine. Fred whipped out a big fucking knife and cut the 8 ball into four piles. Tommy and Nikki snorted two piles each, and Fred said, "Okay, your turn." I was like, "Uh, Fred that was an 8 ball—it's all we had!" Someone else that was down there with us had some blow, threw down a big pile, and we snorted it up. We partied for an hour or so, then headed back to Tommy's room at the Parker Meridien Hotel—more krell, more drinking. Eventually, I staggered home somehow, but I left my wallet in Tommy's room. I called him the next day and told him I left it behind. He left it at the front desk for me with a note that said: "Mity Mouse" spelled like that. T-Bone! There was two nights of this. After awhile it becomes a blur.

1984 was a crazy fucking year. I was still working at IRD in the daytime, a DJ three nights a week at Speaks, was doing too many drugs, drinking way too much, and there were too many girls, plus I was starting my own band, Sweet Pain. The month after the Ratt/Mötley double bill at the Beacon, Twisted Sister and Ratt came through New York City together and played Pier 84 on Manhattan's West Side with Lita Ford opening. I never liked this venue. It was outdoors, on a pier like the name implies.

Manhattan is always a clusterfuck when it comes to parking and getting around, but thankfully Danny from Atlantic Records had the parking pass straightened out. Twisted and Ratt were both on Atlantic and were flip-flopping as headliner on this tour depending on what city they were in. Since this was New York City, there was no question as to who the headliner would be. I headed to Queens to meet up with Bruno, and then we drove to Danny's house. We picked up Danny and Flash, who also worked at Atlantic, and P.A. came along for the party. It was Jay Jay French's birthday, and they had a big cake made saying: "Happy birthday Jay Jay" with the Twisted logo. It was nice, but it was hot as balls, and the cake wasn't looking so good and was sliding around with me in the backseat as Danny drove like a demon to get us there in time. We arrived, Danny gave us all passes, and we put the cake away in a fridge in the hospitality trailer.

We positioned ourselves to watch Ratt start their set. The crowd ate it up as "Round And Round" was big news and all over the radio. Ratt was big and getting bigger and so was Twisted. This was a return hometown show for them. They also had a hot song with "We're Not Gonna Take It" climbing the charts and MTV. They had come a long way since I first saw them in 1978.

Ratt were blazing through their set, and Danny handed me a beer, clinking bottles as we awaited the band's finish. As soon as the set was over, Blotzer and Crosby came bounding down the metal steps of the stage and saw me right away. "Dude!" High fives all around. They were sweaty messes, but they wanted a bump right now! Bruno, P.A., and I went right under the stage with them and gave their sweaty faces big bumps. We stayed under there for a minute or so, bumped up good, and headed to the Ratt dressing room trailer. On the way, I ran into Twisted's road manager, Joe Gerber, and said hello. We reconnected with Crosby and Blotzer, and the party continued. Ratt's road manager, Wally, always pointed us in the right direction. He always took care of us.

We never really hung with the other guys in Ratt. Stephen Pearcy is the singer, and like Vince Neil, he was focused on chicks. Warren is a great guitar player, but mellow and shy. Juan Croucier, we never said more than a pilot hello to. The party maniacs in Ratt were Blotzer and Crosby.

We headed out to watch Twisted tear the place apart. The crowd was theirs, no doubt about it. At one point in the show, Dee told the crowd it was Jay Jay's birthday, and Danny and I brought the cake out onstage. Dee led the crowd in singing "Happy Fucking Birthday," Jay Jay blew out the candles, and Twisted resumed kicking major ass. We eventually made our way home after much partying. Again. It was never dark, the drug use, it was up, fun, and happy. The darkness would come later.

We were not drug dealers, but we had access to them, and the bands loved them, so we brought them. Our connection to the scene was based on us being fans first. We weren't in the business of working with bands, and we didn't work for the record company. We were fans that liked to party, and Mötley and Ratt liked to party too. Plus, we could be depended on to show up with the goods, and fortunately, it was of a very good quality. So once again, I was a facilitator.

This went on, week after week, month after month. Rock and roll, concerts, nightclubs, DJ work, liquor, drugs, chicks, partying—it was a grueling pace. For my age, I was so advanced in some ways (the darker ones) and still a kid in others. When I wasn't working days and doing my weekly DJ gigs at Speaks, I was either seeing my friends' bands or going out to a ton of clubs and attending concerts. I was relentless. I also started my own band, which just added to the insane pace.

In September 1984, I went with Mike Pont to see Ratt open for Billy Squier at the Meadowlands in New Jersey. We once again hooked up with the Ratt guys. Road manager Wally remembered us from past gigs, and we had no problem getting backstage after the show. There was no one really hanging out. Pont and I were pretty much the only ones there. We did connect with Crosby and Blotzer and went in the shower for some bumps. The other guys were kind of wandering around, and I noticed that the legendary sound man, Nitebob, was hanging out too. He was mixing Ratt front of house. I knew who he was, but had never met him. I reminded him of this when I did first officially meet him when he was doing sound for Ted Nugent in 1988. L.A. Guns, who I was working for at that time, were the openers for Ted.

We took some pics with the Ratt guys, had a beer, and left early. We went out and watched some Billy Squier, who was kind of over by this point. After he released the video for "Rock Me Tonite," everyone turned on him. It was so silly. I didn't think it was that bad. But shit, we were chasing bands around that wore more makeup than my grandmother!

A couple months later, Pont and I went to see Hanoi Rocks at The Ritz in Manhattan on November 21st and at L'Amour Brooklyn on November 23, 1984. I really thought they were gonna be big. I think they would have been. Most of us know the story of Vince and Razzle. It was a tragedy for sure. I really don't want to repeat it here, so if you are interested, watch the Mötley movie, *The Dirt,* or just Google it. Pont brought his good camera to The Ritz and took a bunch of great pics, most of them of lead singer Mike Monroe. I think he has one pic of Razzle with Andy McCoy sitting on the drum riser. The show was great. Mike Monroe was like nothing I had ever seen before. You could feel that they were gonna get there. We ended up meeting the Hanoi Rocks guys at L'Amour a couple of nights later, and we talked for a bit. They were nice guys. We had a beer and talked about touring the States. It wasn't that crowded at either show. It was a decent crowd, but they had the rock and roll swagger, that's for sure. You could feel it. The new album that Bob Ezrin produced was so fucking good. Mike ended up hurting his ankle in Syracuse a week later, and they limped through the tour for awhile before having to cancel a bunch of dates. The band flew to L.A. to hang out for awhile, and the rest is history—but they were right...there.

Mötley came back around on August 2, 1985 on the Theatre of Pain Tour. It was the second show of the tour. Bruno and I drove up to New Haven with Eddie Ojeda from Twisted Sister and his bodyguard, Vic. Vic was wild. He had done security for the Stones in 1981 and worked for Freddie Mercury and Queen, among others. The stories he told me about Freddie—oh man. Freddie was a handful. We drove up to the show in my '84 LeBaron convertible. It was August and hot as fuck, so the top was up. A two and a half hour drive on the highway with the top down is not fun. We got to the gig and pulled up to the load-in area. There was a big fence, but Vic jumped out of the car and walked through the main gate and into the stage door. He appeared a few minutes later and got us parked inside the arena. We headed backstage to find the band, which we did. We said a brief hello to the Crüe, Bruno and I got our VIP passes and tickets, and we got some extra tickets and passes for the rest of our crew that was coming up. We hung around for a bit and then headed out to the hotel to leave an envelope for our friends P.A. and Mike Schnapp. Schnapp, at the time, worked in the heavy metal radio department at Combat Records and basically managed my band, Sweet Pain. He eventually left Combat and worked his way up to run the heavy metal/hard music department at Epic Records in the Pearl Jam days and was VP of rock music for EMI, signing the Fun Lovin' Criminals. P.A. is an old friend and also worked at IRD/Relativity and Combat. He was the voice of Major Mayhem, who did all the radio spots for the Combat Records artists. Steve West and Mike Pont also came up for the show and so did the Painettes—that's what we called the teen Sweet Pain fangirls. They also loved Mötley Crüe. This was the second show of the tour, so once again, it was fresh and new for the band, but I could tell it wasn't as loose and fun as the Shout tour. I guess the Vince incident with Razzle might have been to blame. Plus, the tour was two days old. Sure we snorted blow and all, but it was darker. The novelty of it all started wearing off maybe, and it wasn't the same.

I had told P.A. and Schnapp that I would leave the tickets and passes at the band's hotel. I gave them the name and address, but I had got the wrong hotel name somehow, and when I got there and realized it was not the Mötley Crüe hotel, I left a note there for them to go to a different hotel that I thought was it. I had to leave the envelope at only the band's hotel for security reasons. I couldn't just leave it at any hotel. You needed to have someone registered there that you knew. If not, the desk person could just take the tickets and passes, and you would be screwed—no security cameras everywhere in 1985. I left the guys a note to go to that hotel, but that turned out to be wrong hotel also. I then left another note. I got it right with the third hotel. There were no cellphones back then, so you had to leave friggin' notes around town! They eventually got their tickets and passes, and we connected with them at the show. Bruno and I left my car at the band's hotel and took a cab back to the gig. We did the usual pre-show party—blow, drinks, weed. The New Haven Coliseum was an old venue. It opened in 1972. and held 11,000. It was demolished in 2002. The place smelled old. We got in through the backstage entrance and made our way to the floor, grabbing beers on the way through the backstage. We had floor seats, about 25 rows back. The show was good, but it seemed to have lost the dangerous edge. The old songs weren't as raw and punky. There was also a lot of long audience singalongs. It was big arena rock. It was a very slick show, and the new stage outfits and imagery were very Broadway and glam-y. It was the Mötley glam phase. They opened with "Looks That Kill," which was a great opening song choice. Vince was his usual self, "New Haven! How many nasty girls we got here tonight?!" It was a bigger stage with massive stairs at the back, and Tommy aloft in the middle of it all. There were bombs, flashpots, and flames on "Shout at the Devil"—it was a big-time rock and roll show, their first big headlining tour. They had headlined at the end of the Shout tour, but the venues were smaller. This was their follow-up record, and everything was bigger—the venues, the videos, the radio singles, the hype, the imagery. Their cover of "Smokin' in the Boys Room" was all over MTV. It did good on radio, but it wasn't massive. The "Home Sweet Home" video and single would be released later in the year, and that would blow it all wide open—huge MTV video and radio single. I always liked the *Theatre of Pain record,* but it was knocked by a lot of fans, reviewers, and even the band as a weak album. Some of the songs weren't that great, but I loved some of the others. "City Boy Blues" was a fave and of course, "Home Sweet Home." The lyrics to that song are just great.

The band seemed a bit lost on the big stage. It was pretty bare, and there was a lot of room to run around, but Vince did a great job of covering the area, running and prancing around like Peter Pan. Nikki was running around and stuff, but the evil Muppet from the last tour was gone, replaced with a court jester in stripes. He even did a costume change—very Vegas. Tommy did his first big drum riser stunt. The floor of the drum riser would lift up like the top of a box opening, so he would be playing on a 90 degree angle. No one had ever done something like that before. It was a feat to play drums like that. The crowd ate it up. I'll say it again, Tommy Lee is one of the best hard rock drummers ever. He also had added in some drum triggers this tour, samples of different sounds that would play when he hit the drum pads. Mick was

Mick, running up the stairs occasionally and moving a little, doing his the Sweet meets Duane Allman riffs. They brought out Cub Koda to play "Smokin' in the Boys Room" with them. He wrote the song and was the leader of Brownsville Station, who did the original version.

The show ended after much stage talk from Vince about cumming too fast for the guys ("Ten Seconds to Love") and getting a piece of ass in every city in the world ("Piece of Your Action"). The lights came up and Bruno and I headed backstage. We had to get the other guys in our crew and the Painettes backstage also. Vic ended up taking over and running things. Whatever Vic said, went. He gave us the speech: "I work for Twisted Sister, and you are with me, and now you represent Twisted Sister, so what I say goes. You follow what I say?" Uhhhh, okay Vic! The arena was clearing out, and I went out and told the Painettes to hide up top behind some seats until we were able to get them backstage. They hid up there for like 15 minutes in an empty arena. Finally, Vic came out to get them. I was walking Vic out to show them where the girls were hiding. I called out their names, echoing through the empty arena, and they came scurrying down the steps. Vic gave them the talk: "I'm gonna get you back to meet the band, but one of you is gonna be my date tonight!" They looked at me with big eyes, and I gave them a wink. They just nodded as Vic walked us all backstage. Neil Smith, the drummer from the original Alice Cooper band, was backstage hanging out. He lived in Connecticut and came by to see the show. We were with Vic in the bathroom stalls doing blow, bringing other people in to do blow, and generally getting crazy. Eddie Ojeda was in on the fun, and we were all yapping away a mile a minute. It was so crazy, I didn't have time to take any pics at the gig. The backstage party started breaking up, and we all headed over to the band's hotel. Bruno and I grabbed a cab and when we pulled up, there were a million cars trying to park and cops blocking the entrance. They weren't letting anyone in that wasn't a registered hotel guest. The word got out to the fans where Mötley were staying. There were a hundred kids or more there. The Crüe's security guard, Fred, was outside and saw us, and he got us through the cops. He pulled me aside and said, "Nikki's in room 340 and Tommy's in 342. Go take care of 'em." We headed up and got to Nikki's room first. The door was open a little, held open by the security bar. We knocked and Nikki said, "Come innnnn." He was sitting in the dark by himself, the only light was from a lamp with a scarf draped over it, and he was looking scary. He was zoned out. We asked him if he wanted a bump, and he said sure. We all did some bumps and didn't say much. I didn't know it at the time, but it appeared that Nikki might have started with the smack. He wasn't like this on the last tour, at least not from what I could see. We hung for a couple of minutes and then said we were gonna go and would see him later. We walked out and closed the door, walking next door to Tommy's room. We knocked on the door and T-Bone opened it up and said,

"Dudes!" We walked in and there was music playing, "You Dropped a Bomb on Me" by The Gap Band. T-Bone was into the funk! It was a completely different vibe! Tommy was up and partying! There were a few girls hanging out while there was a picture of Heather Locklear on the night table next to his bed. He started telling us about The Gap Band. I already knew who they are from my nightclub DJ days, so we started yapping like madmen about them and funk. The funk drumming is in the Mötley tunes, just listen! We threw down some blow, and we all started hitting it. Eddie and Vic arrived and joined the party. Vic started working the door. Eventually Pont, Steve, P.A., and Schnapp knocked on the door. Vic wouldn't let them in and I had to tell Vic that they were friends and brought back-up party favors. Someone pulled out a bottle of vodka and P.A. threw down more blow. I remembered I had my camera and started taking pics. Nikki must have come back from the dead because even he showed up to the party. Nikki and I took a great pic together and that pic is how I remember Nikki back then. He is looking right through the camera, right through you, with that evil, dark stare. That's how I remember Nikki Sixx. I had an advance tape of the Sweet Pain album in my pocket and gave it to him. We did some bumps and drank through the night. I ended up getting very fucked up. Eventually, everyone started drifting off and leaving. I think Eddie and Vic got a ride home with P.A. and Schnapp, and Bruno left with Pont and Steve. I was a big mess and couldn't drive, so Tommy said I could crash there, and I slept on the floor—or tried to. He was able to go to sleep, which was crazy because we both were partying and snorting blow like crazy. I was wired and awake, laying on the floor looking at the ceiling. Eventually, I couldn't take it anymore and got up and told Tommy I was leaving and driving back to New York. I don't even know if he heard me. I went down to the hotel garage, got my car, and drove back to Queens a hundred miles an hour. I got home and lay awake for hours. The worst feeling. Terrible. Dark and evil.

They came back to the area on August 14, 1985 to play in New York City at Madison Square Garden. After the show, there was no backstage party, but an afterparty thrown by Elektra Records where the band would be awarded gold albums for *Theatre of Pain*. It was in a big loft around the corner from the Garden and was decorated with *Theatre of Pain* artwork along with a guillotine and noose and other torture or death devices to go with the "pain" theme. There was no air conditioning, or very little, just a few big fans, and it was 100 degrees in there. The walls were sweating. I was worried the blow would melt! The band showed up and took pics for the press with their managers, Doc and Doug, and were being Mötley—crazy poses and faces, acting like the gang that they were. They were all dressed up for the event, and it was so hot, I couldn't believe they weren't passing out. They had on long duster coats, chaps over jeans, blazers, and long-sleeve shirts. Jay Jay French from Twisted Sister was there.

I got Richie Ranno from Starz into the party. Nikki loves Starz and probably lifted some things from them, but who doesn't borrow from their influences. Bruce Kulick from Kiss was there—that version of Kiss—not real Kiss. 1985 Kiss. I had to get a lot of people into this party. Let's see: Mike Pont, Kelly Nickels, my girlfriend at the time, my brother, Bruno, the Painettes, and various other people who I can't remember. It was crazy. I was sweating like a pig, trying to make sure the blow didn't evaporate. Fred found me and asked what was happening. I explained my issue with the melting powder. He said, "I'll take care of it," and we went down to one of the band's limos that was idling outside with its air conditioning running and did blow down there—me, Fred, Tommy, and a rotating cast of people. Mission accomplished. We headed back to the sauna that was the party and repeated the limo run a few more times. This went on until the party ended and then we all went out somewhere to drink and snort more. Of course, we ended up in Tommy's room till sunrise.

Mötley Crüe were a big influence on everyone in our circle. They changed the game. They were also one of the first big, cool bands I really got nuts with. I partied with other musicians before and after the Crüe years, but I will definitely say, they were the hardest partying, nicest, and craziest bunch I ever had the pleasure of knowing. I saw them once on the *Girls, Girls, Girls* and *Dr. Feelgood tours*, but by then they were really huge, and it definitely wasn't the same. For me, I will carry those memories and photos of that early time in their career when Shout at the Devil changed the rock and roll game. Everything changes though. Time marches on. Nothing stays the same, except the music. It lives on. Rock is dead, they say? I say, fuck what they say. Rock and roll is a spirit, a rebellion, but it's also the songs. If you ain't got 'em, it don't work. So listen to the songs. They don't change, and they don't disappoint.

Chapter Six - Sweet Pain and 60th Avenue - 1984-1986

Barry, the owner of IRD and now Relativity and Combat Records, liked the music business and the perks that went along with it. We all liked to party and liked hanging out with the bands, in clubs, in theaters and in arenas with some drugs around, etc. Relativity was doing very good with artists such as Robyn Hitchcock, The Brandos, Joe Satriani, and Steve Vai. Combat, the heavy metal label, was doing even better. They were very successful with the thrash and speed metal scene. They signed and had successful releases with Megadeth, Death Angel, The Rods, Possessed, Zoetrope, Nuclear Assault, Exodus, Talas, Dark Angel, and Death. They also had exclusive distribution deals with indie thrash metal labels like Megaforce, Metal Blade, and many European labels. The distributed labels featured bands like Metallica, Venom, Anthrax, Voivod, Celtic Frost, Raven, Mercyful Fate, and Helloween.

Barry knew I had my finger on the pulse of the nightclub scene and that I was in with all the glam bands and he wanted a piece of that, not just to diversify the roster on Combat, but he also knew that a lot of hot chicks liked the glam scene. It was rock and roll. Girls that were into thrash metal were not hot 99% of the time. The old joke was you'd rather fuck the guys at a Motörhead show than the girls. The guys were better looking. We were red blooded males in the music business in 1984. We loved the music, the chicks, the booze, and the coke—we loved it all.

He asked me if I knew of a glam band that fit the bill that we could sign. He wanted to add a band like that to the label. At the time, everyone was already signed from the first wave of the glam scene coming out of L.A.; Mötley Crüe, Ratt, Poison, and W.A.S.P. were already signed. The New York bands that were around were more into that junkie Johnny Thunders, downtown scene, not really glam rock, more like junkie rock, which meant they were unreliable and a headache. Barry said to me, "You should start a band!" So I did with Combat's backing. It was totally a calculated thing. I handpicked the band in late summer 1984, and the main objective was the pursuit of sex, more sex, drugs, more drugs, and rock and roll, even. It was never going to be about precise playing and all that. I was not a real singer, more of a Johnny Rotten than anything else. Sweet Pain was inspired by Kiss, the Crüe, and the Sex Pistols.

I was already friends with Kelly "Blade" Nickels from my late nights hanging out with famed Long Island cover band Hotshot (featuring future Danger Danger member's Bruno Ravel and Steve West). Kelly was the light man and roadie. He got laid more than the band—and the band got laid mucho. He would often leave all the lights on full blast while going off into the equipment truck to get a blowjob. One night, the light board caught on fire from being left on full blast for an hour!

I immediately recruited Kelly to play bass. He looked really cool and totally was the Tommy Lee guy in the band, plus he was my crazy, goofy friend and party bud. He couldn't play all that great at the time, but it didn't matter; he looked the part and would most certainly pull in the chicks. I brought Kelly in to meet Barry, and he said, "Let's do it!" So with myself and Kelly as the core of the soon to be new glam rock sensations, we put an ad in *The Village Voice newspaper* in Manhattan to find the rest of the band. It said something like, "Loud punk/glam band with label deal searching for delinquents to join the gang. Looking for guitarist and drummer who dig Kiss, Starz, Aerosmith, Sex Pistols, and Alice Cooper, and who dress like they mean it," or something like that. We met—did not audition—but met applicants to see what they looked like because we didn't care if they could play. We took their photo with a Polaroid camera and filed them away.

We found Adrian Vance, Scarlet Rowe, and Ronnie Taz already all playing together in a basement in Long Island, waiting to be outrageous and dress like women.

We finalized the lineup in the fall of 1984 and immediately started talking band name, original song titles, and the battle plan. Everyone at the time was into super anal, precise heavy metal.

Precise metal riffing—Yngwie Malmsteen, speed metal, thrash, all that stuff—nauseated us.

We liked Kiss, Starz, Aerosmith, Piper, Hanoi Rocks, Chuck Berry, The Godz, New York Dolls, the Stones, Twisted Sister, Mötley Crüe, Cheap Trick, and the punk rock stuff like the Sex Pistols, The Clash, The Vibrators, 999, Ramones, etc. We wanted to lead the party, but annoy and antagonize people as well, or at least I did. We were basically a cross product of Kiss and the Sex Pistols. How ridiculous does that sound! But to me, that's what we were. The band was thrown together pretty quickly, the songs written very fast, and the album was recorded before we had ever played a gig.

The *Sweet Pain* LP was released in 1985 before the first albums from Poison and Faster Pussycat. We were very New York. We were into booze, sex, and drugs, but we would also kick your ass if we were having a bad day. At least Blade and I would.

We set the tone for in your face glam/punk rock and roll in New York City. When I went to L.A. to mix the record with Randy Burns in late 1984, I went to a gig at the Country Club in Reseda in the Valley. I remember a blonde spiky-haired guy who came up to me backstage and was asking me about Sweet Pain. He had heard about us and was into what we were doing. He later transformed himself into Taime Downe, lead vocalist for Faster Pussycat.

It was my first time in L.A., and, as can be expected, I went a bit nuts out there. Mike Schnapp over at Combat had gotten me a place to stay with some crazy groupie girl named Lisa. I stayed at her house, which if I can remember was in Redondo Beach, a beach town an hour away from the action in Hollywood. In between days mixing the record, I slept at her place, and her friends would come over, and we would do blow and yak and drink and do more blow and yak and drink. Finally, I asked one of the cooler looking rock dudes that was hanging out if he would take me to Hollywood before I lost my mind, which he did. We went to the world famous Rainbow Bar and Grill on Sunset in West Hollywood. I ended up getting in a fight and got thrown out of there. Some dude tried to sit in my booth with the girls I was talking to. I told him to get the fuck up, and he said, "Make me." You can guess the rest of the story. After listening to the dude I was with tell me we should just go back to Lisa's, we headed back down to Redondo Beach, and when we got back, there was a party raging. Lisa wanted me to be her "rocker dude" while I was in town, but she wasn't my type, let's just say. It's the 2020s, so I won't say what I would've said if I was talking to one of my friends from back in the day. It's a new world, and I'm a new person.

We had recorded the albums ten songs in two days. Nine songs were eventually released, and the tenth song, a cover of "Saturday Night's Alright for Fighting" is still unreleased. We had written and rehearsed eight of the songs on the album and went in pretty much knowing the songs, and except for the rap on "I Get My Kicks," everything was rehearsed. We recorded these eight songs with two takes for each song. The rap on "I Get My Kicks" pretty much just spewed out. I had gotten very polluted, and the rap just came out of me on the second take. We were very fucked up making that record, or at least I was. There was a music stand in the studio that was just full of drugs. Wonderful for rock and roll. At the end of the session, we had some time left over, and Kelly sheepishly offered his new song, "Shoot for Thrills." He had just written that song and wasn't sure if he wanted us to try it. He didn't want us to fuck it up! We laid down a quick version of "Shoot for Thrills" and also "Saturday Night's Alright for Fighting," the Elton John song. We did some quick, basic overdubs on "Shoot" and left "Saturday Night" as is, no overdubs, and the cover never saw the light of day. "Shoot for Thrills" was eventually rerecorded by L.A. Guns for their debut album, L.A. Guns, released in January 1988. I think Kelly finally got to hear his song the way he wanted it—or maybe not!

The *Sweet Pain* album was produced by Eric Williams who was in the band the Dancing Hoods. The poor guy. He was an African American rock and roller whose band was on Relativity

Records, so he was part of the family so to speak, and Barry asked him to try to get a record made with a bunch of inexperienced and not great musicians on a very small budget. We recorded it in two days in a garage studio in Island Park, New York, and then I flew the tapes out to L.A. to mix it with Randy Burns at Mad Dog Studios in Venice that used to be a nightclub where The Doors played in the 60s—perfect, insane, Venice, 1960s Los Angeles Doors vibes.

We always did great cover songs live: "Room Service" by Kiss, Cheap Trick's version of "Ain't That a Shame," "I Ain't Got You" from Aerosmith's Live! Bootleg record, Montrose's "Rock The Nation"—loads of classic stuff. Everyone always asked me how we ended up doing a Starz cover, at the time, an unusual choice for a cover song for a new band. Starz never got really big, but we all loved Starz. I met Richie Ranno, guitarist from Starz, at a local record store, Slipped Disc, in Valley Stream. Starz were always one of my favorite bands: classic, well-written songs and an amazing lead vocalist/frontman who wrote the coolest fucking lyrics too. I told Richie about my band and asked him if he would produce Sweet Pain's version of a yet to be determined Starz cover. Richie was always a great guy. He said yes, and we started hanging out and becoming buddies. We chose "Subway Terror" after going through dozens of Starz songs. I really wanted to do "Cherry Baby," but Michael Lee Smith (Starz vocalist) can really sing! I could never cut the vocals on "Cherry Baby." "Subway Terror" suited Sweet Pain the best anyway.

As it turned out, Richie Ranno ended up playing guitar on Sweet Pain's version of "Subway Terror" and also contributed background vocals, as well as producing the track. Richie came and played live with us one night at L'Amour East in Queens. He came up and played "Subway Terror," and we were all so fucked up, so he had a hard time following the song. We were all over the place as usual—sloppy, a mess, so bad—and he was like, *What the fuck!*

The club was packed that night, over 2,000 people. It was an unbelievable night of partying, sex, drugs, and rock and roll too! When Sweet Pain played a gig, it was like a tornado ripped through—casualties everywhere! After the show, I think all 2,000 people ended up in our dressing room! Food and booze flying everywhere, sex and drugs in the bathroom—all in the name of rock and roll decadence!

The new year started off with a wild gig: W.A.S.P., Metallica, and Armored Saint at L'Amour in Brooklyn on January 25, 1985. That night was so packed. You couldn't move an inch anywhere. I met Armored Saint somehow and hung with them on their bus for a bit. Bruno and I were there to see W.A.S.P. though. Man, they were so good for about a year, maybe two. We loved the songs. Great anthemic rock, like a more evil Kiss, but heavier. We ended up hanging with W.A.S.P.'s drummer, Steve Riley, and his wife Mary after the show and partying. When I went to work for L.A. Guns in late 1987, I reminded Steve (now the drummer for L.A. Guns) of that first meeting, and we cracked up! Steve is from Boston, Irish, and had been around the block, so we understood each other, let's say. Boston and New York City are tough cities; East Coast and definitely not Los Angeles.

Bruno needed someone to help pay the rent at his place, so I moved in with Bruno into his apartment on 60th Avenue in Rego Park, Queens in early 1985. It was the height of L'Amour East. L'Amour East is the less famous brother of L'Amour Brooklyn. It was a big club and probably held 1,500 people. It used to be an old supermarket on Queens Boulevard. National acts played there, not as many as in Brooklyn, but you had bands like Twisted Sister, Poison, Keel, and Loudness playing along with the bigger local bands. Bruno and I lived a couple miles away, so we were there all the time. We had some insane times in that apartment. I looked out my bedroom window at the Long Island Expressway. We stayed up and partied all night and slept all day. It was the peak of the craziness for me—cocaine and booze. If there ever was a point in my life where evil and death were creeping under the door nightly, this was it.

We used to go out to a club way out in Suffolk County, out in Deer Park, called the Stage Door. Why we went there, I have no fucking idea, but really we went to see Mike Pont's band, Trouble. They had a weekly gig there. That's where we met the Stage Door chicks. It took at least an hour, if not more, to drive out there. I hated Suffolk county. To me, it was the sticks, filled with hicks. But we went out there a bunch, and I became friends with the coat check girls who were friends with all the bands. I would call one of the coat check girls that I got along with really well and ask her to come hang out with us in Queens regularly. I would call her at 2 AM, or some ungodly hour, and say, "Hey, can you come over? On the way, can you pick up some beer, potato chips, Ring Dings, pretzels, and blow?" She would drive out from Suffolk County, from Deer Park to Queens, over an hour away, bringing us beer, booze, food, and blow. We'd do blow on the glass coffee table—me, her and Bruno—till the sun was up and wouldn't stop until it ran out. Then I would take her to my room, and we would try to have sex—not successful, wired to the gills. The worst feeling. We'd just pass out on the bed naked, and Bruno would stick his head in the door to make sure I was breathing. I'd grunt something to signal I was alive and then he'd go to bed. We would sleep all day until sunset. The coat check girl would be gone when I woke up and then Bruno and I would start all over again.

BRUNO RAVEL: *"I hated when Corky brought her over. She was a gossipy Long Island chick."*

Maybe she was, but Bruno still did blow with us all night!

163

Once the *Sweet Pain* album was released, Schnapp got me radio interviews with stations all over the New York City area. I would go up to the station, they would play the record, I would act like a lunatic on the mic, and we would have fun. These weren't primetime slots; they were heavy metal shows, usually on weekends late night at two in the morning. I did one at K-Rock in New York City with the "King Of Dirt," Mark DiDia. That was the craziest, funniest one. We ended up doing lots of blow and yakking on the radio and playing the Sweet Pain album along with lots of other cool rock and metal stuff: "Rip It Out" by Ace Frehley and "Let It Go" by Def Leppard among them. I took calls from listeners, gave away copies of the album, and was generally out of my mind. I name checked Bruno and also the guy that gave me free high-end sunglasses. It was a free for all. After it was over, we all went to this bar on 8th Street in the Village called Be Bop and did blow and drank until the sun came up. Wired was an understatement. There were many nights of blow and madness with Schnapp in the Sweet Pain days. He usually took care of me and made sure I got home okay, which was every night we went out. Thanks Schnappy!

I was meeting and partying with many rock stars and musicians. I had become friends with Eddie Ojeda from Twisted Sister; he lived in Queens still back then, not too far from me and Bruno. One night, we went to The Ritz in Manhattan to see a show (I can't remember who it was), and we drank and did some blow and generally had a great time. Not like Mötley Crüe crazy, but we had fun. We then came back to my apartment and drank some more with Bruno for awhile until we couldn't stay awake anymore. Eddie slept on the couch. He woke up pretty early because he had to do a photoshoot for Marshall Amps in Manhattan. I drove him home feeling like burnt toast, dropped him off at his place, and went back to the womb of my bed. Eddie is still a friend and was always a good dude, no ego. Our couch was the guest bed for many people back then!

One ridiculously out of control night, my friend P.A. took me to a blues festival at a theater in New Jersey. He was the blues man and had hookups for all the blues shows and knew all the blues cats. The bill was John Lee Hooker, Elvin Bishop, Hubert Sumlin I think, and a bunch of other legendary blues musicians. I can't remember much about it because I was a fucking mess. Vodka and blow all night. We wound up in John Lee Hooker's dressing room, and the only thing I remember is Elvin Bishop just looking at me and shaking his head like, Hmmmm, hmmmmm, hmmmm, and John Lee Hooker saying, "Get that crazy white boy out of here." I wasted that night for sure. I was such a lunatic. John Lee Hooker. I barely remember it.

One night in 1985, we were all going to the club Heartbreak in Manhattan on Varick Street downtown. I was with the guitar player in Sweet Pain, Adrian Vance, and some other people.

Adrian had very distinctive hair: long and black and frizzy, like a mix of Morticia Addams and Cousin Itt. We were standing outside the club, and I looked up the street and here comes Burt Young, Matt Dillon, and Joe Strummer, all walking together, right towards us. I did a double take. Fuck, look at this trio here! Burt Young aka Paulie from the Rocky movies; Matt Dillon, the handsome movie heartthrob from *Rumble Fish and The Outsiders;* and one of the greatest frontmen and rockers ever from The Clash, the punk Dylan, Joe Strummer. They walked right in front of us, and Joe stopped and said to Adrian, "Hey, I saw you on a poster in Shades Records in London!" I couldn't believe it! Joe fucking Strummer recognized the guitarist in Sweet Pain! I almost fainted. Adrian didn't even know who Joe was until I told him later. He wasn't very impressed. I was in awe all night. I had sent some posters to Kelv at Shades Records, as he was the resident glam buyer for the store and also wrote reviews and articles and stuff for some UK magazines. Apparently he hung up the poster in the shop because fucking Joe Strummer saw it! And recognized Adrian Vance from Sweet Pain! I'm still in shock to this day. RIP Joe.

Sweet Pain recorded our album before we had even played a gig. We did things our way! Our first gig was at L'Amour East in Queens on a Wednesday night in March 1985, and we had about 300 people there. We still had our fifth member, Scarlet Rowe, in the band. He lasted two gigs, which were the very first gig and our second gig opening for Ace Frehley in front of 1,500 people a few days later at L'Amour in Brooklyn. After that, he was asked to leave.

Ace had been in retirement, and this show at L'Amour Brooklyn was his first gig after quitting Kiss and going underground. Barry from Combat got us the opening slot for Ace, and we were all stoked. When we got to the club, there were maybe 300 people waiting on line to get in, standing in the freezing cold, holding Ace's solo LP and other memorabilia, and screaming for Ace. Real fans.

We got in the building and asked someone, "Where do we load in? We are the opening band." He told us to go ask that guy, who told us to go ask that guy, who told us to fuck off, to another guy who said, "Who are you?" and on down the line until we finally found the person who could help us. He told us to load in our gear and then go downstairs to our freezing basement dressing room and not to move from there until he told us to. Okay. We were down there for hours, no soundcheck, no food, no beer—nothing. It was freezing cold. Ace's people didn't want anyone around while he was sound checking, which went on for hours. The club kept the fans outside way too long. Until Ace was done sound checking, nobody was allowed in the club. The doors opened late, and the mood was ugly. Thankfully, they let our roadies set up our gear. We finally got the word that we were on in 15 minutes. We got ready, all psyched, and as we walked up the stairs to the stage, we heard the crowd chanting, "Ace, Ace, Ace," louder and louder. They wanted to see Ace, not some opening act they never heard of, especially one that sounded like us. L'Amour used to have a huge video screen that came down in front of the stage and showed music videos while the set change was going on. When we walked up onto the stage, we heard all sorts of stuff hitting the other side of the video screen. We knew we were in trouble. When the screen lifted up and we were announced, we were showered with everything but the kitchen sink. I think they eventually threw that up too. Beer bottles, beer cans, garbage, and even some notes to Ace stapled to lime green tennis balls!

MIKE SCHNAPP: "*Corky was verbally assaulting the crowd and screaming towards any spot where he saw something thrown from. He couldn't really see because of the spotlights in his eyes. He got hit by a flying bottle and got cut on the head. He said something like, 'Oh yeah, that's all ya got?' and started banging a beer can into the cut until more blood flowed. His classic line was, 'Keep throwing those cans and bottles, at a nickel a piece, I'm gonna be rich tonight!'*"

After the show, I went right out into the crowd and fought my way to the bar and had a beer. No one said anything to me. Needless to say, this gig went down in Sweet Pain history as "the war." It was our second gig, and we sounded like a train wreck, but we had everyone in that hellhole watching that stage. Wonderfully insane. Rock and Roll.

I drove home that night with Blade in his crazy 1970s Camaro. It was painted something like a matte black, if I remember correctly, and there were Batman stickers stuck everywhere. The car was all Batman, maybe a Mötley sticker, but the car was banged up. On the way home from L'Amour, the steering wheel fell off! He was trying to screw it back on while we were driving! The nut that held it on had fallen off. It was hilarious, but I almost had a heart attack! We had many nights like this, me and Blade. Crazy, insane fun. Kids.

I was really getting fed up with all the thrash bands calling anyone that didn't look like a filthy methhead a poser. It was a big thing back then: Thrash vs. Posers. I stood up to any of them and would swing a bat at their head if they fucked with me. I'm not saying that this is the recourse I would take today, but back then, that was who I was. But it was so ridiculous. If you didn't conform to what they thought of as metal or rock or whatever, you were a poser. It was usually directed at the glam-y Mötley Crüe and Ratt type bands. I went to a big gig that Combat put together and filmed and released as a live VHS tape called The Ultimate Revenge. It was a thrash mega-show at Studio 54 of all places— hence the title. The bands were Slayer, Venom, and Exodus, three of the biggest and nastiest bands of the breed. It was wall-to-wall leather, denim, stinky sweat, and beer. The air was sticky and steamy. I went to the show because I was on the same fucking label and had worked for the company since 1979, and I said, "Why not!" I went in full Sweet Pain attire and attitude. I got my backstage pass and represented! I ended up getting a "thank you" in the credits of the film!

I hated that thrash shit.

After the gig opening for Ace, we kicked out Scarlet Rowe, and the band was a four-piece. Scarlet was the worst musician out of all of us, and there were lots of other problems with him at the time. The other two guys he came with to join Sweet Pain, Adrian Vance and Ronnie Taz, hated him, and if they say different, they are lying. I'll be nice and leave it at that.

Sweet Pain was now a four-piece. We started to become a very hot draw on the club circuit. We started to draw lots of people to our gigs. We were like a car crash. It wasn't pretty, but you had to look. After a couple of gigs as a four-piece, we were very hot. Whether it was my craziness, the songs, the look of the band, or whatever it was, the formula was working.

Things were about to peak. Drummer Ronnie Taz left after that big L'Amour East gig. He wanted to go live in Manhattan and become a member of one of the Lower East Side Johnny Thunders clone bands that were hip in Manhattan, but didn't mean shit anywhere else. No problem, see ya later. Ronnie eventually ended up joining The Throbs who signed to Geffen Records for one album and were then dropped. They sounded like every other Manhattan band at the time. No one sounded like Sweet Pain. That's how it started, and that's how it was when the band ended. We were truly an original species! After Ronnie left, we recruited Adrian Vance's friend, Jamie Keane, to play drums. We played one gig with Jamie at L'Amour East and then it was Kelly's turn to leave.

Kelly was always the one with the looks and ability to take it all the way. I knew I wasn't a singer in the real sense of the word. I was Johnny Rotten-meets-Alice Cooper, and that was me. Remember, in 1985, punk rock was yet to become a billion dollar moneymaker for the major labels, led by the angst of Nirvana. If you wanted to be in a huge rock band, play arenas, and be a rock star, etc., etc., you went the major label route of commerciality in songwriting and performance with smooth, slick appearances. If you wanted to be huge, that's what you had to do. Sweet Pain were not that type of band! But we were unique, something I care more about. I did not want Sweet Pain to be like every other band around the scene at the time, which were basically Iron Maiden, Metallica, or Dio clones.

I remember one night on the L.A. Guns tour bus, after a gig in 1988 when I was the road manager for L.A. Guns, Phil Collen, the guitarist from Def Leppard, was hanging out. He was in the band Girl with Guns singer Phil Lewis years prior, and he came to see the band. Somehow, Sweet Pain got mentioned, and he said something like, "Oh, that insane glam band from New York? Joe Elliott used to crank that up backstage, right before we went on. Used to psyche us up for the show! They were the Beastie Boys before the Beastie Boys! Fuckin' great stuff!" He was referring to the rap in "I Get My Kicks." Kelly turned to Phil Collen and said, "Well there's the singer right there! Our road manager!" It was a great night. We then had to drive from New Jersey to Florida after hanging on the bus till sunrise. That trip is a book in itself!

I always knew Kelly had the extra something to go all the way. I always knew that. Besides him being one of my best friends, that's why I wanted him in my band. That's what Sweet Pain was all about. He had a certain style, that walking bassline thing. And me and him together, we were nuts, just insane. But I knew he would go on to be the guy, and he did play Madison Square Garden, and I was there. The fucker. I love it!

Kelly told me he was leaving the band one night after rehearsal. He told me he was leaving, that it was getting worse without Ronnie, and he wanted to move on. I knew Ronnie wasn't the greatest drummer in the world, but he had his style, and it all worked when we played together.

I don't think Jamie was ever that comfortable playing with Sweet Pain. It was always a struggle. So when Jamie came in, Kelly knew that was it. Kelly went and joined the Manhattan band, Angels in Vain—who were musically worse than Sweet Pain and so fuckin' pretentious, it was sickening—but they got Kelly to L.A. Angels in Vain went and did some shows out there, and he soon left the band and joined Faster Pussycat. This was 1986, I think. He didn't last with Pussycat though. After getting his leg busted in a very bad motorcycle accident, he went back to New York thinking he was doomed. Then Tracii Guns heard Kelly was out of Pussycat and asked him to join L.A. Guns! Kelly went back out to L.A. and played his first gigs with the Guns on crutches! Tracii knew Kelly had it too.

Sweet Pain continued on with a new bass player, Victor Prestin. It kept getting worse. He really couldn't play. We had put together an album release party at a rehearsal studio in Queens right on the Queens side of the Midtown Tunnel and invited everyone. Victor did something to his hand a few days before the gig and couldn't play. Bruno ended up stepping in and playing bass at the album release party. That night was packed to the gills and pretty insane. I don't remember much, but Bruno told me after the party we went to the bar, Be Bop, in the East Village, and I became "The Stick." The Stick is cocaine. It's what props you up when you are drinking way too much. The Stick props up the booze, but when the coke wears off, The Stick falls down, and so do you, so when you are The Stick, you are so fucking drunk, you don't know what you are doing, but the stick keeps you walking around like a zombie. Horrible. Very dark. Very dangerous. Very stupid. But I had to live through all of this craziness to be where I am at today. I'm just thankful I am still here. It really does seem like this stuff happened to someone else. It was another lifetime ago.

We played gigs and continued on until the summer of 1986 and then I folded the band. I knew it was time to kill it off. It was too many drugs and stuff, too many crazy chicks. We were in Cleveland for a three night stand in some clubs there, and I shacked up with a girl in a Holiday Inn. I was in a separate hotel from the rest of the band and got extremely whacked. No one knew where I was. At the show, I almost got arrested for inciting a riot after some guy jumped onstage and started calling me out. I grabbed a baseball bat from behind the amps and was about to whack him when the cops grabbed my arms and handcuffed me. They let me go, and the show continued—as much of a show as we could muster up at that point.

Sweet Pain's last gig was at the club that started it all for us: L'Amour East in Queens. We played a bunch of other shows after the Cleveland riot, and then we had a show booked at L'Amour East as a homecoming show. Adrian decided he needed to get a nose job and was unable to play that show, which pissed me off greatly. We played the gig with guitarist Jon Sierra from the local band Battalion (Jon later played with Michael Monroe). Jon was a great guitarist, and the Sweet Pain repertoire of songs was not that hard to learn and play. We rehearsed with him once, he played the songs no problem, and then when he got onstage, it was like he had never heard the songs before! He forgot everything from rehearsal. Plus there was a monsoon outside. It was raining cats and dogs, so the turnout was low. After that gig, I called everyone up and told them it was over. We had a lot of fun and shook shit up. That's how I remember it. It was fun while it lasted, but I was getting bored. After Sweet Pain broke up, I stayed away from it all. All the craziness took a backseat. That is, until Kelly called me and asked me to be road manager for L.A. Guns. They had signed with PolyGram and things were looking up chalootz! Did I want to do it? Hell yeah!

But I'm getting ahead of myself here.

Chapter Seven - Relativity Records, Hollywood, L.A. Guns - 1987-1988

After I put Sweet Pain out of its misery, I cut my hair and went back to work for Relativity. Barry hired me as Radio Promotions Director. I stopped the coke—almost. I was killing myself. It was time for a change. Bruno Ravel and I were good friends, but it was tough to live together once I decided to clean my act up. He had Steve West coming over all the time, and they were writing songs and playing loud guitar at 3 AM. He was also a pig. The sink was filled with dishes and pots and pans constantly, mold growing on the dishes. The bathroom was nasty. I love Bruno, he's one of my best and oldest friends, but once I decided to clean myself up, I knew it was time to leave.

I moved out and went back to my dad's house. I became Radio Promotions Director at Relativity in late 1986 and started promoting Robyn Hitchcock and a dozen other artists. I did that for a couple of months, and then I was promoted to Director of Promotions for the Relativity and Combat labels in early 1987. Now I needed to find a radio promo guy to take my place. The office manager at Relativity told me about a young guy named Matt Pollack that worked in a high-end suit store in Cedarhurst and wanted to get into the music business. I went down and met him at the store, Jonathan's, and we talked. I asked him who his favorite band was, and he replied, "They Might Be Giants." Huh?

I was thrown by that answer and thought it was funny, but I figured anyone that can sell 1,500 dollar suits to street smart businessmen can hype records to radio stations. There's a certain art to it. So I hired Matt Pollack to do radio, giving him a callbook filled with the names, phone numbers, and addresses for all the radio stations in the country. I gave him some promo copies of current records we were working and told him to go home and listen to everything. I schooled him on how to call, what to do, and what to say. Once he got the hang of it, I knew he would be a success. When I left Relativity in December 1987, I advised Matt that if he got the chance to jump to a major label, he should take it, and he did. Matt left Relativity shortly after me and went to ATCO/Elektra Records. He then went to V2 with Richard Branson, and he now works for Monotone Management.

When I was doing radio promotion, as a "thank you" tool, I would send the radio stations copies of those hard to find and expensive European and Japanese CDs that we were still importing. The stations would add my records, or sometimes not, but I got relationships with radio stations by using anything I had at my disposal. CDs, t-shirts, books—whatever we had, I would send them as gifts. We had a whole shipping operation in the warehouse and nobody asked, cared, or noticed. I sent the stations everything I could, and we got a lot of adds that way.

We were a brand new label competing against all the big guys—CBS, Atlantic, Warner, etc.—for adds, so it worked a lot of times on the college and small market stations. We were releasing either "alternative" post-punk stuff, weird European electronic music, heavy metal, or hardcore, so it was not possible to get play on WNEW in New York City or KLOS in L.A. during primetime. Yet. But we could get on all the college stations, big and small. And that's what we did.

Eventually, in 1987, the two records that really put Relativity on the map in a big way were *Honor Among Thieves by The Brandos and Joe Satriani's Surfing with the Alien*. I was Director of Promotions at this point, and we hired all the big independent radio promoters: Bill McGathy, Ronnie Rafael, Michael Papale— all the heavy hitters. We started buying ads in *The Hard Report, Gavin Report, and Album Network*, all the weekly radio and music trades. We got play on, I would say, 60% of all the major market big rock stations with The Brandos song "Gettysburg" and also "Honor Among Thieves." It was a great record with great songs and was perfect for the musical climate at the time. Things like John Mellencamp, Tom Petty, etc. were getting big play. The Brandos fit that mold. They landed an opening slot on the very hot INXS tour, which was incredible exposure and helped them land even more radio stations. It was a coordinated effort, sure, but I was the main champion of The Brandos at Relativity. Barry had gotten their demo tape and liked it, playing it for me and asking me what I thought. I said, "Sign them immediately!" Everyone else at Relativity was against it and said it was commercial crap, wouldn't do anything, *blah blah blah*. Most of the Relativity college radio staff, publicists, and press people were all about the underground stuff like the Cocteau Twins, Wiseblood, and Thelonious Monster—who are all great, but wouldn't get the job done as far as taking the label into the same league as Atlantic Records when it comes to getting on the radio. But I knew it was perfect for us. It was rock and roll, and the songs were great. I could hear "Gettysburg" on a station like WNEW in New York. It was The Brandos push that got Relativity rolling in the big leagues.

Relativity also licensed and released the soundtrack to the play *Les Misérables*, which at the time was big in European theater and had just come to Broadway. There was no soundtrack release in the US, so Relativity released it, and it was in every major record chain in the country. Relativity put out so many records, it was mind boggling. It didn't cost a lot to produce these records. A lot of them were licensed from Europe with very little money upfront. You had 90-day terms with the pressing plants, and you always owed them money anyway. They pressed records for you even if you were behind in paying them because they wanted the business. The flow of product into the marketplace was what fed the distribution and that reeled in the cash. The more records out there, the bigger the checks from the giant stores and chains. Product equals cash flow.

We had the heavy metal label, Combat, and a hardcore offshoot, Combat Core. We put out tons of heavy metal and thrash, bands like Megadeth, Possessed, Exodus, Dark Angel, Voivod, Nuclear Assault, Circle Jerks, Agnostic Front, Death, and a lot more. I have to say, the level of insanity that went on with the metal crew, hell, with the whole damn place, was pretty comical and very "mom and pop" in its approach as a record label. I mean, we were an indie, but starting to generate serious cash flow through the distribution end of the business, which most indie labels didn't have. We made and we spent a lot of money. It was loose. The general lax atmosphere in the offices and approach to business were very entertaining and fun, to say the least. Guys like Scott Givens and Megadon kept things lively. The head of the label, Steve Sinclair, was given lots of abuse, and he took most of it. Steve shared an office with the big cheese and owner Barry. Steve was beaten into submission daily by Barry and also by the general grind of the business, but he signed a lot of good bands. He was good at what he did. He used to have a gold album on the wall from Ratt's first indie release EP on Time Coast Records that got them signed to Atlantic. He was involved in that record. That gold album got taken off the wall a lot and used for nefarious reasons in that office. *Click click click.*

The big music conventions were attended and laid to waste. The New Music Seminar was a biggie. It was held in New York City at the Marriott Marquis hotel in Times Square and was very cutting edge in its approach. Labels, record stores, magazines, fanzines, radio stations, nightclub owners, and publicists all attended this "new music" seminar, complete with live music showcases at all the big New York City clubs and venues. There were discussions or panels with a wild cast of characters, people in the hipper end of the music business—heavy duty "industry" people and also guys like Bleecker Bob and nightclub owners Rudolf and Steve Rubell. There were nightclub panels. Everyone would be arguing, fighting, and yelling. It was amazing and very New York City. Relativity had hotel rooms at the Marriott and expense accounts to entertain. It was a free for all. The IRD/Relativity co-owner, Steve Mason, came over from England and was schmoozing at the bar. A lot of deals got done at the New Music Seminar. Records got licensed going both ways over the ocean, bands got signed, people found new jobs, and relationships were made. It was a must attend music convention in the 1980s, and I would say the craziest. It was New York City. It has an energy like nowhere else in the world.

Eventually, as Relativity started to do better and better at radio, I went to every single convention across the country: Gavin in San Francisco, the T.J. Martell Rock N' Bowl in L.A., and on and on, spreading the cheer, the love, and the party. I would take

181

out all the indie promo guys to expensive dinners and schmooze them even more than I had been doing all year. It was business. I would hang out with all of the radio promo guys from all the big labels, especially the Atlantic guys. They had great parties too. They introduced me to a lot of people: program directors at big radio stations, big radio influencers, etc. I put Relativity on the map as a real contender and a real label to be reckoned with. Sure, it was a team effort, but I was on the frontlines, schmoozing the right people, working the trade magazines and influential radio music directors, and helping take Relativity from a small indie label to a big league player. I opened the doors.

Once again, I was a facilitator.

I started going to Los Angeles once a month to schmooze the West Coast indie promo guys that worked for us and got a weekly paycheck. I would take guys like Michael Papale and Kenny Ryback out to dinner and nightclubs and keep the lines of communication open, hyping them on the current hot release and going over radio strategy for the next month, etc.

On one of my many West Coast trips in May 1987, I met the band L.A. Guns, or more specifically, the real brains of the band, Mick Cripps. I would always stay at the Continental Hyatt House or "Riot House" on Sunset Boulevard in West Hollywood—the famous hotel where all the rock bands stayed in the days of Zeppelin, The Who, etc. Legendary rock and roll hotel.

My buddy, Kelly "Blade" Nickels from New York, was playing bass in L.A. Guns by this time, and I let him know I was coming out. They had signed their deal with PolyGram and were recording the album, but they had no money. Their manager at the time, Alan Jones, paid for their apartment rents, rehearsal spaces, band expenses, etc., but the band members had no pocket cash, really. I flew into LAX, rented a car, drove to West Hollywood, checked into the hotel, and called Kelly. I invited him and whoever he wanted to bring to come over and have some drinks. He came over with Mick Cripps and Mick's twin brother, Robert, and we became fast friends instantly. We ended up at the swimming pool on the roof and ordered a case of Corona and a bottle of tequila and drank all day. I ordered some pizzas and fries to give us something to soak up the booze. It was a blast. Here was me and Kelly from New York, Kelly from Sweet Pain and Hotshot, with Mick and Robert Cripps drinking and partying on the roof of the fucking Riot House in the L.A. sunshine. It was what Kelly always dreamed of. He was doing it big time. It was one of those moments that stick with you. Great memory. After a couple hours up on the roof, I looked at the guys and saw their faces were getting burnt from the sun. These guys were vampires for sure—not that they could feel anything. The bottle of Cuervo was empty. It was time to shift gears and make a return to the vampire life—time to hit the bars. I had rented a Caddy DeVille, and we made our way downstairs while the valet brought it around. We stopped by Mick's apartment, and they changed clothes, grabbing jackets and some weed, and we drove around Hollywood drinking in dark places. We started at Barney's Beanery, the Rainbow, and Formosa Cafe and then hit the strip clubs: the Seventh Veil, The Body Shop, and then the Tropicana, the world famous mud wrestling bar that launched a thousand MTV video girls. That place was my least favorite. The typical MTV hair band Hollywood groupie, L.A. stripper-type was launched at the Tropicana. It's like a Halloween costume: Scary Mud Wrestler Hair Band Groupie. But all the bands loved those chicks, and they frequented that place a lot. I never really dug it. We drank lots of tequila and beer and watched chicks mud wrestle. They loved the bands and were all over us. We got so drunk, we lost Mick, and finally found him lying on his back in the parking lot with cars honking, trying to drive around him. We ran over and pulled him out of traffic and put him in the Caddy. I drove Kelly and Mick home to the apartment they shared. They were both plastered. We had been drinking for about 12 hours. I dragged them inside, then I somehow drove myself back to the hotel and passed out.

Wake up call was at 9 AM. I woke up with a hangover, of course, and had to get to a breakfast meeting with the radio guys for Relativity business. I drove over to meet them at some hot Hollywood breakfast place they had picked, valet parked the Caddy, and got to my table outside and waited for the West Coast

184

promo team. One by one, they trickled in. After some toast and eggs and a couple of Bloody Marys, our business finished, and I excused myself and went and collapsed back into bed. I went to see L.A. Guns for the first time later that night at the Troubadour.

I met Mick and Kelly at the show, and we hung upstairs in the dressing room where I met the rest of the band. I had known who Phil Lewis was from his previous band, Girl, from the UK. I was a fan of Girl, so I liked Phil as a frontman already. I met the drummer, Nickey "Beat" Alexander, a legendary Hollywood drummer, having played with L.A. punk heroes, The Weirdos. He also owned the rehearsal studio that both Guns N' Roses and L.A. Guns used: Nickey's Love Palace. L.A. Guns could rehearse there for free. Nice perk.

NICKEY BEAT: *"I got stuck many times unloading the gear at the studio after a gig by myself.*

L7, The Hangmen, GNR—a lot of bands came out of Nickey's Love Palace."

I met the bands namesake, Tracii Guns. It was very much like a Van Halen type of thing, I thought. Tracii GUNS, Eddie VAN HALEN. Tracii definitely gave the band a "metal" edge. There was a period when Robert Stoddard was in L.A. Guns back in the very early days where the band was more like The Dogs D'Amour or The Lords of the New Church. Nickey Beat fit with that type of band; Nickey isn't a heavy metal drummer. And this current version of L.A. Guns was not heavy metal. That's what made it cool.

I met the guys, and we drank and had fun, talking and holding court. The Troubadour is a legendary venue, and it was a trip just being in there. I took some pics with the guys, and we goofed around. There were some girls hanging out that looked very young, and it was all very sleazy. It was something that was very 1980s Hollywood. It was the time. Hollywood sleaze is the sleaziest of them all. I've experienced sleaze in most of the cities in this country, and Hollywood is king of the sleaze. Trust me. Finally, it was showtime, and they hit the stage. I was very impressed. Kelly was still on crutches from his motorcycle accident. He couldn't move around, so he just stood in one spot and moved his top half! They were loud, hard rock and roll. This was my first time ever hearing them, and after a few songs, I knew what L.A. Guns was: sleazy, hard rock and roll with a bit of a punk-ish vibe. Towards the end of the set, I watched as a wild banshee of a man, with a bandana around his head and wearing what looked like a leopard skin fur coat, jumped up onstage and sang a song with Phil. It was Axl Rose. I had heard Guns N' Roses' indie record and was very aware of who they were. Their album was just about to be released, and I had heard their UK single of "Mr. Brownstone" already. The hype on GNR was big, and Axl was on fire onstage with LAG. Honestly, he blew Phil away. Axl was a rock star without trying, but Phil and Axl are totally different types of singers and frontmen, totally different, so it's really not fair to compare them. It was just wild to see Axl live for the first time, that ferocious energy. And what was weird is that the first time I saw Axl sing onstage, it was with L.A. Guns.

After the show, we all hung out in the dressing room drinking and such, and I announced an impromptu party back at my hotel room at the Riot House. Mick, Kelly, and some girls piled into the Caddy, and we headed back to the hotel. I was on one of the top floors, and from the balcony I could see a lot of people pulling up and heading to my room. It got so crazy, that the cops were eventually called. As I watched from the balcony, the LAPD pulled up on Sunset in front of the Riot House. I spun around and told everyone that the cops were on their way up and to clear out, please! Everyone did, grabbing beers from the bathtub as they left. The cops came up, I apologized, and they didn't make a big thing about it. They were just happy that everyone cleared out. I shut the door, popped open a Corona, and turned the music back on. After a minute, there was a knock on my door. It was Axl. He said, "Hey, Beastie Boy, what's up?" (I was in a Def Jam phase, t-shirt and hat-wise). I explained that the cops came, and everyone split. It was a pretty hot night, but Axl still had on that leopard fur coat thing just like a true rock star. He hung out for a few, and we talked a little, and then he left into the night, searching for more fun. The party was officially over, and I collapsed into bed.

I had more Relativity business to take care of tomorrow. I was in L.A. for another day and then flew back to New York.

I kept coming out to L.A. for business and connecting with Kelly and Mick. My room at the Riot House became party central. Kelly got the vampire bites tattooed on his neck when I was in town, once. He was at the hotel the whole time I was in town. All the guys were. It was always a party, every time. We would repeat the pattern of starting the party in my room and then heading out drinking all over Hollywood.

At the Hollywood Tropicana one night, we connected with Bret Michaels from Poison and one of the Poison roadies, Keith Harris. Keith eventually came to work for L.A. Guns in 1988. At the Tropicana, to mud wrestle the girls, you had to bid for the honor. The highest bidder wrestled the girl. You wrestled her in a pit filled with this like cardboard-type flaky stuff that they added water to and turned into a sort of synthetic mud. It was gross. Kelly and Bret both started bidding for Keith and I to wrestle these two girls, and they won! We had to mud wrestle! Drunk! We went in the back dressing room area and put on some shorts that they had there, like when you went to a fancy restaurant and needed a tie, and they had ties for you to wear, the Tropicana had shorts for drunk dudes to mud wrestle in. Who knows what was living inside those nasty shorts, but Keith and I were drunk and didn't care! We stripped down, put on the nasty shorts, and went

188

back out to our seats ringside. When I got in the ring to wrestle, they started the match, and the girl started really beating me up. If I tried to throw her off of me or stop her from kicking the shit out of me, the referee would blow his whistle and grab me and say, "Do not do that." I basically had no defense here and did my best not to get my ass kicked by a crazy Tropicana girl while fucked up on tequila, beer, and weed. After a few rounds of this torture, I finally had enough and just got out of the ring, went in the back, and did my best to clean all the shit off of me and get dressed. When I got back to our seats, Kelly was hysterical. We drank some more and then we got the hell out of there. Back to the hotel, then back to New York in the morning.

I was getting uncomfortable at Relativity by this point. They were moving offices again to a huge complex in Hollis, Queens, and new people were coming into upper management that I didn't gel with. It wasn't the same company that I started working at in 1979. Times were changing. One day, I got a call from Kelly and Mick asking me to be L.A. Guns' road manager. They said I took such good care of them every time I came to L.A., that they wanted me on the road with them. Now that was an interesting offer. I had gotten another offer at the same time to run the heavy metal department at Atlantic Records. I interviewed with the person that would have been my immediate supervisor, and I knew I couldn't work for him and be happy, so the L.A. Guns offer came at just the right time. I said no to Atlantic and went to work for L.A. Guns. I was tired of sitting in a cubicle and living that record "industry" life. Going out on the road across the country was just what I needed. It would turn out to be one of the greatest life experiences I could ever hope for...and almost wound up putting me in the loony bin.

L.A. Guns has been around since 1984. There has been much written about the band, how they formed, who started what, who Axl Rose played with, who played with who, in everything from books to Wikipedia to countless interviews from current and ex band members. It really is a soap opera. I'm not going to try to give you any kind of definitive history of anything, just my story about the time that I knew them and worked for them. A different perspective than what's already been written in other articles and books. There are parts of this book that I had written and worked on 30 years ago.

I flew out to L.A. and started to work for the band on December 28, 1987. I landed at the airport, hopped in a cab, and went straight to Perkins Palace in Pasadena: L.A. Guns were opening for Guns N' Roses. By this time, Nickey Beat was out as drummer, and Steve Riley was in. Before joining L.A. Guns, Steve was in the heavy metal band W.A.S.P. He had been on the road in W.A.S.P. and numerous other bands with major label record deals for a long time. Steve was primarily known as a hard-hitting, double bass, heavy metal drummer. L.A. Guns was now a different band from the one I had heard at the Troubadour, months earlier. They were not a sleazy punk-type hard rock band anymore. They were now a heavy metal band. It's kind of like the way Kiss changed their sound when Eric Carr took over from Peter Criss. The drummer's style really sets the tone for the band, as far as what kind of a band they are.

Nickey told me the following when I first started started working for L.A. Guns:

NICKEY BEAT: *"In L.A. Guns, someone got fired every 6 or 7 months. As it turned out, I guess it was my turn. It could have been anybody, but I guess, spin the bottle, and the bottle fell on me. They had the opportunity to improve the band by getting a real live rock star. Someone from W.A.S.P. already ready to play double bass drums. I'll go ahead and say it: a bit more of a competent drummer. No tempo problems with Steve Riley, as far as I know. I heard that Riley was sitting there talking to Tracii saying, 'Tracii, you got a great band here, but you need a world class drummer. Nickey is not a WORLD CLASS DRUMMER. I AM A WORLD CLASS DRUMMER. You need me in the band because you have a world class band, but you can't do it with a punk rock drummer.'"*

Nickey joined L.A. Guns around the 4th of July in 1985 and was out before Christmas of 1987.

The funny thing is, Nickey worked security for the promoter Goldenvoice at my above mentioned first gig with the band—the double bill of L.A. Guns opening for Guns N' Roses at Perkins Palace. Guns N' Roses wanted the backstage cleared before they went on, and Nickey had to tell L.A. Guns to clear out. Now that's funny. Needless to say, there was a lot of tension backstage at that gig, as there always was and will be whenever there is the combination of Axl, Tracii, and Slash. Tracii and Slash were competing guitar heroes at Hollywood's Fairfax High School, and Axl and Tracii had incompatible personalities.

The very first version of L.A. Guns made a vinyl EP.

NICKEY BEAT: *"It was so bad. It was fucking terrible. That was before I was in the band. That's one of the reasons I never wanted to call the band L.A. Guns. I said, 'Tracii, let me hear one of those records,' and I was like, Oh my God this is fucking terrible. Shit. We are not naming our band after this terrible record. We gotta think of something else. Finally, Mick said, 'Look, we can't think of anything. Let's just use L.A. Guns for the time being, and we will think of something later.' I was like, 'Alright, promise me we will change it later because this is a terrible name.' I was always opposed to the name L.A. Guns in the first place. I thought it was an infringement on the New York Dolls. That's what it struck me as. It was too blatantly ripping off the Dolls, and I hated that. In the very beginning of my version of*

L.A. Guns, when we were a four-piece—me on drums, Mick on bass, Paul singing, and Tracii playing guitar—the four-piece L.A. Guns, we did a few shows around town, and we were getting pretty good. Tracii then flew to New York to play with Cheryl Rixon who was a Penthouse centerfold. Steve Darrow was playing drums for her, and they had some bass player from Ozzy or something like that. Tracii was supposed to be out out there in New York to just do some demos or something like that for her— a quick thing—and we had a gig coming up at the Troubadour. It was gonna be our first time playing the Troubadour, and it was gonna be a big deal because we hadn't played there or the Whisky yet. The Troubadour was gonna be the biggest show we had played. Before that, we were just playing much smaller rinky-dink clubs like King's Palace and Cathay de Grande, just little tiny nothings. Jack Douglas, the big record producer, was supposed to be at the Troubadour that night. He's the guy that did Rocks and Toys in the Attic [classic Aerosmith albums], and we were like, 'Oh my God, we got Jack Douglas coming down, and there's a word out about us,' and we said, 'Tracii, when are you getting back?' He kept stalling: 'I'll be there Tuesday. I'll be there Wednesday. I'll be there Thursday.' He ended up calling us either the day before or the day of the show and said, 'Ya know what? I'm gonna stay in the band here. I quit. You can keep the name. Sorry, but that's the way its gonna be. I'm doing this band. I'm gonna go somewhere with this.' We were like 'WHAT?' That was his thing, 'I'm out, and you guys can have the name.' So I called Duff from GNR because they were rehearsing in my place. I called him up and said, "Look, we need you guys to fill in for us at the Troubadour. Do you want the show? It's headlining on a Friday night.' Duff went, 'Yeah, yeah, sure, we'll do it.' And I said, 'Well, it's tomorrow,' and Duff said, 'Yeah, yeah, we will make some calls. We will do it.' That was the end with Tracii. After that, we got Robert Stoddard in on guitar, and we were still a four-piece."

Tracii eventually was asked back into the band. In L.A. Guns people got fired and rehired so many times, again and again. And it still goes on today!

In a long conversation one night, Mick told me the story of when he met Tracii Guns for the first time. Tracii had just been thrown out of Guns N' Roses (or quit, whatever), but I guess he was still friends with them. Nickey Beat took Mick to a UCLA frat party where Guns N' Roses were playing. A crazy frat party with people jumping in the swimming pool and stuff, and that's where he first met Tracii. There were all these super conservative UCLA yuppies at this party, and here's this band playing the party with Axl walking around, not really socializing, wearing black chaps on with no underwear underneath and his ass hanging out. There was a grand piano in the fraternity hall, and Mick said that he remembered the funniest thing: Axl was sitting down at the piano with his bare ass on the bench playing this piano. Axl just did not give a fuck. Very cool.

Tracii once told me that when he first met Mick, he thought that he was the coolest looking guy at the party. I would agree, even if I wasn't there! Mick always had the best style out of anyone in L.A. Guns. He always looked the coolest. At the time that he and Tracii met, he had just gotten back to Los Angeles from England. Knowing Mick, I would say he was dressed better. He had hipper clothes on than everybody. He had all the English gear on. Before L.A. Guns, Mick had lived in England, and one of the bands he played in while he was there was called The Killer Elite. The band was Mick, Nigel Mogg (future Quireboy), Chris Bradshaw, and Adam Ross, whose older brother is Jonathan Ross, the biggest talk show host in England. After a bit, The Killer Elite changed their name to Faster Pussycat.

Mick eventually left London and headed back to Los Angeles in 1985. The first guy he met when he got back to L.A.was Taime Downe. They started working together, and Mick said, "Let's do a band. I have a good name: Faster Pussycat." But then Mick hooked up with Nickey Beat and Tracii and started working with them, so he suggested to Taime that it would be a good name to use, and Taime kept the name. Nobody was really hip to Russ Meyer then. Hollywood had forgotten about one of their most prolific and iconic film makers. As usual, the British had rediscovered him, like they do with all of the cool, lost, and forgotten American music, films, and art. Taime was really cool because he was one of the guys on the Strip who was hanging out with all these metal bands, but had the whole glam, New York Dolls look. He had the whole New York Dolls gear on, where as all the metal bands had all the stupid studs and stuff. Taime had the whole Johnny Thunders, New York Dolls look down, but slightly more drag.

Robert Stoddard is another unsung hero in the whole history of the L.A. Guns saga. He was like Bob Dylan, that dude. He was a fantastic songwriter, and he started the band The Dogs D'Amour with Tyla, Paul Hornby, and Dave Kusworth. Robert named the band. The Dogs D'Amour always have those acoustic albums—they got all that from Robert Stoddard. He was a guy who looked like he was in The Lords of the New Church, but he would sit down on a barstool with an acoustic guitar and sing all these great songs. He's like a traveling minstrel. He could pick up a guitar anywhere and sit there and play you song after song. He had his own indie albums. Mick told me back in 1987 that he heard about Robert from the Dogs D'Amour guys when he lived in England, but his name at the time was Ned Christie or something like that, and he was the original singer in The Dogs D'Amour. When Mick met the guys in The Dogs D'Amour, they told him, "When you go back to L.A., you gotta check out this guy, Robert Stoddard." So when Mick got back to L.A., he started asking around: "Do you know a guy named Robert Stoddard?" Everybody knew Robert Stoddard from different music circles, not the hard rock sleaze punk circles. Mick hooked up with Robert Stoddard and got him in L.A. Guns. It started out as Nickey, Paul Black, Robert, and Mick playing bass. Robert then left, and Tracii came back into the fold. Mick took the second guitar spot, and that's when Kelly Nickels came in and played bass. After a month of Kelly being in the band, they decided they were not happy with singer, Paul Black, and let him go.

Manager Alan Jones, who is British, knew Phil Lewis from London and flew him over to meet the band. They did one audition, and he became the new lead singer of L.A. Guns. Phil immediately caught Hollywood's rhythm and took to the town like a champ. The band immediately did a sold out show at the Troubadour and got signed to PolyGram right after. Phil was first living at the legendary rock and roll motel, the now long-gone Hollywood Tropicana on Santa Monica Boulevard in West Hollywood. LAG filmed part of their video for the song "One More Reason" at that hotel: the part where Mick gets his throat slit and is thrown in the pool bleeding, killed by a crazy chick! Other parts of that video were shot in Downtown L.A.'s original Arts Distric. "One More Reason" is my favorite L.A. Guns video, in that it is not heavy metal, but punkish and artsy and cool. It totally represents to me what the band was back then. That video was also a contributing factor to the band getting signed.

Phil Lewis eventually moved in and lived with Nickey Beat at "Chez Guns," an apartment complex on Bronson across the street from the Junior High School in Hollywood. It was like Oscar and Felix: Nickey the Animal and Phil this English guy. Nickey used to have pet rat named Rank wandering around the apartment. Phil would wake up, and the rat would be sitting on top of him. Welcome to Hollywood.

In the beginning, Mick and Tracii were running things, then it became too much to deal with. Mick was working for Alan Jones at Let it Rock, a hip English rock and roll clothing store on Melrose Avenue in Hollywood. Alan was kind of managing a couple of other bands, like Charlie Sexton, and one day, Mick said to Alan, "Hey, we need a manager. How 'bout managing us?" Alan agreed, and the first thing he did was get the band a bunch of leather pants from the Kings Road; they were like, *Alright!* Alan was a real loyal, old school-type manager. He was one of the guys. He went all the way for the band, but it was Steve Riley that forced him out. One of the biggest regrets Phil, Tracii, Mick, and Kelly had about L.A. Guns was sacking Alan Jones. He was the guy that got the band their record deal, him and Vince Ely from The Psychedelic Furs. They were working together and got the band the deal. Vince Ely was working with Alan Jones, and those two were going around shopping L.A. Guns to different labels. Alan Jones was in a band in London in the 1960s called Amen Corner. They opened for Hendrix and Cream and people like that.

Vince Ely was hanging out and working with Nickey Beat on drumbeats and stuff, also. Vince Ely from the Furs was very instrumental in getting them signed.

When Steve Riley joined the band, he had just come out of W.A.S.P. and was used to the big high-powered management team at Sanctuary. He didn't think Alan had the industry cred—which he didn't. It became a power struggle. Riley wanted control of the band. Alan was a hands-on manager: he was with them all the time, protected them, and went the distance for them. By having some big industry guy like Allen Kovac—some guy who never ventured out of the office as the manager—Riley could assume more control of the band, which he did. But Steve's input and push were very valuable. He had years of experience on the road, doing big arena tours, and he had interacted with lots of big management companies as well. That was all very helpful. The band collectively leaned on him for assuming a leadership role, mainly because no one else wanted to be bothered. Kudos to Steve for taking on that role.

I remember a story I heard about when they recorded the first album at the Village Recorder in Santa Monica. Stevie Nicks was recording next door, and she would never show up. She had the whole big studio lockout—ten engineers sitting around all the time, all day long. LAG would come in and say, "She show up?" "Nope." Then one time she showed up at like two in the morning, all coked up, and couldn't sing. They didn't see her again for three weeks; the clock ticking. The guys were like, Yeah, rock and roll. Pink Floyd was on the other side of them at the same time. They had three semi-trucks full of equipment backed up to the Village Recorder with their own gear. LAG asked the Floyd, "What do you even use the studio for? You have more equipment than the studio!"

Mick knew Arthur Kane, ex-bassist of the New York Dolls, who was his next-door neighbor in Hollywood for years, since 1985. L.A. Guns opened some shows for Arthur around Los Angeles when he did a small tour with his former New York Dolls bandmates Johnny Thunders and Jerry Nolan. Mick and Kelly knew Arthur, but it was mainly Mick's brother, Robert, that was really friends with Arthur. Arthur lived right next-door to Mick and Robert on Holloway Drive. This girl named Chris Amarow that used to take pictures of the band was friends with Arthur too, and she introduced everyone. It just so happened that Arthur lived right next door to Mick and Robert, so they were friends ever since.

One time, L.A. Guns were playing the Palladium in Hollywood, and Robert Cripps came to the gig, along with his and Mick's friends Henry and Arthur Kane. Arthur had just started drinking again after being sober for awhile, so they all got really fucked up. They totally cleaned out the backstage liquor. Arthur and Henry took all the whiskey! Every bottle! Later on that night, so the story goes from Henry, they all went back to Robert's. In Robert's apartment, he had a big huge closet that had no door, and just had like gypsy beads hanging down for a door. Henry said they were so fucked up, as they were talking, Arthur put his hand down against the beads, like the beads were the wall, and just fell into the closet onto the floor. They woke up the next day with brutal hangovers, and Arthur just got up, walked to the liquor store, and started drinking at 9 AM. Whiskey, again, in the morning. Arthur was a bad alcoholic. When he started drinking, the only way he stopped drinking was the hospital. He was now off the wagon and drinking again heavily, and it caught up to him in a crazed incident. He accidentally fell out of his window and fell three floors down onto the driveway of the Holloway House Apartments and broke his legs. After Arthur recovered from this life-changing injury, he stopped drinking for good and became a devout Mormon, working at the Mormon Temple on Santa Monica Boulevard.

In 2004, Arthur finally got to live his dream of reforming the New York Dolls. The surviving original members of the band got back together and did a show in the UK, which was put together by Morrissey for his Meltdown Festival. However, the reunion was cut short. On July 13, 2004, only 22 days after the reunion concert, Arthur thought he had the flu and checked himself into a hospital in Los Angeles. He was diagnosed with leukemia and died within two hours. The Mormon Temple treated him well and gave him the respect he deserved. It really sucks how Arthur died. I had the great opportunity to hang with him a couple of times to smoke a little weed and just chat. He was always a gentleman and always had an amazing story to tell. RIP Arthur "Killer" Kane.

Nickey Beat moved up to Hollywood in 1977 when punk was starting. Before punk, he was into Kiss. He moved up to Hollywood to become a rock star, not a punk rock star.

Nickey had long hair, but it just so happened that the first band he joined up with were a punk band. The night before his first gig with the punk band he had just joined, he went to see Iggy Pop, and Iggy had the Sales brothers as the rhythm section with David Bowie sitting on the side playing keyboards. Nickey said, "Oh my God, this is a valid thing, this punk," and the next day, he chopped his hair off. He was in a punk band. What the fuck, was he going to be the one weird looking guy in a band that all had short hair? He would have stuck out. He wanted to go with the flow and all that. Then, punk exploded. As far as Nickey's background, that's just where people got to know him from: the punk scene. He was in all kinds of bands before punk rock, lots of Top 40 bands. He was in an all-chick half-lesbian Top 40 cover band that played in a lesbian bar in Orange County. Tracii had asked him come out and audition for Guns N' Roses when he was still in that band. The first time Nickey saw Guns N' Roses was at the Troubadour, and it was Axl Duff, Izzy, Tracii, and a guy named Rob that was in the very first L.A. Guns. The next thing he knew, there were auditions for a drummer, and he came and auditioned for Guns N' Roses, thinking nothing about it. They called him up and wanted him to do it, but Nickey had already told Stevo Jensen that he was going to be in Stevo's band, Stevo's New Improved Vandals. Tracii then called him up and wanted to put a band together with him and this guy Mick.

Nickey made sure that L.A. Guns were a black-haired band. Anytime they got a new member, they only got guys with black hair or told the guys they would have to dye their hair. Like, "When you come audition, I don't care what color your hair is, but if you end up in the band, it will be long and straight and black."

Nickey Beat played drums on the first L.A. Guns album on PolyGram, but he was out of the band before the album was released, and Steve Riley's picture and name are on the record.

The final and definitive "classic major label lineup" of L.A. Guns was now set:

Mick Cripps, Tracii Guns, Kelly Nickels, Phil Lewis, and Steve Riley.

There were many members before and after this version, but this is the one that wrote the songs and made the albums that keep the current versions going, no matter what they might say to the contrary. Mick Cripps was a very influential part of the whole process. Nothing really went ahead, unless Mick said okay. He was the brains, really, behind the early days of the band. He got them a manager and got the band signed. Kelly and Mick wrote a lot of songs with and for L.A. Guns. Everyone thinks it's all Phil and Tracii. That might be true now, but the band and the people that wrote and recorded the first three L.A. Guns albums were more than just those two. The first three albums are the ones that matter. The golden days with PolyGram with the big industry machine pushing them. That's what made them into a band that had success and can still keep going, riding off the name and the songs on those first three albums.

Since the band was going on the road in January, I temporarily lived with Mick and his brother, Robert. Kelly used to live with Mick, but he moved out to the "Chez Guns" complex on Bronson. Mick lived on Holloway Street in West Hollywood, right across from Tower Records. The day I got there, Mick's cat, Fathead, pissed nasty cat piss all over everything in my suitcase—I guess Fathead was not happy I was moving in! I had to go out and buy all new clothes and a new suitcase. I would only be there for about a month, which was a good thing, as the night before we were leaving to go on tour, there was minor earthquake, and the place shook a good shake. I was not used to earthquakes.

I can deal with a lot of things, but not Mother Nature's wrath! She's in control! I was happy to hit the road.

The band had a New Year's Eve gig booked at the Troubadour in West Hollywood. After the gig, roadie Frank asked manager Alan for money to buy blow for the band, but really it was for some of the band and the crew. He got it, and we all started doing lines. I was up all night and ended up at Steve Riley's apartment watching football on New Year's Day. Steve, his wife Mary, and I were gacked. I then went over to Chez Guns and found myself doing blow with a crucifix that mysteriously broke under its own power the next morning. I stopped doing cocaine then and there. I had been slowing down a lot, but this incident made me quit for good. I just was sick of it, and there was no way I could take this band around the country while doing cocaine—and for the record, L.A. Guns was not a big drug band. There were moments of course, but the guys were content with weed and beer; maybe a little Jack Daniel's once in awhile. They were not into heavy drugs at all. In 1988, Tracii didn't drink or smoke weed or anything— the other guys did. Kelly and Riley were big weed heads, Mick liked to drink beer, and Phil did whatever Phil did, which could be anything at any time. I have a strong constitution, and when I make up my mind to stop something, I stop. I had done enough coke for two lifetimes. I just thank God that I had the internal willpower to stop myself. Didn't need rehab. Just two or three really bad nights gave me the internal power to stop. When I'm done with something, I'm done. It's such an evil drug. That's the last time I did it: January 1, 1988.

For the next couple of weeks, we did pre-production, advancing of gigs, and preparing for a year on the road. The album, L.A. Guns, dropped January 4, 1988. We set up a gig for the album release party at the Los Angeles Police Academy. After soundcheck, the guys were in the police gym playing basketball on the hardwood floor in Beatle boots, and the cops told 'em to get off. It was very weird doing a gig in the police academy. We were all smoking weed and drinking on police grounds and generally being a rock band—pushing the envelope. Arthur Kane came with his wife, Babs. The whole Hollywood scene was there. The label hired some mud wrestling chicks from the Tropicana that were dressed in police uniforms with their boobs hanging out all over. All of the record label people from PolyGram were out in full force. PolyGram was a huge label and had lots of power. They had Bon Jovi, Def Leppard, Cinderella, Scorpions, and Kiss. They were a serious rock label. The new booking agent, Jim Rissmiller, and his staff were also schmoozing the room. A lot of press was there. Everyone was stoked—the future looked awesome! We played shows on the West Coast for most of January: the L.A. area, San Francisco, Phoenix, etc. I drove everyone in a Winnebago for some of these shows and said a prayer before every drive. The guys would be drinking and yelling and blasting music in the back. Trying to keep a giant rolling shoebox on the road while a rock band is going nuts in the back was not easy. I don't know how the bus drivers do it!

The new booking agent, Jim Rissmiller, and Rissky Business then took over, starting with the first show of the first real tour in Austin, Texas on February 14, 1988 at the Back Room.

The No Mercy Tour was on the road, and I was the road manager. The rest of the crew was Frank Fuccile, production manager and tech; Timmy Doyle, drum tech; Kent Holmes, Tracii's guitar tech; Keith Harris, Kelly and Mick's tech; and Carson Price, sound man. The merch guy rode on the bus with us as well. Twelve guys on the bus; tight quarters was an understatement.

Everyone was in great spirits, but I sensed the immediate difference in the four new guys who never toured before and the veteran drummer, Steve Riley. Sure, Phil Lewis had toured when he was in the band Girl in the UK and had also played Japan, but the touring was very limited and nothing like touring America. Steve was older than everyone; he played in a version of Steppenwolf way back, and recorded and toured with national acts Roadmaster, The B'zz, and W.A.S.P.—and now the Guns. That divide and difference made it uneasy at times. The four newbies would have slept on the bus with no hotel rooms or showers if you said that's how it would be. They didn't care; they just wanted to rock. Steve wanted not just hotel rooms, but good hotel rooms. That's one example. Steve was also the only band member with not only a girlfriend, but a wife. That complicated things. I had known Steve and his wife, Mary, from when Steve was in W.A.S.P. They were both very nice to me always, and I have never had a personal problem with Steve or Mary. But that difference, of an older, seasoned, experienced drummer with a wife, on tour with four horny, partying, younger guys without girlfriends on their first tour just created an unfortunate tension. It was an issue for me, that's for sure, but I was being paid to deal with it, so I did, and I did a good job under the circumstances, I must say. For the band, it really wasn't a big issue at the time. Everyone was too excited, too positive, ready to make it. But things did blow up big at times—big. Later on, everyone bickered and fought, it got physical, and the damage was done. But for now, it was the first tour, so things weren't too bad—yet.

We played every club in the country two or three times over, worked our way up to opening for Ted Nugent in theaters, and AC/DC and Iron Maiden in arenas. We were pirates, out on the road with no mobile phones or computers, no debit cards, and no GPS. Money had to be wired back and forth via Western Union: wiregrams. I had a fanny pack with ten grand in it, brass knuckles, a big folding knife, four rolls of quarters, a bottle opener, weed, and condoms. We had a paper map and a bus driver who used to drive for Iron Maiden—besides being Iron Maiden's driver, he was the giant Eddie monster onstage every night.

Warren, God bless him, did some insanely long drives back then. It wasn't regulated like it is now—how many hours you are allowed to drive. It was insane how those drivers got away with some of those super long drives we did. No way you could do that today. Warren almost drove off a mountain in a blizzard on a 20 hour-straight drive from a Galveston, Texas spring break show to Denver, Colorado. His eyes looked like Rodney Dangerfield after those long drives speeding on whatever he took to stay awake. I sat up with him that time in the snow, pure whiteout conditions, and got him through it. We almost all died. It was scary as hell.

Another time, we drove straight from New Jersey to Fort Lauderdale, nonstop, 21 hours, and did a gig when we got in. I was always the first one up in the morning just so I could sit up with the driver and keep an eye on him—if I even went to sleep at all. The stress was unbearable at times.

The tour bus is something that has been mythologized over the years and with good reason. It's where everything goes down. It's the band and the road crew's home for a year. But let me tell you, it's no fun after a couple of weeks. And if you saw what went on in there night after night, you wouldn't ever want to sit down in a tour bus ever again. Unless you are someone very big, like say, Lady Gaga, who would be pretty much alone on the brand spanking new bus with her assistant, it's disgusting. We had 12 people on there, and in 1988 that could have meant you were on a bus from 1980 or older. It was the band's first tour; we weren't getting the newest most modern bus. You live on that fucking thing, and the smell from the last band that had it still lingers in the air. The thing smells terrible and is never clean. It's a friggin' petri dish.

Here's some examples from which I speak:

The bus always smelt like beer, piss, and nasty girls. The smelly, disgusting couch in the front of the bus was the worst. That thing saw more liquids squished into it, that no amount of steam cleaning could ever do anything to rid the bus of the smell. Food, beer, whiskey, smelly chicks—Tracii had relations with a "fan" on that couch, and it stunk for a week. Gross, man. Tracii would fuck chicks in the back of the bus and then run to the front and grab a bottle of Jack Daniel's, pouring it on his pecker to kill off the germs—like that would work! Dirty clothes everywhere, mostly Tracii and Phil's. Trash everywhere. The floor covered in broken glass, candy, chips, rags, and shit. Cigarette butts everywhere. Smoke so thick after a gig when there was 20 people on there; fans, chicks, band, crew—whoever. Even after the bus driver had the thing steam cleaned and sanitized, it would return to a complete shambles after a day or two. The back of the bus was like a dark medieval dungeon of filth and excrement. It was it's own little compartment, and you could lock the door—it was usually taken over by Phil—but everyone used that back "lounge."

The so-called "bathroom" was really a tiny, smaller than a broom closet room with a plastic toilet that resembled a Porta John and a small sink with water that barely trickled out. The rule is always: don't shit in the toilet, but not everyone follows the rules. The smell of piss and that nasty smelling sanitizer that they use in Porta Johns was always there.

The bunks, all 12 of them, were coffin-like boxes that were claustrophobic and inhuman. Mick would say that when he woke up in the morning in the bunk, it was like that Three Stooges train short where they would spring up and knock their heads on the ceiling of the bunk. He would come to, and his first thoughts were, "What the hell insanity is going to occur today!" It was horrible, never quiet, and you can never get any rest in those coffins. There is always someone up making noise, or people walking around, going to the bathroom, or snoring like wounded animals. Disgusting.

Ahh, the old tour bus. It was fun. For awhile.

Weed. I became a weedhead while working for L.A. Guns. I did drugs in my life, but I never smoked. I have never smoked a cigarette ever. I had smoked a little weed here and there, but didn't like smoking anything, really. But in L.A. Guns, Steve and Kelly were the weedheads and through being with them every day, I became a weedhead too. We smoked every day for a year. Kelly, Riley, most of the crew, and I smoked weed nonstop. We were always rolling joints nonstop. First thing we did in the morning was smoke a fatty. We wouldn't even get out of the bunks—we were all passing joints while still in bed! When we got to a town, the first thought wasn't about the gig—it was where was I going to get weed. The bus drivers drove while smoking weed! TRUE! Total insanity. To be clear, if I got weed, it was for the band, and of course, for me too. But if I didn't have it for them, it would not be a happy day!

Tour Diary Excerpts: No Mercy Tour 1988

ATLANTA · February 18, 1988: *The tour rolls into Atlanta, GA for the first time at The Masquerade club. I had to deal with a crazy wino that kept trying to climb on the bus and into the luggage hold underneath. It got physical, unfortunately. The club was small with a balcony, and it was packed. The show was cookin'. I saw some old Georgia friends, and we hung on the bus after the show.*

BALTIMORE · February 21, 1988: *First time at Hammerjacks.* [Hammerjacks was a legendary rock club that every band that was on the same circuit as us played a couple times a year. When you saw Hammerjacks on the itinerary, you were like, *YEAH!* It would be packed with people, there would be tons of wild chicks there that wanted to meet the band, and there would be lots of drinking. It was definitely a party at Hammerjacks, for sure.] *After the gig, I was settling up with the* club, getting paid, and getting the band some beer and Jack Daniel's for the bus—the usual. I finished up, and when I walked out the door of the club towards the bus, I saw that the thing was shaking and bouncing. I was like, "What the fuck is going on in there!" When I got to the bus and opened the door, there were probably 30 people inside, music blasting, people smoking, drinking, spilling booze everywhere. Chicks dancing around half naked, band members right in the middle. We pulled out of there as the sun was coming up. The bus smelled. Bad.

NYC · February 24, 1988: *Hit my hometown of New York for the first time at the Cat Club. We were staying at the classic Mayflower Hotel on Central Park West. We ran into the actor Michael V. Gazzo when we were leaving for the gig, and I stopped the band and went up to Michael and asked for his autograph. He was so nice and asked me my name. When I told him, he kind of chuckled and said, "Michael Corcione! Ahhh, where you from?" I said, "Cedarhurst out on the Island." He replied, "Ahhh, the Five Towns." He knew. I thanked him and went back to the band and started getting them in the cars for the ride to the soundcheck. They said, "Who the fuck was that!" I said, "THAT, my friends, was Frank Pentangeli from The Godfather!" Steve and Mick and Kelly looked at me in awe! [We watched all the old movies on the long bus rides and The Godfather was certainly one of them.] At the gig, I had to make the promoter at the club get better mics for Steve's drums, as they weren't proper drum mics. Steve insisted.*

It was chaos for awhile watching the promoter run around like a chicken with his head cut off trying to borrow mics from other clubs so the band could soundcheck. That night, the club was packed to the rafters. I saw many old friends, including Richie Ranno from Starz. Didn't go to sleep for 36 hours.

LONG ISLAND · February 27, 1988: *First Long Island gig at Sundance out in Suffolk County. Place was wall-to-wall. Oversold. Saw many old friends, people that Kelly and I both knew from his days as a roadie for Hotshot. It was a wild and hectic tornado of a night. We all got pretty drunk and watched the sun come up.*

DETROIT · March 3, 1988: *Saint Andrews Hall. [My dad was here in Detroit in "college" again, and I went to visit him.] The promoter gave me the runner for the afternoon. [The runner is a kind of a gofer-type person who works for the promoter.] She drove me the 45 minutes each way to see my dad. Turns out her dad was the "dean" of the college. Talk about a crazy coincidence. Or was it?*

GALVESTON, TEXAS · March Spring Break: *Gene Loves Jezebel were on the bill and wanted to borrow Steve's drums. That didn't go over too well with Steve. [The person that was handling their band was a friend I knew from the Relativity days, Mark Kates.] I hated to be an ass about it, but Steve would not agree to* *anyone borrowing his drums ever. Not anyone. Maybe John Bonham. So I had to deal with that situation all day. Sorry Mark.*

DENVER · March 15, 1988: *The hotel we stayed in was right across the street from a place called Shotgun Willie's. We thought it was a steakhouse. It looked like a Wild West steakhouse kind of place. After we checked in, I went over with one of the crew to get some food and walked into a very large strip club. Okay! We had a day off today and then the gig tomorrow. I went back to the hotel, informed everyone that, no, it isn't a steakhouse, it's a strip club! Everyone went over there and pretty much stayed over there until showtime the next day. Everyone got laid in Denver. The crew, the bus driver—everyone. It was wild.* [The girls were all over the place, and they absolutely loved the new breed of MTV bands like Mötley Crüe, Def Leppard, Ratt, L.A. Guns, and GNR. A few of the girls that were hanging out with us had just been filmed at McNichols Arena in Denver in February for the Def Leppard video "Pour Some Sugar on Me." In the video, you can see them all dancing in the front row. I guess the Leppard boys found Shotgun Willie's too! Needless to say this was a fun two days.]

HOLLYWOOD · March 25, 1988: *Palace Theatre. Ozzy showed up backstage to check out L.A. Guns. [He was considering having them open his new tour in a few months. Ozzy was managed by Sharon Osbourne, daughter of Don Arden who ran*

Jet Records in the UK and also ran most of the British music business. Phil Lewis was in the band Girl before LAG, and they were on Jet Records, so Ozzy knew Phil.] He and Zakk Wylde showed up backstage and said hello to the guys before the show started. Ozzy was a nervous wreck. He ate an apple and asked for a Coke. I got him a can, and he asked me if there was booze in it. I said, "No sir," and he said, "Are you sure? Because I can't have any booze man." As he was saying this, there's a piece of apple on his lip, and I am trying to assure Ozzy that I did not put any booze in his Coca Cola, debating if I should tell him about the piece of apple on his face. [A photographer quickly appeared and snapped a pic of Ozzy and the Guns that ended up in some rock magazine.] Ozzy watched the show from the wings and after 15 or 20 minutes, he pulled me aside and said that he had to leave, but to have Phil call him tomorrow at the Sunset Marquis. [L.A. Guns never got an opening slot on an Ozzy tour.] I later found record producer Rick Rubin wandering around outside by the stage door after the gig and asked him if I could help him. He had a pass on and said he was supposed to talk to Tracii about possibly producing the next record. I led Rick upstairs to the dressing room, and him and Tracii sat and talked. [Nothing came of that either. We were in Hollywood for a few days, and then played Anaheim on March 30th.]

TULSA · April 8, 1988: *Cain's Ballroom. Kelly gets to play on the same stage that Sid Vicious did in 1978. Mick woke me after* *an hour of sleep to go find a magic store to look for magic tricks.* [We did this in a lot of cities, find a magic store. Mick was always up earlier than everyone, and I was always appointed his minder on these early morning excursions through strange downtowns.]

CHICAGO · Friday and Saturday April 15 & 16, 1988: *The Thirsty Whale.* [New crew addition Scotty Daggett shows up to work. He was an old friend of Steve's, someone he had toured with in the past. Scotty was an alcoholic trying to get clean of drugs and booze. He had just come out of rehab, and Steve got him work. He was to be the production manager and also a guitar tech.] *We are at the gig, and Scotty was supposed to have arrived already. I start asking around to see if anyone has seen him. I run into Keith, one of our techs in the club, and he says, "I think he's on the bus. You might want to go see what's going on." So I head to the bus, walk on, and it's empty, but the door to the back lounge is closed. I walk to the back and knock and hear a voice I don't recognize say to come in. I walk in, and our new production manager and a girl are having a party with ice cubes. She is spread open on the back couch. He sticks the ice cubes in, and she pops 'em out across the room. Nice to meet ya. It's your first day of work and this is how its gonna start?* [Scotty didn't last very long. Maybe a week. He was so shaky, he couldn't string a guitar. He was not ready to be out on the road. But the two gigs at The Thirsty Whale in Chicago were wall-to-wall people. Real rock and roll. Insane shows. Chicago was always good to the band.]

217

FLORIDA - April 20, 1988: *Two days off in Plantation, Florida. Then we open the tour with Ted Nugent at the Sunrise Theatre on April 22nd, followed by a gig at a waterpark, Water Mania, in Kissimmee, Florida on April 23rd. Sunrise Theatre gig was great, nice to be on a bigger stage.*

On the way to the next gig at Water Mania, the bus broke down. We were stranded on the side of the road. Warren was trying to get help on the CB radio. We all piled out of the bus, as it was hot as fuck, and Warren couldn't run the generator. So we had no AC, and we got off and threw a fucking football around in the hot sun. That lasted about 90 seconds, and we just got back on the bus and waited. And sweat. Eventually, some fans that had seen us at the Sunrise Theatre the night before, saw the bus on the side of the road and pulled over to see if we were okay. They were heading to the gig at Water Mania, and they were driving a van! What luck! Some of the crew had driven the equipment truck and were already at the show. So the rest of the crew and I got a lift from the fans to the gig. We would also send help. We get to the gig, and I see it's a giant pool! The band is playing to people on floats in the water. That's a first! The crew get the gear set up and get everything ready. We have some time before I need to panic. Thankfully, Warren had contacted someone on the CB that sent help, and the bus got fixed. Now there is about 20 minutes to showtime. I'm standing on the stage at the highest point, sweating and pacing, watching for the bus to drive into the backstage area. With 15 minutes to spare, the bus comes pulling in, the guys change their clothes, the intro tape is rolling, and they run onto the stage and almost skid off into the pool! The stage is kinda damp and slick. The band was like, What! Their eyes were wide open when they walked on to the stage and saw the crowd was in a giant pool! Floating on tubes and stuff and the band is playing to them. So bizarre! But Ted was awesome to us. The legendary Nitebob was doing sound for him. Derek St. Holmes was in the band playing guitar and singing too, so it was like old Ted. We were all psyched. Except maybe for Mick. He wasn't a Ted guy really. I mean, Kelly and I used to go see Ted Nugent at Nassau Coliseum on Long Island back in the day. And Tracii and Steve loved him. "Great White Buffalo" and all that. On opening night, Ted came in the dressing room to say hello to everyone. Ted's a tall guy, and he just strutted in like Tarzan and said, "Hey boys! L.A. Guns! I like that name! Guns! Let's rock and roll."

ATLANTA - April 24, 1988: *Fox Theatre. I had family come by to see me: my mom and sister and another young fan that was the son of someone my mom worked with. The Fox is a legendary venue, and it was a thrill to work on that stage.*

MEMPHIS - April 26, 1988: *Memphis. The local PolyGram rep takes us to Graceland. We pay our respects to the King.* [This started Kelly's Elvis fixation. We listened to Elvis on the bus every day for a few days until Tracii couldn't take it anymore. Then it was back to the usual playlist of Bad Company, the Stones, Zeppelin, The Cult, etc. But Mick would always throw on some Kraftwerk once in a while and just piss everyone off—maybe not Phil. You need to change it up sometimes, man. We live in a heavy metal rock and roll bubble; let's listen to other things, please and thank you.]

TOLEDO - April 29, 1988: *Toledo, Ohio: Sports Arena. Money was tight, checks were on hold, and per diems being held back.* [The management of the money by the office was erratic at best. And out on the road, I was the guy holding the cash that was being used to pay for everything. Some of the guys in the band would just demand I give them money, or they would hijack my fanny pack that I kept all the cash in. They would say, "We are going out to eat. We are taking the cash." I would say, "You just can't take it." They would say, "Its our money, and we are taking it," and they would go out to lobster dinners and steakhouses and strip clubs. Some of the guys just took the money. I had to start sleeping with the thing on my waist.]

SAGINAW - April 30, 1988: *Saginaw, Michigan end of tour with Ted at Wendler Arena. After tonight's show, Ted invites us out to an end of tour dinner at a steakhouse in the woods of Michigan. Ted and his road manager drove a car to the steakhouse. [Ted would fly everywhere on tour and rent a car in* *each city.] So we are in our bus following Ted's car: I am sitting in the front seat next to the driver, the curtains are pulled open, and all the guys are looking out the front window, excited and hyped from the gig. As we are following Ted, we see some kind of animal run out in front of Ted's car. Was it a fox, raccoon, dog, or cat? I don't know, but I do know that Ted whipped out a pistol, hung his arm out of the passenger-side car window, and shot the damn thing. One shot. We were wide-eyed. When we got to the restaurant, Kelly said, "Nice shot, Ted!" and Ted replied, "I should have stopped and scraped it up. We could have grilled it!"*

PORTLAND, MAINE - May 1, 1988: *Two days off in Portland, Maine. We are now opening for AC/DC. It's the start of the tour, and there are two days of pre-production for AC/DC. We stayed at our hotel and drank and smoked weed or visited the gig, excited as fuck. [Mick starts me wearing the wrestling mask.] Last time we were in Hollywood, Mick and I went to the store Wacko on Melrose. They sold all kinds of cool and bizarre stuff, and I bought a wrestling mask just to have it. I always loved the old masked wrestlers as a kid and thought it was cool, so I got one. Mick and the guys wanted me to do an intro for them on this tour, in the biggest venues they've played yet. Big arenas, two nights sold out in a lot of cities. Mick said, "You have to wear the mask!" I became "Lord Humongous from the wastelands of Hollywood."* [I'd put on the mask and my L.A. Guns leather jacket, go out with my giant Maglite, and do the intro. The sound man, Carson, would put an effect on my voice that made me sound like a monster. The intro music was from The Lost Boys, "Cry Little Sister," and at the end of that, I would bellow, "Hello my sick puppies! It's time for you to kneel before the Hollywood Vampires! From the wastelands of Hollywood, California, please welcome, L.A. Guns!" I did that every night on that tour. Hahahaha! We were pumped for two nights sold out at the Cumberland Civic Center. We had not done a tour this big before. We had to get our new giant backdrop hung up every night by the AC/DC crew. There were some union halls, and it had to be handled a certain way. So thankfully, the crew were very nice to us. We needed a bar to hang the backdrop, and their carpenters got one together for us. We used their light tech to do our lights and also their monitor guy. They couldn't have been nicer to us. Much respect to AC/DC and their crew.]

BOSTON: *Two nights sold out in Boston at the Centrum arena. Steve Riley's hometown. [A lot of his family came down and it was always fun in Boston.] Great seafood restaurants. We ate good, drank well, and hung with some of the locals for a few days. I have to say, that the band is on fire right now. They always sound good, but they have been playing live five nights a week for the last four months, and they are locked in and kicking ass. Steve is a powerhouse drummer, man. Standing there in the wings, watching him bash the fuck out of the drums every night, locked in and in a groove is something I will never forget. It felt like power.* [The whole band would just rip your head off, right from

222

the opening song, "No Mercy." They were tight as fuck, and when they were onstage like that bashing it out, it was the only time I think they were happy. It was what they were supposed to do. All the traveling, waiting, boredom, drama, bad food, and bad habits—it's all tolerated so they could play 38 minutes a night. Wild, when you think about it that way. Onstage, the guys were doing their job, doing what they were put out on the road to do. Offstage is where the problems began.]

CANADA: *Two nights up in Canada in Ottawa and Hamilton, Ontario. The band had dumped all their weed before we entered Canada, and now Steve and Kelly and the crew were on a search for the goods. Before they did something risky and stupid, I ended up connecting with someone through the merch guy who knew a guy, etc., and found myself in some dodgy apartment trying to buy weed and hash. There was danger in the air. I felt it as soon as I laid my eyes on the place, but I got it done—and got the fuck out of there. Hash was in abundance in Canada. I came back with so much, everyone smoked it constantly until we had to cross back over into America.*

DETROIT: *Joe Louis Arena in Detroit. Phil didn't soundcheck. He was feeling a little under the weather.* [It was hard for Phil to keep his voice together, touring nonstop and such. It's such a physical drain, and you have to work very hard to stay healthy. It's tough to do. So if Phil didn't want to sing the soundcheck to save his voice for the show, I would sing a couple songs with the band. We would do "S.O.S. (Too Bad)" by Aerosmith and some other cover song. It was wild singing in an arena! Even if it was empty and all the lights were on!]

NEW JERSEY · May 20, 1988: *Brendan Byrne Arena, Meadowlands. This was a crazy couple of days. A lot of friends were at the gig. My brother was there, Bruno Ravel—everyone. When I checked into the hotel in New Jersey, there were about a hundred slips of paper waiting for me at the front desk with messages to call people. But that would have to wait. Mick Cripps was getting married. Mick and Shawn got married at City Hall in Downtown Manhattan today, and he played the gig that night. Angus Young from AC/DC gave Mick his limo to use for the day as a wedding present. Alan Jones had sent me a box of suits for the guys to wear to the wedding. I think only Kelly went. I was supposed to go, but there was so much shit going on it was impossible. At the same time that Mick is getting married, Tracii decides he wants a new backline. He bought three Marshall stacks from Manny's Music on 48th Street in Manhattan.* [Manny's was a great store which, sadly, is no longer there. Tracii arranged all of this at retail price at one of the most expensive stores in Manhattan, at the last minute, and had it delivered to the arena.] And to top it all off, PolyGram decides to give the band an award. The band's debut album had been out since January, and it was almost gold. Almost. So they decided to present the band with a 3/4 gold album. It looked like a fucking pie chart from middle school. Whoever decided that this was a good idea was wrong because the guys were furious. It was the most ridiculous thing ever. Kelly, especially, was pissed. And they had to pose with that stupid plaque with the PolyGram heavies. Scott Koenig was there with Mike D from the Beastie Boys. [I was friends with Scott. He worked for Rush Management and managed the Beasties. I got Scott and Mike to come up to the party that PolyGram had set up to take a photo with the guys. They came to watch AC/DC, but I got him to bring Mike up for a photo. I had known Scott from the Relativity days. We had traded records, CDs, merch, and stuff back and forth and had become friends. I was into the Beastie Boys heavy in 1986 and 1987 and had the inside track to everything from Scott. At the end of this gig, I think I had been up for two days with about four hours sleep. If you could call it sleep.]

LOUISVILLE · May 24, 1988: *Freedom Hall, final show of the tour. Live radio broadcast, and I get the pie in the face. The AC/DC crew pulled all their end of tour pranks on us. They hit me in the face with a couple of cream pies while I had the mask on and was doing the introduction. Then they had a giant, inflatable Godzilla that was attached to a rope that they would hang down from the lighting truss up above. They would dangle it in front of Phil, and he would kick out at it. They did a bunch of other harmless, but distracting stunts too. The show was being* recorded for a *Westwood One* live radio broadcast that would be sent out to radio stations all over the country, so the band was a bit on edge, and to have all these pranks going on didn't help. After I got hit with the pies in the face, I had to run to the side and take the mask off and find a towel to wipe my eyes because I couldn't see. The bad had just started the set, and the stage was slippery from the whipped cream all over the floor. Phil was having a hissy fit about it. Why didn't I clean it up right away, etc. I couldn't fucking see, that's why! I had to wipe my eyes before I could wipe the stage floor. But I understood that Philip was just on edge and trying to sing well for the radio recording. [The opening song, "No Mercy," from this taping, complete with my interrupted-by-a-cream-pie-in-the-face intro, was issued as a B-side on the "Rip and Tear" cassette single and also on the promo vinyl 12" single of "Rip and Tear."]

LONG ISLAND · May 27, 1988: *Showcase.* [We played a club on Long Island called Showcase. It was only open for a short time.] *No one knew anything about the place. None of my friends back on Long Island knew anything. We played the gig; everything was great. It wasn't well promoted. [It was an off-night, like a Tuesday, and there were probably only a hundred people there.] They paid us ten grand cash. Took it out of a briefcase that probably had more than a couple hundred grand in it. This club was definitely a laundry. They had to be washing money in that place. You could just tell.*

SOUTH AMBOY, NEW JERSEY · June 1, 1988: *Club Bene. Phil Collen from Def Leppard came down and jammed with the band on "Hollywood Tease."* [Phil Lewis and Phil Collen were in the band Girl together in the early 80s in London, and "Hollywood Tease" was a Girl song that L.A. Guns had rerecorded for their debut album. This is the gig that Sweet Pain somehow got mentioned on the bus after the show, and Phil Collen was telling us how Def Leppard listened to the song "I Get My Kicks" before they went onstage to psych themselves up for the show! Kelly Nickels pointed at me and said, "Well, there's the singer right there: our road manager!"]

HALLANDALE, FLORIDA · June 2 & 3, 1988: *The Button South. We have a new bus driver now named Billy, and after last nights gig in New Jersey, he drove to South Florida, 21 hours straight through, and when we got in, we did a gig that night. Some of the guys from Anthrax and Metallica must have been playing somewhere close by 'cause they came down to the show and wound up in the dressing room afterwards. A lot of drinking and crazy Florida chicks. Kelly pushed a groupie into the pool the next day after the gig. She had on her full get-up: makeup, teased hair, heels, barely there clothes. She was parading around the pool, being all cool and snooty, and Kelly just shoved her in.*

MIAMI · June 5, 1988: [Miami in 1988 was still like Scarface. The place was dangerous and rundown. It was not like it is today.]

After the gig while we are loading out, Tracii got his prized Les Paul guitar stolen. It was a quick hit and run. I immediately started talking to the promoter and his people, trying to suss out who it might have been, etc. Usually those kinds of thieves hit every gig that comes through town, so they are known to everyone. After about 15 minutes of talking to the promoter, we figured it out. The word went out, and we tracked the thief down, got the guitar back, and gave him a thank you upside the head.

IRVINE, CALIFORNIA · June 8 and 9, 1988: *Irvine Meadows Amphitheater. We are playing a club somewhere in Florida and get a call that we are picking up the Iron Maiden tour. Immediately. Fly out to Irvine, California right away. Guns N' Roses were opening the tour and pulled out. They weren't digging the whole idea of playing in front of a giant glacier every night.* [The new Iron Maiden album and tour were called Seventh Son of a Seventh Son, and the album imagery had ice and a glacier in there. Because the glacier onstage was so monstrous, it was visible behind the opening band every night. You couldn't avoid the thing. Axl was also having issues with his voice, which I think was the main reason, but I'm sure there was some other drama going on as well. They left the tour, and the promoter wasn't happy. There were two nights sold out at the big outdoor venue, and a lot of the tickets were sold because Guns N' Roses were on the bill. The venue was about an hour and a half from Hollywood, so it was sort of a hometown area show for GNR.] *The promoter*

228

came up with the brilliant idea for the Guns N' Roses guys, minus Axl, to jam with the L.A. Guns guys on a couple of songs to appease the fans that bought tickets to see GNR. This was not a good idea to begin with. [Add to the fact that we had to fly out to Irvine right away, rent gear, and do the shows—remember we were in Florida. The truck with all of our gear would have to drive from Florida and meet us at one of the later shows on the West Coast, so we flew into LAX and went right to the gig. We had arranged to have a rented backline from SIR delivered to the gig for us—amps, drums, etc. The gear was not their "A" gear. It wasn't in great shape, and the amps were having issues.] So we do our set, the amps are cutting in and out, and the sound is shit. Then, when it was time for Duff, Slash, and Izzy to jam with us, their amps were cutting out too because it was the same shitty rented gear we had from SIR. After the show, they accused us of sabotaging them. Or at least Slash did. We had a big pow wow after the gig: their manager, Dougie Goldstein, Slash, and me. I think Adler was there too. [It was all bad blood going back to Fairfax High School. Slash mentions this incident in his book, and he said we sabotaged him. But I was there, and it was the gear, man. We had the same issues with the gear, and our sound was shit too. But I understand his frustration—Tracii could rub you the wrong way sometimes, especially if you were another musician. But I always respected Guns N' Roses. On the occasions that I spent time with Axl and talked with him, he was always cool, and we always got along. He knew me from a year or so ago when I would come out and stay at the Riot House in Hollywood. We once had a long conversation in New York City in the VIP room of a club called Spodee Odee in 1989. We talked about band things, Tracii, why he couldn't be in a band with him, etc. He said he liked Tracii, but he couldn't be in band with him. I thought that was interesting. I met Steven Adler a few years later when Kelly, Danny Berger, and I rented his house up in the Hills for awhile. I never got to know Slash or Duff. Izzy, I hung with a couple of times. But GNR were the real deal. That time, 1987, 1988, 1989—they were on fire.

When I was going out to LA in 1987 and had just met the L.A. Guns guys, I heard a story about the guitar solo in "Sweet Child O' Mine." We were all hanging out one night, and someone said that Slash was inspired by the solo in the song "Baker Street" by Gerry Rafferty. If you listen to both solos, they are pretty similar in feel and structure, but I'm not a musician, and I don't know Slash, and I don't know if that story is true, but that's what I had heard. And this was before "Sweet Child O' Mine" was on the radio. It was very early times. It wasn't a big hit yet. But I love that "Baker Street" song! I think the guitar player that played the solo on the record ended up getting his own record deal just from that solo. At least that's what I heard.

With Iron Maiden, we did the remaining dates on the tour that GNR had pulled out of. We played San Diego, The Forum in L.A, Phoenix, Albuquerque, and Denver.]

PHOENIX: *A kid grabbed Tracii's guitar when he was hanging it out over the security pit. I saw the kid grab his strap and start tugging it hard, and I crouched low and ran across the stage and did a baseball slide into the pit, grabbed the kid's arm, and told him to let go. He was screaming at me over the wailing music, saying "No," and "Fuck you." I whipped out my giant Maglite that I carried on my belt and wailed into the kids arm hard, and he let go. Tracii looked down at me like, Wow! [It was all guys in the audience on that tour.] The Maiden audience is mostly dudes every night anyway, but it was especially rowdy tonight in Phoenix.*

Barstow, California

After that short Maiden leg ended, we headed back to L.A. to film the video for the new single, "Electric Gypsy," out in the desert in Barstow, California. It was 105 degrees, and we filmed all day. We were there probably 14 hours. The band borrowed bikes from some local L.A. bikers, and the biker guys stayed on the bus all day with their girls, drinking and hanging. At one point, I went on the bus to get something, and they were watching animal porn, bestiality stuff. I was like, Jesus! Can it get any lower than this! The band and PolyGram made the video using the same director, Ralph Ziman, from their earlier clips, "One More Reason" and "Sex Action." The video that he did for them before they got signed, for the song, "One More Reason," helped them to get a record deal. That video to me is what L.A. Guns are supposed to look and sound like. THAT is L.A. fucking Guns. Ralph was a friend of the band and Alan the manager, and I think he did the videos really inexpensively. I don't think the band had insurance for the "Electric Gypsy" shoot, and some of them looked pretty shaky on the bikes, riding back and forth next to a rolling freight train. I remember that became an issue at one point. There was some drama for a bit. It all got calmed down, and we ended the day safely, gave the bikers back their bikes, said goodbye, and hit the road, as I plotted with the bus driver to get the bus sanitized and steam cleaned at the next available opportunity.

Hollywood

After the video filming, we all stayed in L.A. for a few days to take care of some business at the office and do some promo stuff for PolyGram, etc. We stayed at the Holiday Inn on Highland in Hollywood. Kelly got me drunk and took me out to get a tattoo. We went to Sunset Strip Tattoo right across from the Riot House. I just picked something off the wall: a flying dragon breathing fire. Kelly calls it my little dinosaur. Compared to the ink the guys have, and all the other bands who were covered in tats, mine was like a little nothing. After I got the tat, we ended up at Gladstones on the beach in Malibu eating oysters and drinking more beer and tequila. The band also did a gig at the Cathouse in Hollywood while we were in town, which was an unorganized mess as it usually is when doing a gig in those types of places—same at the Cat Club in NYC—subpar sound and lights, etc. Very hip and cool venues—the hip spot to be—but production-wise, not good. When it was time to head back out on tour, we were all loading up onto our freshly steam cleaned and sanitized bus, and Tracii was on the front couch watching a porno. Steve and his wife, Mary, got on the bus, and Steve had an issue with Tracii watching the porno in front of Mary. It was like a respect thing. Well, they got into it. Tracii was going on about this being a fucking rock and roll tour, etc., blah blah. Steve was like, "Listen bro, you can't watch porno in front of my wife. That ain't cool," and he was pissed. Steve has that Boston accent, and he was mad; you could tell by the tone of his voice. There was some pushing, only a little bit. Steve would have killed Tracii in a physical fight, so it was never going to go there, but it went on and on for hours and delayed the bus leaving. Tracii was the one that wanted Nickey Beat gone and got Steve into the band in the first place. So stupid. What a way to start the new leg of the tour.

There was not one thing we could do that would not result in some kind of mishap, fight, commotion, or meltdown. Right now, it was Steve and Tracii going at it. Sometimes, it was one of the other guys. No problems with Phil; he was pretty easy to deal with, except for his kleptomania. Kelly, I knew from the old days in New York back in 1983, so we were tight, and we would room together. We just had fun all the fucking time. Easy times with Kelly. I actually roomed with either Kelly or Mick, depending. And I must say though, that Tracii always did his job and was always on time, which for a road manager is a huge plus! He was also generous with his money and nice to fans. He did have to deal with a lot of stupid interviews asking about Guns N' Roses. That band was exploding, and that's all that the interviewers wanted to talk to Tracii about. I'm sure it was very frustrating to have to answer those questions, but it's all part of the deal: the deal with the devil, the devil being the contract you signed to be able to be on a major label and hopefully become a rock star.

My entire memory of this time on tour was like being in a tornado 24-7. There was no sanity. Everything was impulsive, knee-jerk mania. There were only rare moments when everything was calm. There was always someone that needed to be reeled in: the roadies idiocy; the bus driver hadn't slept in 24 hours and is still driving; the paychecks were bouncing; Phil stealing a gun from a pawn shop in Texas, and I had to save his ass from going to state jail for ten years; Kelly hurting his fucking leg again; I having to remove some chick that had been on the bus for a few days and wouldn't leave; the manager, Alan, passed out on the front couch holding an empty bottle of vodka; Tracii mooning the audience when we opened for AC/DC, essentially stealing guitarist Angus Young's shtick; having to move Steve's hotel room three or four times because it was either near the elevator, ice machine, soda machine, etc.; Tracii deciding to buy a whole new backline of amps from Manny's Music in New York City at retail prices on the day L.A. Guns opened for AC/DC at the Meadowlands, which was also the same day that Mick got married at City Hall in Downtown Manhattan. It goes on and on.

We finally left Hollywood and went back out on the road after the porno watching incident between Tracii and Steve and hit the clubs again. You are always playing clubs while waiting for a bigger tour to do, like opening for a bigger band in arenas or theaters. We were playing a club somewhere, and I got a call at the hotel after the gig with the news that we got a co-headline tour—or so we'd been told.

The Vinnie Vincent Episode

We got a co-headline tour with Vinnie Vincent. On a co-headline tour, usually the bands share equal billing in all advertising and equal stage production, etc. Vinnie Vincent was in Kiss for a second; he was in the band for one tour in 1982, the very last one when they still wore makeup. He is revered by some Kiss fans because he was in the "makeup" era and had his own makeup design, the Ankh Warrior. Ho hum, gimme a break. Then he was on the *Lick It Up* album, which was the first Kiss album after they took the makeup off. Vinnie thought he was Mick Jagger or something because of this. Delusional. He was eventually fired from Kiss, but because he was in Kiss, he was able to get a solo record deal. The tour was contracted as a co-headlining tour, but Vinnie had other ideas from the get-go. We only did three gigs with him: July 7th at The Vic Theatre in Chicago, July 8th in Taylorville, Illinois, and July 9th at Harpos in Detroit.

The entire three days were a nightmare from start to finish. Vinnie was acting like he was the biggest rock star on the planet. He wore a big pink wig and had tighty-whitey underwear on under his spandex, and you could see his underwear lines. He looked like a little kid or something. The guy was sooo not cool by any stretch of the imagination. Vinnie had issues with everything; the drum riser being one of the main ones. I'm sure there was jealousy with Tracii also; the guitar hero wankfest competition crap. But usually it was always about the fucking riser.

Right from the get-go, Vinnie and his people wanted to have a meeting with me to "straighten things out." Vinnie was such a dick, and his road manager was an even bigger one. We met at The Vic Theatre in Chicago at soundcheck in the afternoon, and they didn't want to soundcheck until the theater was cleared of everyone, us included, which is complete bullshit to be pulled by any band, especially someone like Vinnie Dickhead. Of course, his soundcheck went on for hours, and we barely had time to put our gear onstage. We had the drum riser discussion, and they wouldn't strike their drums, so we had to set up in front of them, which left very little room. Everyone was pissed. We did the gig and then got the hell out of there. On the bus ride, Steve Riley was in my ear about the drum riser and what needed to get done at tomorrow's gig, going on and on all night. I kept rolling joints and smoked until I couldn't keep my eyes open and passed out on the couch.

The second show was in Taylorville, Illinois. The same crap happened. I had arranged a meeting at the venue with me, Riley, Vinnie, and Vinnie's road manager about the drum riser issue. They were being assholes again, and I thought the vein in Steve's neck was going to explode; he was so mad. They wouldn't budge, saying they were the headliner, when we were told by our agent and contracts were signed stating it was a co-headline tour. They were definitely fucking with us. We had power outages in the middle of the set, equipment went missing, no stage room, they wouldn't strike the drum riser—all kinds of stuff was pulled. Everyone was pissed. We did the gig and got out of there. Same talk with Steve on the bus ride, but more heated. We were all drinking, and the talking about it got everyone riled up. It was Mick, Kelly, and Steve that were pissed. Tracii and Phil stayed out of it. I was bracing for the inevitable war that I knew was coming, but was powerless to stop.

We get to Detroit and the venue, Harpos. It was the third and last show we did with him. The tour was supposed to be like two months. We were all miserable, and the band wanted out of the tour. I was told to come to yet another meeting with Vinnie and his people at their hotel. It was about 30 minutes away from the gig, and they told me to take a cab there, and I could ride back to the venue with them on their bus. I took a cab out there, met with them, and the meeting went nowhere. I think they just wanted to pull a power trip because when it was time to leave, they said I couldn't ride on the bus with them, sorry. I had to find a payphone and call a cab to get back to the gig, which is not like calling an Uber today. It took over an hour to get a cab out in the suburbs of Michigan to take me back into Detroit. I got back to the gig, and the band asked me what happened. I gave them the story, and Steve, Kelly, and Mick were mad and getting madder. They were fuming. We did our set, and amps were unplugged mysteriously again, lights went out—all kinds of shit. I was ready to kill the pink wig-wearing bastard and his chickenshit road manager.

The guys got through their set, and then we went immediately to our bus out back. Everyone was stewing. The drinking started. We sat there waiting for the crew to break down and load up for an hour or so. Steve disappeared somewhere with the promoter. Phil was not around, which wasn't unusual. Tracii was in the back lounge of the bus with a girl. Kelly, Mick, and I were hanging out in the front lounge of the bus drinking. The crew was out by the truck talking to some girls. Our bus driver was still at the hotel sleeping, but was supposed to be arriving soon. Vinnie's set ended, and immediately his crew started loading stuff out to his truck. We were on the bus, parked outside by the loading dock, drinking beer, smoking weed, and watching as Vinnie's crew loaded out. Kelly was in the front of the bus with Mick, sitting on the couch, and I was standing by the door. We were all watching out the front window. Every time Vinnie's guy walked out towards their truck, he was mouthing shit back and forth with Kelly, "Fuck you" type of suggestions. When the guy walked out and told Kelly, "Blow me," making the "blow me" motion with his hand, Kelly pushed me out the door onto my back, and in a few long strides, jumped onto the back of Vinnie's truck. Kelly's leg was still messed up from his motorcycle accident, but he didn't care. He was going to kick some ass! Mick followed him out the door and into the fight, and I quickly got up to go make sure my guys didn't get hurt or hurt anyone else too bad! Kelly has those long arms, like Frankenstein, and when he swings, man, you better watch out! Some of our loyal road crew, drum tech Timmy D. and guitar tech "Chief," jumped into the truck and got in the mix also. They had our back! Everyone was having a huge brawl in the back of Vinnie's equipment truck, beating on Vinnie's roadies because Vinnie wouldn't come out of his bus, so the crew took the beatdown. There were like five or six people inside the truck fighting. Someone had Mick's hair and was yanking it really hard, and I cracked their hand with my Maglite. The guy yelped like a wounded animal and let go. Once I got it all separated, I looked out to the back of the truck, and there were a bunch of fans looking in at this spectacle with open mouths. They must have thought, *What the hell is THIS!* Tracii didn't get involved, staying on the bus. Steve was so stressed, pissed off, and frustrated because he wanted to punch Vinnie in the face and couldn't, so he got a bottle of Jack Daniel's from the venue promoter after the show and was passed out drunk in his bunk. He didn't see or hear any of this. I don't know where Phil was, but no one expects Phil to fight anyway. Needless to say, we were thrown off that tour. Without being told, I knew the tour was over.

After the fight, I got everyone on the bus and told the driver to drive back to L.A. He asked me if I was sure. I said, "Oh yeah." As soon as we got out of town a ways, I had the driver stop at a truck stop, and I got off the bus and called the office back in Hollywood. Alan had already heard what had happened and was mad. What could I do? This was an unreasonable situation. The tour was forced and not a good match of bands to begin with. Vinnie was a dick. Unreasonable. I had to fight for my guys. That was my JOB. There was nothing else I could have done. I told Alan I would call him in the morning and headed back to the bus. When I walked on, Steve was getting out of his bunk still looking drunk, saw me walking in, and said, "Hey Cork, are we at the hotel?" I had to tell Steve what happened and he was like, "WHAT!" I told him the story, and then Kelly, Mick, and the other guys got back on the bus and talked about the brawl for the next two hours. We had to drive home from Detroit to L.A. It took us three days. No hotels. Complete misery the whole way. We had to keep touring to keep the cash flow going, and there was no more tour, which meant money would be tight, so no hotels. Alan was a great protective manager. He got the band signed, went the distance, was loyal, and was one of the guys, but the organization was lacking. The cash flow was not flowing at times. I was stressed out to the max. I had called the office back in L.A. after the very first Vinnie gig and told them I didn't think it was going to work because of all the issues, which I presented as a long list. I was told to keep it together and keep that tour on the road no matter what—don't let it end, smooth it over—and now we were coming home after three gigs.

I thought that ride was never going to end, just flatlands across the Midwest—nothing. It was awful. We stopped a bunch for fireworks and stupid shit. The air conditioner wasn't working right, and we were drinking the whole way home with no tour. Miserable. We had nowhere even to live! We went to the Franklin Plaza Suites in Hollywood off of Highland and lived there for a month. I thought I would have a rest and a break at the Franklin Plaza Suites for awhile, but it got even crazier once we got there. All hell broke loose! Mick disappeared into this room with his new bride, pregnant with their future son, the entire time we stayed there. I didn't see Mick much, hardly at all, once we got to the Franklin Plaza. Later on, Mick told me he didn't remember seeing me much either. He was in a daze. It was a moment of temporary peace and calm for him away from the insanity.

Once we checked in, I got everyone settled, and saw Flavor Flav from Public Enemy come screeching out of the garage driving a topless Jeep, grinding gears the whole way down the street. He rented this car and didn't know how to drive a manual shift transmission. I had to jump in and show him what to do. One night, I remember seeing Flav jumping out of a window. The most surreal scene.

Andy McCoy from Hanoi Rocks was living next door to us as well—Andy on one side and Flavor Flav on the other. We had no money because we had no tour; paychecks were bouncing. Everything was based off of tour income, so everyone had no money. It was dire. The drinking and weed smoking went into overdrive. We met two girls that lived down the hall that had the best weed I think I've ever smoked. They told us that once a month, they went and stayed the weekend with an older gentleman friend in San Francisco, and he would entertain them, and they would entertain him, before he would give them money and the best weed. I smoked a joint of this stuff, and when the phone in the room rang, it looked like it was jumping off the table. Serious shit. Needless to say, they supplied us for free the entire time we were there. We were going out to clubs every night because we could always drink free in all of those places. In Hollywood, L.A. Guns were hometown rockstars. If we had no money, we would hit the nightlife and see what turned up, then head back to the Franklin Plaza to more weed and drinking—and trouble.

I was sharing a suite with Kelly and Timmy D., the drum tech. Timmy wasn't there a whole lot—I think he stayed with a girlfriend, mostly, so it was me and Kelly. The Franklin Plaza Suites were just that: mini suites. The suite had a master bedroom and two beds in the living room that doubled as couches, plus a kitchen, living room, dining room, and bathroom. Kelly, of course, got the master bedroom. By this point, I was only sleeping about three hours a night, anyway. I would have slept on nails. I mean, doing this job with these lunatics, you have to be the last one to bed and the first one up everyday. You have to make sure all the band and crew are in their rooms and not out doing stupid shit like skipping out on checks at Denny's; throwing long fluorescent light bulbs out of the windows of the hotel like spears, shattering on the ground and making lots of noise at 3 AM; or stealing guns from pawn shops. Once I knew that everyone was passed out, in their rooms or bunk, etc., then I went to sleep. I always had to be up early to deal with the office and any of the many other requests that were asked of me, so three hours a night is about right.

Into this mix, Kelly started seeing Sharise Neil, wife of Mötley Crüe's singer, Vince Neil, on the secret. I, of course, had to facilitate the whole thing and get her in and out of our suite every night on the quiet. More stress. That went on for a couple of weeks, probably every other night. I think she and Vince might have been separated—but still. It was very covert, the whole thing. I think there was a second rockstar girlfriend that Kel was messing with too. That kind of stuff went on all the time in Hollywood and the scene in the 80s. Most of those girls would bounce from rockstar to rockstar. Sharise was cool, though. Kelly had lots of chicks hanging around, but not too many married ones. I was stressed about it because if it got out and blew up, it could possibly hurt the band—which it did. Vince was in a huge band with a lot of power. L.A. Guns lost some tours because Vince made some calls. Once he found out she was seeing Kelly, Vince sabotaged some things for the band, an unfortunate casualty of the rock and roll chick wars. By this time, I had been sleeping three hours a night and smoking weed and drinking beer every day for the last nine months. I was toast. I really loved the guys and did everything I could to take care of them, but everyone has their breaking point.

One day I came in the door after being out at the office trying to get everyone's checks straightened out so we could eat. The crew was threatening mutiny after the Vinnie Vincent debacle and not having any money. I walked in, and Kelly and Timmy were shooting fireworks off on the balcony—bottle rockets and stuff that they had bought on one of the ten million stops we made on our trip back from Detroit after getting thrown off the tour. Shit was whistling and whizzing everywhere. I was in no mood. I yelled at them to stop, and Kelly was like a little boy caught with his hand in the cookie jar. They lit off a few more before finally ending the war on the neighbors below us. They then proceeded to pick me up and drag me into the bathroom, throwing me into the shower and turning the ice cold water on me. When they threw me in, I hit my head on the faucet. It hurt like hell and was the straw that broke the camel's back. I snapped. I punched a hole in the wall of the shower and pretty much let off some steam. Kelly and Timmy looked at me wide-eyed. I had enough. Everyone left me alone for a day or so, and I thought a lot about my situation and decided to quit. I couldn't do it anymore. I was on the road for eight months straight. I loved the guys, but there was too much tension and stress. I had to go home and regain my sanity. I hated to do it, but I had to for my health.

Chapter Eight - The Clubs Again, L.A. Guns, Crumble Pie, Grunge - 1989-Present

I left the No Mercy Tour and flew back to New York. Once I got home, I got in bed and slept for a month. Literally. I started eating better and working out. Once I was fully rested, I started thinking about what I wanted to do. I always loved to DJ. It really is the only thing that I really wanted to do in my life and really went after and made happen. Everything else I've done kind of fell in my lap. It was all good timing. I have also been a DJ for over 25 years. I know it better than anything else I've ever done. I still love to do it. I will always be a DJ.

I started asking around to see who would be interested in starting a new rock dance club. I made a deal with a club that had disco and new wave nights in Franklin Square, Long Island—now they would have a rock dance club every Wednesday night called Hot Rocks. I was inspired by the Cathouse in L.A. There wasn't a club like that in the New York City area. The timing was right, which is very important when starting a nightclub. It did well right away. As a DJ, I treated it the same as I would if I was playing disco or new wave. I made people dance, but now by playing only rock songs that had a groove—no heavy metal guitar wank and no thrash—rock and roll: Mötley Crüe, The Rolling Stones, Aerosmith, The Cult, Guns N' Roses, plus songs like "All Right Now" by Free, "Hair of the Dog" by Nazareth, "I Was Made

For Lovin' You" by Kiss, and "Round And Round" by Ratt. We did great promotions and lots of giveaways. I started making mixtapes when I played every night and started giving them to the office. They would make a cassette cover for it, reproduce them, and give them out free to the patrons. We did them as thank you gifts to the loyal club goers. I would add in some new songs that the record labels were pushing, if they fit my playlist, as a thank you to them for helping me out. I started issuing a Hot Rocks Top 20 Playlist that the office had professionally printed. It had the Top 20 songs, some pictures from the club, and it listed new promotions and events. Eventually, the Top 20 sheet became a little booklet. It got upped to glossy paper, and we added more pictures and started doing album reviews and featuring new releases for the record label, as well, as a bubbling under chart with newer records or bands. There were a lot of bands and a lot of records coming out every week back then. CDs were in full swing. The labels were spending money. The industry machine was rolling. The *Hot Rocks Top 20 sheet* was a great marketing tool, and all the record labels loved it because we gave bands exposure and were also partnered with local rock radio stations like WBAB to do co-promotions. Once again, we were helping to break records. The sheet got mailed out to all the people on the mailing list, including club patrons, record labels, print media, radio, and various music industry professionals.

We did a big party for RIP *Magazine*, which was, at this point in time, the leading rock and metal music mag. They were based out of L.A. and were part of the Larry Flynt publishing empire, so it was the hip rock magazine in the 1990s. They had done a party in L.A. that was a huge event with all the L.A. rock stars in attendance. I wanted to do a New York party, and I was very friendly with the advertising director at *RIP*, Mike Mathison, and had done a lot of business with *RIP* when I was at Combat Records. We set up a New York RIP party and invited a ton of bands and record company reps, media, etc. We sent limos into Manhattan to bring whatever rock stars were on the East Coast to the party: Mike Monroe from Hanoi Rocks, guys from Great White, Sebastian from Skid Row—a bunch of bands. *RIP* did a great feature in their next issue with a nice photo spread.

The success of Hot Rocks led to me getting a call from the people that owned a similar type of club, Avanti, in Bayside, Queens. The club was in the basement of a building on Bell Boulevard. They also owned a printing business that was upstairs above the club. They printed flyers and mailers for all the nightclubs in the area. There were two or three printers in the area that had all the club business in New York City, which was a nice chunk of change every month. They, of course, printed flyers for all of their own club nights for free. It was great set-up, as printing was the lifeblood for the nightclubs back then. It was very expensive, and a big cost every week. You did regular mailings to your mailing list—names that you collected every night. A girl would walk around with a clipboard and get everyone's name for the mailing list. You printed handouts, cards, and flyers every week and gave them to sub-promoters who handed them out in the street, at the mall, or put them on car windshields in all of the big parking lots. It was very competitive. If you put your flyers on the cars in a competing club's parking lot, you could have a big problem. Guys had gotten their jaw broken for putting their flyers on cars in another club's parking lot—forget about in the club. If they caught you in the club handing out flyers for another club, you would end up in the hospital.

One of the guys that worked at the printer was a rock guy named Nicki Camp who was in the New York City band, Lover, back in the day and also promoted clubs. He heard about Hot Rocks, came and checked it out, and wanted to do the same thing at Avanti. I went and met with Nicki and the owners of the club, and we made a deal to do the same thing I was doing at Hot Rocks. We called it Raw. We perfected the meet-and-greets at Raw. We would send a limo to pick up a band we had already arranged with to come hang out, drink for free, and meet fans—and girls. We did this with a lot of bands: L.A. Guns, Warrant, Danger Danger, Bang Tango, etc. Most we didn't pay, but a few we did. We paid Ace Frehley from Kiss to come down and sign autographs for an hour. We had concert after parties, meet-and-greets, birthday parties for guys in bands, etc. I was the DJ and set up the promotions at both Hot Rocks and Raw. I connected with all the record labels, and we did many cool co-promotions. With any new album release, we always did free CD and poster giveaways, free t-shirts, and raffles for bigger prizes like custom leather jackets and guitars. As far as serious promoting goes, radio was still very important back then. It was another tool that you used to get the word out about the club via paid commercials. Hot Rocks and Raw bought a lot of commercials on the local rock stations. I would go and sit in with the guy that made the radio spots and put them together with him. I would supply the music, we would create the copy, and then put it together. Those 30 second radio spots were a huge part of launching both Hot Rocks and Raw, along with many other clubs of all types all over the Long Island and Queens area.

Raw was a success from day one, packed out every Friday night. After a few months of Raw kicking ass, Nicki asked me if I wanted to DJ on Sundays at Limelight's Rock N Roll Church night in Manhattan. He had been promoting there for awhile, and the DJ was not playing the right music. He was playing some rock, but also some house music and club music. He couldn't get the crowd to dance playing just rock songs. He just didn't have the feel for it. I was in a unique position, having started as a disco DJ way back in 1978 and also being a huge rock fan. I just knew which rock songs to play and which not to. I knew how to stack songs, making sure I had a powerhouse two-hour set for the prime of the night. I did not easily break new songs into my playlist. They had to meet certain criteria. I was very picky. Remember, it wasn't a heavy metal club; it was a rock and roll dance club. I wasn't a heavy metal DJ; I was a rock and roll DJ. For example, even though in the early 90s Metallica was huge, I only played their one song, "Enter Sandman." That's the only Metallica song I ever played because it had a groove and fit my playlist. None of their other songs did. It was about dancing, not headbanging. Limelight also had live bands perform on Sundays: the biggest local and area bands, as well as lots of national touring talent. I worked at Limelight for almost six years every Sunday. Some of the bands that performed while I was working there include: Pearl Jam, L.A. Guns, White Zombie, Rage Against the Machine, Marilyn Manson, Tool, Blind Melon, Bad Brains, Buzzcocks, Eddie Van Halen, Vince Neil, Stephen Pearcy, D Generation, Kix, and UFO—the list is long.

Once I got back home to New York, I was getting back into the Manhattan club scene and started making the rounds again. Within a month, I had the lay of the land, and dove in headfirst. L.A. Guns came through and played The Limelight a couple of months after I left their employ. Mick Cripps asked me to meet them at the airport, and he would ride into town with me. When I showed up at the gate to meet them, they couldn't believe how healthy I looked. Honestly, it was probably the best shape I had ever been in. I gave the guys a high five, said hello, and helped them with their bags. Some things never change. Mick and Kelly Nickels rode with me into Manhattan. I gave all the guys presents from my massive t-shirt collection—some real cool t-shirts. There is a pic out there somewhere from backstage at Limelight that night, and they are all wearing the t-shirts. Mick, Kelly, and I hung out and smoked some weed and drank some beer like the old days. They were in town for another day to do press, and then they headed back out on tour.

The Limelight was a super hot club. Peter Gatien, the owner, was the club king of New York City. He had the four hottest mega clubs in Manhattan: Limelight, The Tunnel, the Palladium, and Club USA. Limelight was his first New York City club, and he had six nights a week going there, all doing the business. Peter always said that his biggest night for alcohol sales was Sundays with the rock and roll crowd. Peter had started in the nightclub business up in Canada promoting Rush at his first club, a rock and roll place back in the early 70s, so he understood rock and roll. Limelight and Peter are usually always associated with the house music, techno, and rave scenes and with the Club Kids and drug busts and all, but Peter knew about rock and roll.

At Limelight, I met and became friendly with the notorious Arthur Weinstein (RIP). Arthur was a former club owner and now the lighting director, among other things, for Peter at Limelight.

Arthur was a true New York City legend. In previous years, he had opened an after hours club, the Jefferson, that was the place to be at 5 AM. He also owned the pre-Studio 54 celeb hangout, Hurrah, and had opened the club, The World, down in Alphabet City with August Darnell from Kid Creole and the Coconuts. Arthur was friends with Studio 54's owner, Steve Rubell, as well as anyone and everyone that worked in "nightworld." Arthur either liked you or he didn't. He liked me, and we became friends. He schooled me about ambient mood lighting (which he was a master at), as well as what it took to make a real party, even when the club might be slow on an off-night. To kick off every night at Limelight, we would smoke a joint and have a drink. Then, at the end of the night, he would take over the dance floor lighting, and I would play his favorite songs while he would work the lights. I played "More" by The Sisters of Mercy, "She Sells Sanctuary" by The Cult, "Lost in the Supermarket" by The Clash, and "Sympathy for the Devil" by the Stones, and Arthur had some fun. Art always gave me the straight story whenever there was club drama going on, which was every minute of every day. He would let me know who to tell to fuck off and who to listen to. I mean, Limelight was open six nights a week, and each night had its promoters and DJs, sub-promoters, and hangers-on etc., etc., and there was always drama going on. He helped steer me around it. Arthur was one of two people at Limelight that I could call a friend: him and Shawn Brophy, the sound man. Art was a music fan, and we went to see the Stones together at Giants Stadium, Mick Jagger solo at Webster Hall, and also Kraftwerk at the Hammerstein Ballroom, among other nights out. When my son, Jagger, was born in 1994, he gave me a little Mercedes car for him that he could sit in and pedal around when he got older. It was very well made and obviously an expensive item. Art got it from some rich dude he knew that was cleaning stuff out and getting rid of things. He hauled that thing to the club and gave it to me. I put it in my car at the end of the night and brought it home. Art was the king of nightworld in my eyes. There was no one Arthur didn't know. Art was a controversial figure, but he was the real deal. When the book *The Last Party* by Anthony Haden-Guest was released, I picked it up because I was interested in reading about the history of the 1976-1996 New York City club scene, and Arthur is in the book quite a bit also. I brought it to the club, and he signed it for me: "To my friend Mike, the party is never over. Your friend, Arthur 4-19-99."

There will never be another Arthur. I am proud to have been his friend.

Through working at Limelight, I started getting work at Peter Gatien's other clubs. I worked at all four of his clubs at one time or another. One of Peter's main people in the office, Monica, liked me and helped me get work. I made it easy for everyone. I was their resident rock, lounge, and special event DJ because I was very flexible as to what types of music I could play. I could work at almost any type of event or private party. If it called for Sinatra, jazz, rock, disco, house, lounge, Top 40—whatever they needed, I could do it. Most of the DJs at Limelight only did one thing. They played house or techno or drum and bass or industrial, etc. I could do it all because I loved all types of music. Before Peter lost everything, he was set to do the nightclub in the Olympic Village for the 1996 Olympics in Atlanta. One of Peter's first nightclubs in America was a disco in Atlanta in the late 1970s, also called Limelight, so he had connections in Atlanta. They wanted me to DJ that club at the Olympics for them. They needed it to be mainstream, but not too much, and no drugs. They knew I could do it. But then came the pressure from the mayor of New York City, Rudy Giuliani. They made an example out of Peter. He was arrested, his clubs closed down, and he was deported. The Olympics project didn't happen, and Peter's reign was over. New York City nightlife would never be the same. It was the end of an era.

Working at Limelight was a conduit to a lot of things for me. I was back in the New York groove, so to speak, and ended up promoting and doing DJ appearances at many other clubs. I met new contacts, reconnected with a lot of old record company friends, and started going to dozens of concerts. I was very excited about the whole Britpop thing that started coming out of the UK with Oasis, Suede, The Verve, Pulp, etc. I saw Oasis every time they played in New York City. Each time, they played bigger and bigger venues. I think I saw them five times from their first US show at Wetlands in 1994 to the Academy and Roseland shows to the Paramount Theatre under the Garden. The last time I saw them was out at the Jones Beach Theater on Long Island in 1996. I saw The Verve a few times as well on the *A Northern Soul and Urban Hymns* tours. The Verve and Oasis are, to me, the last of the great rock and roll bands.

One night I was at a club called Spodee Odee, which was in an old standalone building, an old house I think it was, on West 23rd Street. It was probably a Monday, which I think was their big night. I ran into some people I knew at the bar that said Axl Rose was upstairs in the VIP area. I ordered a beer and talked to a friend for awhile. Eventually, one of the promoters of the weekly party came by to say hello and gave me a few drink tickets. We talked music for awhile, and then he walked me up to the VIP area. Actually it was the VVVIP area: the deepest inner sanctum, through multiple rooms and doors to a small room where the heaviest VIPs would assemble, away from the unwashed masses in the normal VIP room. I walked in, and Axl was sitting on a couch. I walked over and said hello. He had that look of surprise on his face like, *What are you doing here?*, and I sat down next to him, and we clinked glasses. We talked about all kinds of stuff, but the conversation drifted to Tracii Guns and L.A. Guns and why Axl couldn't be in a band with him, etc. It wasn't an angry thing, just very matter of fact. I never saw Axl be unreasonable, angry, or agitated. Anytime I saw him, he was always very cool with me, and it was very chill.

In late summer 1989, L.A. Guns released their new album, *Cocked & Loaded*. They had switched management from the guy that got them their record deal, Alan Jones, who had protected them and looked out for them—their hands on manager—to Allen Kovac, who was managing Richard Marx and some other mainstream artists who I can't remember. Allen was an industry guy, and he was what Steve Riley wanted, someone with more cred and industry power, who wasn't going to be out on the tour bus with them all the time. Kovac rarely appeared out on tour. This gave Riley more leverage to make the decisions and run the band. They hit the road with a much bigger production this time: two big 18-wheeler trucks for the stage, sound, production and gear, and two buses for the band and crew. They were headlining theaters and small arenas, bringing out full production, ramps, staging, lights, PA—the whole rig, which they had to pay for. There were two opening acts, Tora Tora and Dangerous Toys, who drew no one to the shows and did nothing for the package, as far as credibility or sales. It was a little over the top. I mean, their first album only went gold. They weren't at the big, multiplatinum sales level yet, so to be spending money like that was too much too soon, in my humble opinion.

Mick and Kelly had called me and said that they didn't like their road manager and asked me to come out on the road and just hang out and have fun with them, which I did. I showed up in Austin for the tour opener, and then stayed for the Houston show. I hung out for a week, then went home. Mick called me all the time complaining about things, joking really, but not.

About a month later the tour got to New York City, I connected with Mick and Kelly again, and we hung out. They were playing The Ritz, which at the time, had moved Uptown to the old Studio 54 location. Mick pleaded with me to go out on the road again, so I did. I can't ever say no to Mick! I left with them after the show at The Ritz and travelled with them for about ten days: Philly, Boston, Providence, Wilkes-Barre, Poughkeepsie, Clifton Park, and Baltimore at Hammerjacks. I just took care of the guys and helped out their poor road manager. He was a nice enough guy but not "one of the boys," so to speak. He was from the Kovac office and had been out on the road with a bunch of wimpy-ass bands.

As usual, there was some more insanity in store for me. In Wilkes-Barre, Pennsylvania, we were staying in a hotel that was old train cars. It was pretty cool, but weird at the same time. After the gig, we were at the hotel, but were all out hanging on the now newer, but still smelly tour bus with some girls and fans. Everyone was talking, listening to music, drinking, smoking weed, etc. All of a sudden, Kelly starts arguing with some girl on the bus. It got louder, and then she stood up. He then stood up. She took a swing at him and connected. He grabbed her by the hair and started dragging her to the front of the bus, and I grabbed her and maneuvered her out of the bus after much yelling, punching, and kicking. She fell out of the door onto the ground. I told Kelly to stay on the bus and took her and walked her away. We are walking towards the parking lot, when she stopped, turned, and looked at me coldly, right in the eyes, saying, "You will pay for this," before walking away into the night. I believed her. After that rumble, the party broke up, and everyone went back to their train cars to go to sleep. The next morning, we woke up, started getting dressed, and carried our bags to the bus. As I approached the bus, I saw a note taped to the door. It said something like, "You have violated the coven of the 13th Territory of Pennsylvania witches," and that we would all pay for the desecration and disrespect of their territory and authority as witches, etc., etc. It was written by hand in a looping Old World-style font. It looked serious. It was scary as fuck. I showed the guys in the band, and they were all wide-eyed. We all hoped that we didn't have a curse put on us for all time.

At the next gig in Poughkeepsie while the band was onstage, the bus was broken into, and a lot of stuff was stolen: video cameras, boomboxes, personal bags containing personal diaries, and videotapes. There was a lot of crazy stuff on those videotapes. Needless to say, the band were freaked out. Apparently the security guy that was stationed to watch the buses, conveniently, "wasn't around" at the exact moment that someone came to break in. Was it the witches of Pennsylvania? A random occurrence? An inside job? We will never know, but we all said a prayer in between cursing the damn witches for the break-in. My time on this leg of the tour ended in Baltimore at Hammerjacks. Another insane night in Baltimore. It does get tired after awhile. I got picked up there after the gig and went back to New York. I loved the guys and missed hanging with them, but the road life was not for me, at least in long doses. The tour continued on, and the band ended up having a minor Top 40 hit with the song "The Ballad of Jayne" and a second gold album. Things were looking up for L.A. Guns, but the 90s were on the way, and unfortunately, things were about to change drastically for the Old Guard rock and roll bands out there.

On June 25, 1991, the third L.A. Guns album, Hollywood Vampires, was released. It was a true move to a more mainstream commercial rock sound, and they hoped to have a big hit with it.

On August 27, 1991, Pearl Jam's album, Ten, was released.

On September 24, 1991, Nirvana's Nevermind album and the Red Hot Chili Peppers album, *Blood Sugar Sex Magik,* were released.

The old school heavy metal and glam bands were done, overnight, just like that. Everything changed. Bands that rode in limos, fucked groupies, wore custom-made stage clothes, and sang about "Cherry Pie" were over. A couple of the more organic, real bands were able to get around this shift in the rock landscape, mainly Guns N' Roses and Metallica. Guns N' Roses were so big that they were able to hang on. They weren't a hair band anyway. They were much more punk rock, raw, and street than Warrant, Winger, or Poison. Metallica was a dirty heavy metal thrash band, more like Motörhead than Iron Maiden, so those two made it through. Everyone else was dead. A L.A. Guns and Pearl Jam at Limelight gig poster from 1992 that is promoting two different shows is a good example of out with the old, and in with the new. L.A. Guns couldn't fill theaters and small arenas anymore. They were on their way down, so they were back in the clubs and played Limelight on April 5, 1992. The following week, Pearl Jam played Limelight on April 12, 1992 on their first album tour. It was so packed that it was a fire hazard and an over the top and incredible show. They were on the way up, of course. If you were Mötley Crüe, Poison, or Warrant, you were done. Sure, you could hang on for another year or two, but the golden days were gone.

The cracks in the L.A. Guns machine had started back in 1988, but were now really starting to show themselves after the stress of knowing that they were yesterday's news, and that a new scene was eclipsing them. 1991 and *Hollywood Vampires* was the end for the "classic" one for all, and all for one L.A. Guns.

The A&R man for L.A. Guns was Bob Skoro. He signed them to PolyGram, believed in them, and was their main man at the label. Bob was a good dude. He had to deal with rock star tantrums from the band sometimes, which was a nightmare for him, but he was loyal to the band. His end with L.A. Guns was not a pleasant one.

I had heard from various members of the band about the restaurant meeting in 1991 that L.A. Guns had with their A&R man, Bob Skoro, that really became the end for the band. The story was that Bob Skoro took the band out to dinner at an upscale Italian restaurant on Melrose. It started out as a victory dinner because *Hollywood Vampires* was near gold, but Steve Riley was pissed that it wasn't platinum and thought the record company wasn't doing enough—something like that—and it got ugly. My sources said that they thought Steve was going to punch Bob. Manager Allen Kovac wasn't there. Riley was really stoned and was in bad mood again and started having a go at Bob for God knows what. The conversation deteriorated because Bob talked over Steve, and Steve freaked out. He stood up from the table and started yelling at Bob, threatening to take him outside and beat his ass. The whole restaurant went silent. Of course, it was beyond embarrassing and uncomfortable. Bob was really scared. But supposedly Tracii, Mick, Kelly, and Phil Lewis got everything cooled down. Then right afterwards, Bob came up to Mick and Phil outside the restaurant and told them that he quit, and somebody new at PolyGram would be handling them. It ended up being Davitt Sigerson. That's when their career was officially over. Everything was violence. It was insane.

In 1991, L.A. Guns were on tour with Skid Row in Europe and that's when Steve Riley got a little loose with his hands and swatted Phil in the face with a newspaper. It was a silly little thing, but probably not for Phil. It was the end of Riley for awhile. Again, what I heard from the guys in the band was this was when Riley was at the height of being very demanding. They were on tour with Skid Row in Europe on the *Hollywood Vampires* tour, and Steve was really getting on everyone's nerves, especially Phil's. For some reason, he was really pissed at Phil. I guess Steve's attitude was, there's Sebastian (Skid Row singer) out there wailing every night, and Phil was struggling, ya know. Phil is a much different kind of singer than Sebastian. He isn't a wailing screamer type of vocalist, and Steve was all over Phil about it. He was on the phone all morning with Jim, their road manager. Steve's room wasn't right, and Jim couldn't get his room changed, so he was all pissed off. They were down at breakfast, and Jim was on the phone with Steve all morning, with Steve laying into Jim, saying how come they couldn't stay longer and get some sleep, yada yada. Jim said, "Hey, we gotta roll." Steve wanted to change all the plans, and Jim had to tell him, "Hey, it's not our show. We have to stay on track with the Skid Row guys," so Steve was all pissed. Mick and Phil were having breakfast, and Jim came down and said, "You guys better watch out. Steve's on the warpath." They were like, "Oh just forget it. Don't worry, Jim, never mind, forget it," and he must have thought, "Oh thats easy for you guys to say."

They were just hanging out and having breakfast, and they look over and see Steve coming towards them, looking pissed. He came over and kind of just sat down and joined Mick, Phil, and Jim. He was sitting opposite Phil, and he had his rolled-up newspaper in his hand. Phil said, jokingly, something like, "What's the matter Steve, didn't you sleep well last night?" Steve looked at him and said, "No, you fucking kid," and went, whack, and hit Phil right in his fucking forehead and face with the newspaper. None of the guys could believe it. Phil just sat there and said, "Hey, what's the matter Steve?" Steve was going on with Jim about his problems, and then Phil got up and left. Phil caught up with Mick later and told him, "I can't do this anymore. I can't be in the band with him anymore." There were three more shows left on the tour, and Mick and Kelly tried to calm Phil down, like, "Hey, please just grin and bare it. Let's get to the end of this thing, get through it, and we will just figure it out." He said, "Alright."

The next day, Phil said, "When we get back to L.A., I'm quitting the band." They said to him again, "You can't do that." Phil gave the ultimatum, saying, "I can't be in the band with him; either he goes or I go." They thought they had calmed him down. When they got back to L.A., Phil again said, "That's it. I can't play with Steve," and they had a meeting and threw Steve Riley out. They got their manager, Kovac, to fire him. He said something like, "Hey, you can't smack the lead singer in the face with a newspaper. It's totally out of line. Don't contact the band. It's over." They had to pay him off, as well. He still made out okay. Steve always made more money than everybody, probably because he was older and more experienced! He didn't write any songs back then, but when Steve joined the band, Tracii and Phil cut Steve in on their publishing. He had nothing to do with the first album, not one iota. Phil and Tracii generously gave him some of their royalties as a thank you for joining the band, but he really did nothing on the first record. His picture is on the back cover, but that is the sum total of his involvement on that album. Steve wasn't able to put down his recording mark with the band until they recorded their second album, *Cocked & Loaded.*

When L.A. Guns finished touring *Hollywood Vampires*, they didn't do anything for about two years. That's when Mick started doing Crumble Pie

In summer 1992, I got a call from my good friend Mick, asking me to put together a short East Coast tour for a band he was playing in called Crumble Pie—except now they are called Operation Werewolf. And then when they came East, they would be called See No Evil, Hear No Evil, Evil Knievil. Huh? "What are you talking about?" I replied. "Oh it's a new band we started for fun, and we figured it would be cool to take the band East for some shows." Crumble Pie had been playing the Hollywood clubs with a regular gig at the Coconut Teazser. Since I had worked for L.A. Guns as tour manager on their first tour in 1988, Mick knew I could get the job done.

I got the band, and Nicki Camp booked nine shows with no breaks in between—nine one-nighters. This should be fun. We played the Limelight in New York City, Baltimore, Staten Island, Long Island, Philadelphia, New Haven, and L'Amour in Brooklyn. Griff and Spike from The Quireboys were in the band, and I knew them from when they opened for the Guns in the States and figured it would be a blast. Oh, it was a blast: nine days of rock and roll, drinking, insanity, and laughing, a lot of laughing. I met the guys at the airport with the passenger van and was introduced to Doni Gray, the drummer (who also was in the band Burning Tree with Marc Ford), and erstwhile harp player and singer, Steve "Boysee" Counsel, who, I might add, was a real "character," as we say in New York. Keith Brown was the quiet one—at least there WAS a quiet one! Quireboys bass player Nigel

Mogg came along for the ride—and the booze—and the birds. And of course, Mick was in the band playing guitar and keyboards. We travelled, all nine of us, in a passenger van, which I drove. A second van carried the gear and was driven by Eddie Javaruski, the roadie and sound man.

Spike complained all day, every day about his back: "Corky, I need some Doans for me back," was all we heard every day. Spike thought he needed the back pain medicine Doans. He thought he hurt his back. It was his kidneys and liver achin', more likely! After the last gig of the tour, when we were walking back to the van, I found a pack of Doans on the windshield. Somebody finally got Spike his Doans!

The only show that was recorded was at the Rage club in Baltimore, Maryland on Friday September 4, 1992. Why other shows weren't recorded, I don't know. Maybe it was the fact that the band was more interested in making sure I had enough booze for them was part of it. Anyway, I gave the sound man a blank cassette tape and asked him to record the gig. And what a gig it was. This gig was show number eight, and the band had been playing straight with no breaks for the last week. They were "cooking," as they say in jazz land.

The band played songs that they enjoyed playing. It was FUN! They fed off each other onstage, conjuring up the devil from the crossroads nightly, while knocking over every round of drinks that was brought to them. "More drinks!" Spike would say to no one in particular, and he got them every time. They cared not who they were playing to or where they played. As long as there was electricity and alcohol, it was all good. The band switched instruments often and jammed on obscure cover songs, as well as original tracks. Songs like "Gang Bang" by The Sensational Alex Harvey Band, "Miss Judy's Farm" by the Faces, and "Slave" by the Stones. Doni sang the McCartney song, "Maybe I'm Amazed." Every member was a multi-instrumentalist, and every member took turns on vocals. The lineup was: Spike, lead vocals; Guy Griffin, guitar and vocals; Mick Cripps, guitar, Fender Rhodes piano, and bass; Keith Brown, bass and piano; Steve Counsel, harmonica, vocals, and acoustic guitar; and Doni Gray, drums and vocals.

This was one of the most enjoyable times I have ever had on the road. There was no pressure from anyone. No record labels. No publicists. It was done for pure rock and roll fun and mayhem. Is there any other way?! After nine days on the road, we dropped the band at Kennedy Airport and bid them adieu. Then I went home and slept for three days.

In 1992, L.A. Guns put out the *Cuts* EP during a two-year break just to put something out there. It was all cover songs. I think it was a contractual thing. They also got a new member, a drummer named "Bones." Then, after falling out with Phil, Tracii quit or was fired, depending on who you ask, so Mick, Phil, and Kelly did the *Vicious Circle* album without Tracii or Steve Riley. Mick has told me that *Vicious Circle* is his favorite L.A. Guns album, and that Phil really did a great job writing songs with Steve Dior and the producer, Jim Wirt, was his favorite producer.

MICK CRIPPS: *"We had half of Crumble Pie on that record. Griff [Quireboys guitarist Guy Griffin] played on a track. Boysee [Steve Counsel] was on a couple of songs. Doni [Gray from Burning Tree] played drums on a couple of tracks. Steve Dior [The Idols/London Cowboys] did a lot of the backing vocals with Phil. He wrote a couple of songs with Phil and I, as well. Tracii came in when we were done and overdubbed some guitar. PolyGram didn't even know Tracii was out of the band, and when they found out, they flipped. They didn't know anything. I got Tracii back in the band. Tracii rejoined the band after we were nearly finished with the album. He added his guitar parts, cowrote a couple of new songs with us, and we were able to deliver it to the record label, very satisfied with the outcome. But we didn't even have an A&R guy at that point. After Hollywood Vampires, we had a couple people who kind of handled us, then we did Cuts, and no one claimed us. We went like two or three years with nobody at PolyGram representing us or anything. A total mess. I don't even think we had Kovac managing us at that point. Chaos. So Tracii had to come back, or we'd get sued by PolyGram. Nickey Beat played drums on a song, Myron Grombacher too. Riley came back* at the end and was on a song. It's such a hodgepodge of players. Bones disappeared halfway through the record—that's why there are so many drummers on it. We filmed a music video for the song "Long Time Dead" and used it as the opening number on tour in 1995. I think Riley only came back at the very end of the recording. He played on one song. It was me, Phil, Kelly, and Bones, and then Bones left. He only did the first few songs, then disappeared, so we had to get other drummers. Tracii came back, and then Riley came back because we had to tour the record. It came out in the beginning of 1995, and we did a really good four-to-five months of touring, and then I quit the band and went to work at Zomba. LAG then got dropped from PolyGram. Kelly left, and then Phil left. That's when Tracii did Killing Machine, and they did a new version of L.A. Guns with some awful metal singer in 1996/1997. Then Phil came back in 1998, and I got the whole original lineup together to do the three Cleopatra records in 1999 through 2000—three records in 12 months. We did a few months of touring, made good money, and then I left again. Then Kelly left again and was replaced by Muddy, and that was it. Depressing. It totally crumbled into mayhem and bad feelings. I remember Kelly and I sitting around all depressed at Phil's house when it was all over, and we were getting fucked up, drinking, talking about how our style of music was over and grunge and industrial music had taken over. And Phil said, "Yeah, it's like the end of vaudeville." Ahhh hahaha! I will never forget that.

Hahahaha! I was in L.A. Guns from 1985 to 1995, and then again from 1999 to 2001. That was it for me. That was enough!"

The big Halloween gig at Webster Hall in Manhattan with Bones on drums in 1993 was the last thing I was involved with for them. I got L.A. Guns to play the show, and Nicki Camp got the other four bands on the bill as support: D Generation, The Voluptuous Horror of Karen Black, the Lunachicks, and Sticky. Bones had been hired as the new drummer in L.A. Guns, but it was at the end really. Steve eventually came back, and they did other records with other labels, but the magic was gone, the moment, the time. Gone with the wind. Now it's just Phil and Tracii on one side, and Kelly and Steve on the other, with Mick in the middle, always neutral, always diplomatic. The smart one. There are now two versions of L.A. Guns. Two versions still going, still playing, at the same time. Talk about confusion. Like I said, it's a soap opera. So on it goes.

Rock and roll as we know it is over. Grunge killed the Mötley Crües, Poisons, and Warrants of the world. Rock was merging with techno to become "industrial" with bands like Nine Inch Nails and Ministry. Rap was merging with rock, exemplified in bands like Rage Against the Machine and Limp Bizkit, to create an even wider spectrum of what we call rock music. Add in the lightweight indie college stuff like R.E.M. and Counting Crows, who were all capturing a piece of the market share, continuing to fracture and splinter the music world. And ultimately, real rock music got heavier and heavier. Heavy metal was lightweight now. Slayer, Cannibal Corpse, and Pantera attacked your senses like a sledgehammer to the skull. With the advent of Pro Tools and digital recording, bands could now produce heavier, more insane music using the new computer technologies. The old Sunset Strip era was still locked in the analog world. Records were now being mastered differently to appeal to the dance floors. Techno, house, and industrial dance music were exploding. The new, heavier rock bands started using this new technology to make the sub-bass more intense and make the high-end pierce your ears like a knife. There were no more girls dressed up and pretty at the front of the rock shows anymore; it was all dudes dressed in cut-off cargo shorts and combat boots, moshing and slam dancing. No more girls at rock shows at all really, and if there were, they were all the way in the back, so they didn't get pummeled in the mosh pit. The front row of the Limelight now looked way different than just a year before. Scary, sweaty dudes now dominated the crowd. The music industry pie was shrinking for the old rock bands, especially the hair metal scene. Then, when it all got too big, as trends alway do, and Cobain left us, and Woodstock '99 destroyed what hope you had for the emerging generation of kids—the huge hip-hop scene killed off what was left of grunge and took over. And it's been hip-hop, pop ever since. And here we are.

Of course, the club, Hot Rocks, eventually closed. Raw hung on awhile longer, and then closed too. Limelight and Peter Gatien were getting harassed and attacked by Mayor Giuliani and the government. The rave days were ending. A Club Kid murder and too many bad drugs killed it off. Peter Gatien was deported to Canada. The clubs were done in New York City and all over the metro area. They were over. Finished. Times were changing. Again.

I married Maryann in 1993, and my son Jagger was born in 1994. My life was on a different trajectory. I was still doing DJ work and promoting clubs, even managing a local New York band called Rosary Violet. But I was also trying to transition into something more 9-5. It was not an easy transition, but I wanted to get out of the nightlife. That life is subhuman: late hours, drugs, alcohol, sex, dark and slimy people. Just breathing in the thick humid air in one of those mega clubs is enough to make you feel like you inhaled the breath of Satan. So it was on my radar to try to break free of nightworld. But I had to pay the bills, so the club work would continue for a little longer. In 2002, I received the news that my wife, Maryann, was diagnosed with cancer. This was a shock and a major jolt for me. She was sick for a year, and the last few months were very bad. She fought all the way though. Never gave up hope. She passed away in 2003, and I raised my son, Jagger, by myself from the age of nine until his graduation from high school in 2012. All of his grandparents were a big help in raising him, as well. It was so rewarding watching him grow up, of course, but we also had a lot of fun. We did many cool things and took many great trips. I'm happy he remembers all of those good times we had. I can only imagine how the pain of losing his mother has affected him. Hopefully one day he will heal from that trauma. I pray for him every day. I have done my best to be a good father and be there for him, and I'm very proud of the man he has become. Once Jagger graduated high school in June 2012, he left for college on the West Coast in California, while back in New York we all went through Hurricane Sandy. That pretty much did me in, as far as New York went. I left there in early 2013 and went out in search of myself. I had been through a lot of traumatic times in my life as a kid and spent years living a wild, ego-driven, and abnormal lifestyle—abnormal, as far as my definition of it. I was partying hard for 15 years. I had seen and done too much, too soon. My early childhood and my family issues had affected me in ways that I had never even imagined. I was in pain, trying to numb myself and possibly hurt myself, unknowingly. I needed to slow down and focus on healing those parts of myself that were keeping me on a repeated cycle of old, outmoded, and ineffective behavior. I needed a rebirth. I wandered the country for awhile and then found the light I was looking for in Los Angeles, in a place I never thought I would return to, much less find something good in. But I did. My love, Becca aka The Kid, has healed me and helped me to find my true path. She's helped me to love myself, to work on healing myself, to grow, and to evolve. She inspires me to be the best version of myself I can be. Work-wise, I've always been a knock-around kind of guy. I've done a lot of different things for work in my life, 25 years of it in the music business. I was lucky and driven. I set out to be "in it" and hopefully be able to survive and pay my bills. I never approached anything I did with the attitude of how much am I getting paid. Maybe I should have, but things would not have worked out for me the way they did. It all happened the way it was supposed to. Since the music days, I have had to do other "straight" work to provide for myself and my loved ones, doing jobs that I was good at, but I didn't love. It was just a means to an end. Straight jobs. There's no fun in it. Sucks out your soul. That's when I decided to finally finish my book that I had started writing 30 years ago. The craziness is now all over for me, and I can look back and acknowledge it all. I can look at it through a different lens and examine it for what it was. I'm happy to have lived long enough to be able to do this at all, honestly. But then again, I always felt invincible. I still do in some ways, but I am much more cautious than I used to be. And I like my slow and relaxed lifestyle. It's kind of like the end of *Goodfellas.* I get to live the rest of my life like a shnook—not really, but you get the idea. Life takes you down many roads, and I finally am at the point where I wanted to do it. To finish it. I wanted to leave these stories for posterity and get them off my chest once and for all. It's like therapy. So I have told the tales, and there are still some more to tell, but that's for another book. Now, I work daily on lifting my consciousness to higher levels, connecting with my inner spirit, and to heal and love myself so I can ascend higher. It's all about working on the inner you. It all starts there, every bit of your happiness. I thank God, the universe, and my guardian angels for giving me the opportunity to experience life as I have and for keeping a watch over me, guiding me safely to the present moment. Thank you for allowing me to see. I promise to use the knowledge wisely.

Thank you to: Thank you to: Jagger Corcione, Becca "the Kid" Fisher, Mike Corcione Sr., Franne Corcione, Jennifer Corcione, Joyce Corcione, Stacey "Shmendrek," Bruno Ravel, Steve West, Mike Pont, Scott Levitt, Mitch Pfeiffer, Mick Cripps, Ian Cripps, Shawn Cripps, Kelly Nickels, Robert Cripps, Nickey "Beat" Alexander, Alan Jones, Barry Kobrin for giving me the shot, Michael "Spud" Chandler, Paul "P.A." Aaronson,, John Sciortino, Tommy Lee, Nikki Sixx, Rich Fisher, Doc McGhee, Fred Saunders, Robbin Crosby (RIP), Larry Braverman, Bart Dorsey (RIP), Richie Ranno, Uncle Ralph Greco, Mike Schnapp, Paul Di'Anno, Rod Smallwood, Danny Buch, Joe Gerber, Uncle Ralph Greco, Peter Gatien, Shawn Brophy, Arthur Weinstein (RIP), Frank White, Dave Plastik, Lynn Felderman, and Andrew Horn (RIP) and Sarah Smith.

And to the memories of: Maryann Mari, Jonathan Corcione, Alex Corcione, Caine Dominici, Vincent Corcione Jr., Donnie Richardson, Sean McCarthy, and John Capitano

Bands

Lynyrd Skynyrd

Edgar Winter

Kiss

Foreigner

Cheap Trick

Tom Petty

Sex Pistols

Piper

The Brats

Hotshot · NYC

Wowii

Lover

Murder Inc.

Falcon Eddy

Twisted Sister

Swift Kick

Lipstick

Diamond

The Kidds

U2

Billy Squier

Kid Blue

Mötley Crüe

Ratt

Duran Duran

W.A.S.P.

My Top 250 Songs Ever ...

In No Particular Order

1. "You're No Good" - Linda Ronstadt
2. "Superstar" - Carpenters
3. "Kashmir" - Led Zeppelin
4. "Fox On The Run" - Sweet
5. "What Is Life" - George Harrison
6. "I Got the Blues" - The Rolling Stones
7. "Baker Street" - Gerry Rafferty
8. "Bring On The Night" - The Police
9. "Reflections" - The Supremes
10. "Harmony" - Elton John
11. "Bittersweet Symphony" - The Verve
12. "Jackie Blue" - The Ozark Mountain Daredevils
13. "Break It to Me Gently" - Brenda Lee
14. "Take It On the Run" - REO Speedwagon
15. "Night Moves" - Bob Seger
16. "Wake Up Everybody" - Harold Melvin & The Blue Notes
17. "Firestarter" - The Prodigy
18. "American Girl" - Tom Petty
19. "Magnet and Steel" - Walter Egan
20. "You and I" - Rick James
21. "One of These Nights" - the Eagles
22. "You're So Vain" - Carly Simon
23. "Maggie May" - Rod Stewart
24. "Shambala" - Three Dog Night
25. "How Long" - Ace

26. "The Letter" - The Box Tops

27. "Looks That Kill" - Mötley Crüe

28. "She Sells Sanctuary" - The Cult

29. "Mannish Boy" - Muddy Waters

30. "I Wanna Get Next To You" - Rose Royce

31. "You Make Me Feel (Mighty Real)" - Sylvester

32. "C'mon and Love Me" - Kiss

33. "Save a Prayer" - Duran Duran

34. "Ashes to Ashes" - David Bowie

35. "Year of the Cat" - Al Stewart

36. "Vienna" - Billy Joel

37. "The Magnificent Seven" - The Clash

38. "Miss You" - The Rolling Stones

39. "Wichita Lineman" - Glen Campbell

40. "That Smell" - Lynyrd Skynyrd

41. "Date With the Rain" - Eddie Kendricks

42. "New Gold Dream" - Simple Minds

43. "Another Place, Another Time" - Jerry Lee Lewis

44. "Hot Burrito #1" - The Flying Burrito Brothers

45. "No More Mr. Nice Guy" - Alice Cooper

46. "I Want Your Love" - Chic

47. "Rocket 88" - Jackie Brenston

48. "Bitch" - The Rolling Stones

49. "Roadhouse Blues" - The Doors

50. "Rhiannon" - Fleetwood Mac

51. :Rikki Don't Lose That Number" - Steely Dan

52. "Hold It Now, Hit It" - the Beastie Boys

53. "Kodachrome" - Paul Simon

54. "That's the Way of the World" - Earth, Wind & Fire

55. "Eminence Front" - The Who

56. "Fist City" - Loretta Lynn

57. "Superstition" - Stevie Wonder

58. "Fooled Around and Fell in Love" - Elvin Bishop

59. "Machine Gun" - Commodores

60. "Dream Weaver" - Gary Wright

61. "All Mixed Up" - The Cars

62. "Cuban Slide" - The Pretenders

63. "Downed" - Cheap Trick

64. "Pull Up to the Bumper" - Grace Jones

65. "Ride Like The Wind" - Christopher Cross

66. "Numbers" - Kraftwerk

67. "I Just Wanna Have Something To Do" - Ramones

68. "52 Girls" - The B-52's

69. "Never Say Never" - Romeo Void

70. "Magic" - Olivia Newton-John

71. "Ghost Town" - The Specials

72. "Close Up the Honky Tonks" - Buck Owens

73. "Two Sevens Clash" - Culture

74. "No More No More" - Aerosmith

75. "Pretty Vacant" - Sex Pistols

76. "Sin City" - AC/DC

77. "Love Will Tear Us Apart" - Joy Division

78. "Goldfinger" - Shirley Bassey

79. "Step On" - Happy Mondays

80. "The Tears of a Clown" - Smokey Robinson & the Miracles

81. "I Don't Love You Anymore" - Teddy Pendergrass

82. "Dim All the Lights" - Donna Summer

83. "Don't You Want Me" - The Human League

84. "Into The Groove" - Madonna

85. "Pretty in Pink" - The Psychedelic Furs

86.   "It's Only Make Believe" - Conway Twitty

87.   "Suspicious Minds" - Elvis Presley

88.   "Situation" - Yaz

89.   "Keep on Smilin'" - Wet Willie

90.   "Good Golly Miss Molly" - Little Richard

91.   "It Won't Be Long" - The Beatles

92.   "Hit Me With Your Rhythm Stick" - Ian Dury and The   Blockheads

93.   "Angel Eyes" - Frank Sinatra

94.   "I'll Never Grow Up, Now" - Twisted Sister

95.   "Precious" - The Pretenders

96.   "Don't Stop 'til You Get Enough" - Michael Jackson

97.   "And the Cradle Will Rock…" - Van Halen

98.   "Fire Island" - Village People

99.   "Whiskey Bent and Hell Bound" - Hank Williams Jr.

100.   "Punky Reggae Party" - Bob Marley

101.   "Move On Up" - Curtis Mayfield

102.   "Candy" - Iggy Pop

103.   "Stone in Love" - Journey

104.   "All Along the Watchtower" - Jimi Hendrix

105.   "Running On Empty" - Jackson Browne

106.   "Hell Bent for Leather" - Judas Priest

107.   "Look Sharp!" - Joe Jackson

108.   "Come as You Are" - Nirvana

109.   "Aquarius/Let the Sunshine In" - The 5th Dimension

110.   "Bad Time" - Grand Funk Railroad

111.   "Isis (Live Boston 1975)" - Bob Dylan

112.   "In the City" - Joe Walsh

113.   "Feelin' Stronger Everyday" - Chicago

114.   "Shot In The Head" - Marcus Hook Roll Band

115.   "La vie en rose" - Grace Jones

116. "Nights on Broadway" - Bee Gees

117. "Cars" - Gary Numan

118. "The Cisco Kid" - War

119. "La Grange" - ZZ Top

120. "Blue Monday" - New Order

121. "Ship of Fools" - World Party

122. "Prove It All Night" - Bruce Springsteen

123. "Moody" - ESG

124. "Since You Been Gone" - Rainbow

125. "Axel F" - Harold Faltermeyer

126. "Girls Talk" - Dave Edmunds

127. "Got To Have Loving" - Don Ray

128. "Bark at the Moon" - Ozzy Osbourne

129. "I'll Be Good to You" - The Brothers Johnson

130. "I Was Made For Lovin' You" - Kiss

131. "Live Forever" - Oasis

132. "Home Sweet Home" - Mötley Crüe

133. "Uncle Albert/Admiral Halsey" - Paul McCartney

134. "No One Gets the Prize/The Boss" (12" single) - Diana Ross

135. "D-I-V-O-R-C-E" - Tammy Wynette

136. "Light My Fire" - The Doors

137. "The Night They Drove Old Dixie Down" - The Band

138. "Couldn't Get It Right" - Climax Blues Band

139. "Clampdown" - The Clash

140. "I Want You Back" - The Jackson 5

141. "The Air That I Breathe" - The Hollies

142. "Mr. Brownstone" - Guns N' Roses

143. "Wanted Man" - Ratt

144. "Fool for the City" - Foghat

145. "Stop This Game" - Cheap Trick

146. "If You Could Read My Mind" - Gordon Lightfoot

147. "Luckenbach, Texas (Back to the Basics of Love)" - Waylon Jennings

148. "A Girl Like You" - Edwyn Collins

149. "Primary" - The Cure

150. "It's a Long Way to the Top (If You Wanna Rock 'n' Roll)" - AC/DC

151. "Evil Woman" - Electric Light Orchestra

152. "Give Up the Funk (Tear the Roof off the Sucker)" - Parliament

153. "Tuesday's Gone" - Lynyrd Skynyrd

154. "Ooh Las Vegas" - Gram Parsons

155. "Easy Loving" - Freddie Hart

156. "Mama Tried" - Merle Haggard

157. "Cat People (Putting Out Fire)" - David Bowie

158. "Cities in Dust" - Siouxsie and the Banshees

159. "Heart of Gold" - Neil Young

160. "Last Night I Wrote a Letter" - Starz

161. "Mandy" - Barry Manilow

162. "Fan Club" - The Damned

163. "Dynomite" - Bazuka

164. "Get Down Tonight" - KC and The Sunshine Band

165. "On My Radio" - The Selecter

166. "It Only Takes A Minute" - Tavares

167. "Russian Roulette" - The Lords of the New Church

168. "Life During Wartime" - Talking Heads

169. "For the Love of Money" - The O'Jays

170. "Don't Leave Me This Way" - Thelma Houston

171. "Rock and Roll" - Gary Glitter

172. "Gypsys, Tramps & Thieves" - Cher

173. "Champagne & Reefer" - Muddy Waters

174. "Kinky Afro" - Happy Mondays

175. "After Dark" - Pattie Brooks

176. "Mystify" - INXS

177. "Electrical Storm" - U2

178. "Native New Yorker" - Odyssey

179. "Shame" - Evelyn "Champagne" King

180. "On Broadway" - George Benson

181. "If I Can't Have You" - Yvonne Elliman

182. "The Logical Song" - Supertramp

183. "Now That We Found Love" - Third World

184. "The Way We Were" - Gladys Knight & the Pips

185. "Feel Like Makin' Love" - Bad Company

186. "Waterloo" - ABBA

187. "My Mistake (Was to Love You)" - Diana Ross & Marvin Gaye

188. "Gold Dust Woman" - Fleetwood Mac

189. "Atlantic City" - The Band

190. "Time Waits for No One" - The Rolling Stones

191. "A Woman in Love (It's Not Me)" - Tom Petty and the Heartbreakers

192. "New York State of Mind" - Billy Joel

193. "California Dreaming" - José Feliciano

194. "Angel From Montgomery" - Bonnie Raitt

195. "Sorry Seems to Be the Hardest Word" - Mary J. Blige

196. "Lido Shuffle" - Boz Scaggs

197. "I'm so Lonesome I Could Cry" - Hank Williams

198. "Sick and Tired" - Chris Kenner

199. "Black Coffee" - Humble Pie

200. "He Stopped Loving Her Today" - George Jones

201. "Satin Sheets" - Jeanne Pruett

202. "What's Made Milwaukee Famous" - Jerry Lee Lewis

203. "Isn't It Time" - The Babys

204. "Photograph" - Ringo Starr

205. "Found A Cure" - Ashford & Simpson

206. "Miracles" - Jefferson Starship

207. "Delta Lady" - Joe Cocker

208. "Whatever Gets You Thru the Night" - John Lennon

209. "Chloe Dancer/Crown of Thorns" - Mother Love Bone

210. "Sway" - The Rolling Stones

211. "Driver's Seat" - Sniff 'n' The Tears

212. "Slave" - The Rolling Stones

213. "Together Again" - Buck Owens

214. "You Keep Me Hangin' On" - Rod Stewart

215. "You'll Never Find Another Love Like Mine" - Lou Rawls

216. "Vertigo & Relight My Fire" - Dan Hartman

217. "Uptight (Everything's Alright)" - Stevie Wonder

218. "Seasons of Wither" - Aerosmith

219. "Turn the Beat Around" - Vicki Sue Robinson

220. "Melody" - David Johansen

221. "Thank You" - Led Zeppelin

222. "The Hardest Part" - Blondie

223. "The Flame" - W.A.S.P.

224. "Photograph" - Def Leppard

225. "Calley Oh" - Billy Squier

226. "Homosapien" - Pete Shelley

227. "(Don't Fear) The Reaper" - Blue Öyster Cult

228. "Come On, Come On" - Cheap Trick

229. "Night Time Is the Right Time" - Ray Charles

230. "Modern Love" - David Bowie

231. "Ode to Billie Joe" - Bobbie Gentry

232. "Family Affair" - Sly and the Family Stone

233. "More Than a Feeling" - Boston

234. "On the Radio" - Donna Summer

235. "Love Hangover" - Diana Ross

236. "What's Going On" - Marvin Gaye

237. "Long Train Runnin'" - The Doobie Brothers

238. "Mrs. Robinson" - Simon & Garfunkel

239. "I Wish It Would Rain" - The Temptations

240. "Young Hearts Run Free" - Candi Staton

241. "Bernadette" - Four Tops

242. "I'm In Love with My Car" - Queen

243. "If You Can't Rock Me" - The Rolling Stones

244. "Do You Feel like We Do" - Peter Frampton

245. "Legalize It" - Peter Tosh

246. "One More Time" - Lynyrd Skynyrd

247. "Let It Ride" - Bachman-Turner Overdrive

248. "Free Ride" - Edgar Winter

249. "Deuce" (Alive! version) - Kiss

250. "Here Comes the Sun" - The Beatles

Printed in the USA
CPSIA information can be obtained
at www.ICGtesting.com
LVHW070859051123
763053LV00035B/3